Ottoman Children and Youth during World War I

Contemporary Issues in the Middle East
Mehran Kamrava, *Series Editor*

SELECT TITLES IN CONTEMPORARY ISSUES IN THE MIDDLE EAST

Colonial Jerusalem: The Spatial Construction of Identity and Difference in a City of Myth, 1948–2012
Thomas Philip Abowd

Democracy and the Nature of American Influence in Iran, 1941–1979
David R. Collier

Iraqi Migrants in Syria: The Crisis before the Storm
Sophia Hoffmann

Islam, Arabs, and the Intelligent World of the Jinn
Amira El-Zein

Law of Desire: Temporary Marriage in Shi'i Iran, Revised Edition
Shahla Haeri

Making the New Middle East: Politics, Culture, and Human Rights
Valerie J. Hoffman, ed.

Political Muslims: Understanding Youth Resistance in a Global Context
Tahir Abbas and Sadek Hamid, eds.

Shahaama: Five Egyptian Men Tell Their Stories
Nayra Atiya

Ottoman Children and Youth during World War I

Nazan Maksudyan

Syracuse University Press

First Edition 2019
19 20 21 22 23 24 6 5 4 3 2 1

∞ The paper used in this publication meets the minimum requirements of the American National Standard for Information Sciences—Permanence of Paper for Printed Library Materials, ANSI Z39.48-1992.

For a listing of books published and distributed by Syracuse University Press, visit www.press.syr.edu.

ISBN: 978-0-8156-3627-4 (hardcover) 978-0-8156-3645-8 (paperback)
978-0-8156-5473-5 (e-book)

Library of Congress Cataloging-in-Publication Data
Names: Maksudyan, Nazan, 1977– author.
Title: Ottoman children and youth during World War I / Nazan Maksudyan.
Description: First edition. | Syracuse, New York : Syracuse University Press, 2019. | Series: Contemporary issues in the Middle East | Includes bibliographical references and index.
Identifiers: LCCN 2019001349 (print) | LCCN 2019008420 (ebook) | ISBN 9780815654735 (E-book) | ISBN 9780815636274 | ISBN 9780815636274 (hbk : alk. paper) | ISBN 9780815636458 (pbk : alk. paper)
Subjects: LCSH: World War, 1914–1918—Children—Turkey. | Children and war—Turkey—History—20th century. | Children—Turkey—Social conditions—20th century. | Orphans—Turkey—History—20th century. | Orphanages—Turkey—History—20th century.
Classification: LCC HQ792.T9 (ebook) | LCC HQ792.T9 M35 2019 (print) | DDC 303.6/6083—dc23
LC record available at https://lccn.loc.gov/2019001349

Manufactured in the United States of America

To my mom and dad, Meri and Vartan,
for truly loving their children,
and the children of their children,
as much as they loved each other

Contents

ILLUSTRATIONS

Maps

TABLES

ACKNOWLEDGMENTS

I HAVE WRITTEN THIS BOOK thanks to a fellowship from the Alexander von Humboldt Stiftung that enabled me to finish my research and writing in the course of 2017 and 2018. I am grateful to Leibniz-Zentrum Moderner Orient for hosting me during this period. I profited greatly from the productive academic environment at the institute, together with the insights and knowledge of my colleagues, particularly Ulrike Freitag, Nora Lafi, Heike Liebau, Katrin Bromber, Katharina Lange, Nitin Sinha, Ali Nobil Ahmad, Sanaa Alimia, Malte Fuhrmann, and Larissa Schmidt. I am also very lucky that my colleagues at the Centre Marc Bloch, Markus Messling, Leyla Dakhli, Franck Hofmann, and Catherine Gousseff, welcomed me not only as a colleague but also as a friend.

I had the chance to discuss earlier versions of this work with friends and colleagues, who have shared their erudition and expertise with me. I am particularly thankful to Taner Akçam, Yiğit Akın, Mustafa Aksakal, Beth Baron, Ben C. Fortna, Chris Gratien, Mischa Honeck, H. Şükrü Ilıcak, Oliver Janz, Hans-Lukas Kieser, Rober Koptaş, Kathryn R. Libal, James Marten, Inger Marie Okkenhaug, Manon Pignot, Kent F. Schull, Talin Suciyan, Vahé Tachjian, Erol Ülker, and Keith D. Watenpaugh.

I am also grateful to Boris Adjemian, the director of AGBU Nubar Library (Paris), and Vahé Tachjian, project director and chief editor of Houshamadyan, for permitting me to use amazing photos from their wonderful archives. I sincerely thank Raymond Kévorkian for letting me use his wonderful map of Armenian deportations and Kerem Halıcıoğlu for working on the map to change place-names.

Words are insufficient to describe my gratitude to Gülsün Karamustafa. I am extremely happy and lucky that Vasıf Kortun introduced me to her, and thanks to her kindness and generosity, her beautiful work *The Monument and the Child* is the cover of this book. A book that struggles with structures of adults and agencies of children could not have been visualized in a better way.

My bighearted, beautiful friend Başak Deniz Özdoğan was very generous to help me dig in the Ottoman Archives through the uncataloged files of the Directorate of Orphanages (MF.EYT.). The brilliant Ali Bolcakan helped me access rare books in the University of Michigan Library. I also thank my good friends Gökçe Akyürek, Seçil Alabucak, Hilal Alkan, Volkan Çıdam, Esra Demir, and Hilmi Tezgör, with whom I always find love and understanding.

The biggest hug goes to my family. My loving husband, Ali Ilıcak, gave me the push when it was the time to leave the work aside and *resist* during the Gezi resistance in 2013, and he also encouraged me when it was the time to *leave* so that I can safeguard my scholarly work. My dearest sons, Ara Fikret and Nazım Aren, were my only joy and happiness during brutal 2015 and 2016 in Turkey. They were also my hope and strength to start a new life as a forty-year-old exile in Berlin. Thanks to them, I can easily say "home is where your children are." I cannot possibly express my indebtedness to my mother and father, Vartan and Meri Maksudyan, who gave me love, strength, and self-esteem all through my life. My favorite and only sister, Sibel, is my best friend and better half. I hope I can write a third book dedicated to her.

And thank you, Berlin—you became my home and provided me the peace and freedom to think and write!

A Note on Transliteration

THROUGHOUT THE BOOK I have used the anglicized versions of most Ottoman Turkish and Arabic words rather than writing them in italics or transliterating them, the criterion being inclusion in the *Merriam-Webster English Dictionary*. Hence, I use *agha*, *bey*, *ghazi*, *mufti*, *pasha*, *sharia*, *ulema*, *vizier*, *wakf*—but *efendi* instead of *effendi* and *kadi* instead of *cadi*. In place-names I follow English spellings as well, except for place-names that constitute part of the name of a book or a publisher in the notes; hence, Istanbul but İstanbul Üniversitesi.

Transliterations are based on a modified version of the system used in the *International Journal of Middle East Studies*. Modern Turkish orthography has been used for the transliteration of Ottoman Turkish with certain modifications. In the main body of the text and in the identification of authors, I avoid all the diacritics associated with transliteration, namely, underdots on consonants and macrons on vowels. The exception is the use for ‘ayns and hamzas when they appear in the middle of a word, which I indicate with an apostrophe (‘). Since modern Turkish no longer uses hatted vowels (â), I also omitted most of them from the text.

Ottoman Children and Youth during World War I

INTRODUCTION

The Children's Version

AKIRA KUROSAWA's amazing film *Rashômon* (1950) tells a story from twelfth-century Japan, in which a samurai and his wife are attacked by the notorious bandit Tajomaru, and the samurai ends up dead. Tajomaru is captured shortly afterward and is put on trial, but his story and the wife's are so completely different that a psychic is brought in to allow the murdered man to give his own testimony. He tells yet another completely different story. Finally, a woodcutter who found the body reveals that he saw the whole thing, and his version is again utterly different from the others. The film reconstructs the "same story" from the perspective of these four different actors-witnesses, bandit, wife, dead husband, and woodcutter. Although each witness sincerely believes in the truth of his or her testimony, all these individual versions remarkably contradict one another. So *Rashômon* asks the intriguing question of who is telling the truth. Or else, whose version is truer?

Following the analogy, depending on the questions and interests of the "interrogator" and also the cooperation and frankness of the "witnesses," the historian is able to recover only a version of the "event" and eventually only a partial history. This book is the product of the conviction that enumeration and multiplication of accounts relating to the same events, eras, and processes contribute to an enriched perception and comprehension of the essentially misty substance of history. This book, focusing on the testimonies of children and youth in the

First World War, strives to regard children as legitimate witnesses to construct a new history.

From a global historiographic perspective, the initial works about the Great War were political and military analyses, attempting to construct a chronological and event-based account of four years of war. In the decades immediately following the war, numerous volumes were published on different fronts of the war, day-to-day analysis of the political administration, and causal relations between actions and reactions. In time, diplomatic and political history literature became more and more voluminous, though there was a shift in the aftermath of the Second World War. New research agendas took into account demographic developments, economic trends, the social effects of mass mobilization, and the role of capital accumulation and imperial rivalry in the outbreak of the war. These works were the early attempts toward an "economic and social history" of the First World War. In the 1980s, the passage to the cultural turn was quite smooth and had its echo in the historiography of the Great War. Historians became more interested in what happened to different groups of ordinary people during wartime. They focused on the home front and civilians and on issues such as memory, discourse, and "war culture." Histories taking into consideration the role of women, and then children, were produced in the past couple of decades, in line with the enlargement of the actors and scenes.

From Military to Social History of the Ottoman Great War

As Erik J. Zürcher notes in his 1996 article "Between Death and Desertion: The Experience of the Ottoman Soldier in World War I," there has been an attempt in Ottoman historiography since the 1970s "to write the war's social history, to concentrate on the war experience, viewing the experience of the First World War from below, through the eyes of the men who served in the trenches, or people who drove the ambulances, the women who filled the shells in the factories."[1] Zürcher's several essays on the Ottoman conscription and the resistance against it have contributed greatly to our understanding of the social aspects of the military dimensions of the Great War, in this way bringing military history in touch with the everyday experiences of ordinary people.[2]

Yücel Yanıkdağ's research on prisoners of war (POWs), malingering, mental illness, and soldiers' fear, courage, and masculinity is an alternative (social) reading within an essentially military experience.[3] He discusses war and medicine in terms of the wider sociocultural context and in this way transcends the boundaries of military life and the temporal boundaries of wartime itself. As frequently used by social historians of World War I, the documents relating to POWs have the power to capture soldiers' voices. Interrogations of Ottoman POWs and letters to Ottoman POWs and newspapers produced within the prisons have been important to write war's history from below.[4] Wartime diaries of the Ottoman soldiers, which have been for a long time considered to be extremely rare, have also recently become quite numerous and one of the main sources for Ottoman historians specializing in First World War studies.[5] These sources were used to enter the life of the ordinary soldier in the trenches.[6]

These works can be called *milito-social* histories, where the main actors were only men and soldiers and the narrative was mostly set in the front. Beşikçi also conceptualized his recent work on deserters as a military problem becoming a social issue.[7]

Militarization and Propaganda

Historical research on mobilization, the militarization of society, and the changing features of the wartime state apparatus has contributed to our understanding of the social aspects of the war. It has provided a glance into the home front and civilians, albeit focusing on military history. One of the pioneers in the field, Mehmet Beşikçi's *Ottoman Mobilization of Manpower in the First World War* (2012), discusses how wartime mobilization turned the Ottoman state into a more centralized, authoritarian, and nationalist entity. As I will discuss in more detail in chapter 3, the militarization of society had a huge impact on the lives of the children as well. Ottoman Muslim children were part of the military mobilization through the formation of paramilitary scouting organizations.

Works on mobilization and militarization also underline that the Committee of Union and Progress (CUP) government exerted strict control over the public sphere and associational life, if not directly shaped voluntary initiatives.[8] Public activities and visibility were limited to fund-raising for military activities, propaganda aimed at mobilizing the home front, and philanthropy for soldiers' families and other "deserving needy." Arts and propaganda were also deeply intertwined in the period. Literary propaganda along with painting and cinema were also used as sites of mobilization.[9] The National Defense League played an active role in mobilizing visual culture for propaganda purposes. The league's commissions during this period include Mehmed Ruhi's postcard series on mobilization, presenting the entry into the war within a festival ambience and as a convivial gathering. His postcards also featured many children, who were depicted not only as happy and supportive of their male relatives' conscription, but also as integral to the Ottoman war effort.[10] However, researching wartime propaganda material and public events exclusively might be biased in exaggerating the extent of the militarization and nationalization among ordinary people, given the authoritarian pressures over the press and public opinion. Moreover, non-Muslim Ottomans are completely silenced and invisible in these sources.

Relevant for the purposes of this book, Muslim children and orphans of martyrs (*evlad-ı şüheda*) and soldiers became the primary objects of state philanthropy for propaganda and nationalist purposes. Family members serving in the army transformed children's public identity and reconstructed their relationship vis-à-vis the state. *Evlad-ı şüheda* became a catchphrase and an unavoidable refrain both in the press and in state discourses pertaining to children. It was as if the war made every man a soldier and every child an orphan of a martyr. The foundational myth and admission criteria for state orphanages (*darüleytams*), as discussed in chapter 1, make it clear that every new institution had to matter within the tight boundaries of war and mobilization. The state also put children into a hierarchy with reference to family members in the army. Through organizations such as the Orphans and Widows Aid Fund (Eytam ve Eramil Sandığı) and through state subsidies for soldier families (*muinsiz aile*), children were rewarded both as the living legacy of the dead and as symbols of sacrifice and heroism. Through material and symbolic gestures for their families, the state appeared to pay tribute to deceased fathers. Symbolic honoring took the form of medals, memorials, and ceremonies.

Home-Front Suffering

The interest in the home front and the daily experiences of ordinary people expanded the field of the Ottoman social history of World War I quite significantly. The First World War was a different experience from earlier forms of war effort. Both contemporaries and historians described it as a "total war" that required the most comprehensive mobilization of all members of society, regardless of age or gender, as well as extensive resource allocation for the war.[11] Millions of men were conscripted and served for longer terms in the military. The war lasted nearly four years for the Ottoman society, from October 1914 to November 1918. However, many problems having their origins in the war continued to have an impact in the postwar period.

The impact of mobilization on a massive scale, its disruptive effects for the society and economy, and other catastrophic effects of the war—in other words, "home-front suffering"—have become a new popular part of Ottoman history over the past decade. In her pioneering work, Elizabeth Thompson offers a detailed discussion of wartime famine, diseases, and mortality in Syrian provinces of the Ottoman Empire. The extreme requisitioning powers of the government of grain and livestock put the agricultural products and farm animals at the disposal of the Ministry of War. Farmwork ceased with the depletion of the workforce. Lack of mechanization, labor shortages, and requisitioning of animals caused a sharp decrease in agricultural production. By 1916 economic infrastructure was devastated, rationing was extensive yet insufficient, and food shortages turned into enormous famine in parts of the empire. Melanie Tanielian has focused on the issues of food shortages, famine, and disease in Beirut and Mount Lebanon.[12] After Elizabeth Thompson's inspiring work *Colonial Citizens*, there has been new research on how certain localities experienced the war as a social unit. Çiçek's book on Syria under Cemal Pasha's governorship, Martin Strohmeier's work on Medina, and the work of Yuval Ben-Bassat and Dotan Halevy on Gaza and Jaffa are among these works.[13] Yiğit Akın's recent book *When the War Came Home* (2018) is the most exhaustive account of the experience of the war on the Ottoman home front. Akın provides a detailed account of mass mobilization and the destruction it caused on the home front in the form of shortages, large-scale suffering of civilians, population displacement, and ethnic cleansing of non-Muslims.

All these works have been a great inspiration in developing the understanding that the agency of different sections of civilians became increasingly visible owing to the harsh circumstances of the war years. As discussed in more detail in chapter 4, the war's devastating impacts on children not only made them readily discernible in archives and contemporary press, but also opened new channels for them to exert agency. The survival sagas of Armenian children are situated within this paradox of harsh circumstances and empowerment.

Women's War

As the idea of the "total war" came to encompass the unarmed and nonbelligerent sections of the society as well, women's experiences of the First World War also grew into a new field of Ottoman social history. Women, as heads of households with no males present, as workers producing for the ever-increasing demands of the army (such as manufacturing uniforms, shoes, and linen), or as founders or members of voluntary associations, started to have more contact with the state and complained about more intrusion into their daily lives.[14] Nicole A. N. M. van Os's works from the 1990s onward have focused on how Ottoman Muslim women contributed to the military effort as civilians through associations, journals, and other public appearances. Her research on the impact of direct financial aid to soldiers' families (in the form of a monthly "separation allowance") discusses Muslim women's relative empowerment vis-à-vis the state, although the distribution of aid was stained with injustice and corruption.[15]

Akın's research based on Muslim women's petitions also underlines that women's petitions and telegrams were a new mode of interaction between Ottoman Muslim women and state authorities based on a perceived understanding of mutual obligations and expectations. Referring to themselves as soldiers' wives and mothers, Ottoman Muslim women complained bitterly about pervasive poverty and hunger, state requisitioning and confiscation, and the harsh wartime taxation policies of the government. Elif Mahir Metinsoy's recent book *Ottoman Women during World War I* also focuses on the suffering and the agency of Muslim women, aspiring to give voice especially to "ordinary women," as opposed to works on elite segments of society. One exceptional work on the lives of Ottoman women during World War I is Zeynep Kutluata's dissertation, which differs from most of the above-mentioned works in its multireligious definition of the adjective *Ottoman*. Her chapter on the petitions of Armenian women who demanded justice and amnesty for their arrested and deported family members is a rare example in Ottoman historiography of giving voice to Ottoman non-Muslim women and situating the genocide within the war chronology.[16]

As I have noted in my previous book, historians of children and youth are especially indebted to feminist historical scholarship. Within the historiography of the First World War as well, the efforts to construct new narratives that treat women "as historical subjects" have been opening the way for historians of children and youth in order to construct a proper historical identity for children, one that recognizes their agency.[17]

Situating the Armenian Genocide within World War I Historiography

It is noted in World War I historiography that the war blurred the boundaries between the military and civilian realms, bringing together soldiers' experiences at the front with the daily life of people on the home front.[18] Nevertheless, the divide between the actual fighting and the home front was not so clear for Ottoman societies during the war.

Ottoman Anatolia appeared geographically distant from the warfront, yet the Gallipoli campaign changed the configuration in western Anatolia, large tracts of eastern and northeastern Anatolia became a war zone between the Ottomans and the Russians, and war raged over Palestine through 1917 and beyond. If one includes the rebellions (such as in Hijaz in 1916), occupations (of Iraq after 1917), deportations and massacres of Ottoman Armenians, Greeks (*Rums*), and Assyrians, and lawlessness reigning throughout the empire, the war was also on the home front.

Large segments of society suffered from forced displacement, ethnic tensions, and massacres. The deportation and massacres of non-Muslims brought another dimension to the home-front experience. The state waged a war against its own citizens. Uprooted Armenian refugees were everywhere, on the roads, hiding in the villages, piled in camps. Civilian Muslim populations became perpetrators and took part in violence and looting. Çetinkaya claims that atrocity propaganda and boycott movements, initiated during the Balkan Wars, were yet another "front" in the "total war," playing a vital role in the demonization of enemies (both within and without) and, thus, in legitimizing the elimination of Ottoman non-Muslim communities.[19] Enmity and fighting were transferred from the war front to the home front.

The new research on the Armenian genocide increasingly advocates the necessity of situating it within the historiography of World War I as well as part of European, if not world, history.[20] The research and findings of this book attest to the fact that it is impossible to write a children's history of the Ottoman First World War without allocating a significant portion to the lives, experiences, and agency of Armenian children. The fate of the genocide orphans, specifically discussed in chapter 4, is quite central to the general narrative arc of the book.

Children as Pawns

Despite serious weaknesses, the Ottoman state succeeded in mobilizing hundreds of thousands of civilians on short notice, building an army of about 2.9 million troops.[21] Children, especially young boys, were not exempt from the war effort, combat, and fighting. It is difficult to ascertain the number of underage soldiers in the Ottoman Army. However, in October 1916, the government passed a temporary law for the "correction" of registered birth dates of "actually military age" children.[22] The heads of enlistment offices were given the authority to conscript those boys who "seemed" suitable for military service. In this period, it is likely that a large number of boys as young as fifteen or sixteen were conscripted into the army.[23]

The combatant states not only conscripted child soldiers, but also developed and promoted the idea of mass heroism to tap the economic resources of child laborers and consumers. Children of both sexes assumed the places vacated by grown-up men. These war workers were not laboring children but little adults. Teenage boys and girls were called upon to assume responsibility for absent adults and sacrifice for the nation, but they also figured as independent agents. Ottoman children between the ages of eight and sixteen were extensively involved in the realms of agriculture, manufacturing, and shopkeeping. Many children were employed as farmworkers, as "soldiers of the soil," since food was a necessary weapon. Indeed, school-age children were already working in agriculture extensively on the eve of World War I. However, as the war meant the total mobilization of adult men, the younger population became the main labor force. Child labor in the industrial sector also became indispensable. In the coal mines of Zonguldak, the manpower shortages already evident during the Balkan Wars became worse during the world war. After 1915 those individuals available for "unskilled" mine work were "children, old men, malingerers unfit for military service."[24] Children in industries requiring semiskilled work were also of vital importance. Official and semiofficial organizations, such as the Islamic Society for the Employment of Women and the Society for the Employment of Wives and Children of Veterans and Martyrs, founded at the instigation of the War Ministry, encouraged the recruitment of women and children in the urban manufacturing sector.[25] Armenian boys and girls working as laborers (*amele*) in the yarn factory of Adana were exempted from deportation orders until replacements could be found from among the Muslim child population.[26]

Children also appeared in propaganda and mobilization efforts as symbols of virtue, sacrifice, and patriotism (see chapter 3). Through novel forms of representation, such as boy scouting, they were portrayed as icons of heroism, nationalism, and ideal citizens to mobilize the population for the war effort. *Evlad-ı şüheda* in particular became public figures, frequently portrayed in state discourses of war propaganda, moral discourse, and literature as courageous, patriotic members of the nation (see chapter 1). New official celebrations were organized around and about children supposedly to create awareness about the needs of children, but also to make use of them in war propaganda. A newly introduced Students' Feast (Mektepliler Bayramı) was first celebrated in 1915, while an additional Children's Feast (Çocuklar Bayramı) was organized in 1916.[27] Children took part in official ceremonies, such as the sultan's inauguration anniversary and the welcoming of German emperor Wilhelm II (1859–1941) in Istanbul. They marched in front of soldiers, sang military songs, and offered flowers to higher officials.[28] By propagating images of children's alleged enthusiasm for war, the Ottoman state hoped to encourage mobilization. The "nationalist spirit" of children would purportedly reinforce selflessness and courage in soldiers.

Children as Agents

The historical and cultural perspective toward children in a society is one of the most important pillars of the discrimination against children. In the eighteenth century, the romanticist movement upheld the prevalent claim that children are vulnerable, innocent, and ignorant and idealized them as singular beings, as if they were irrelevant in society. Since childhood is viewed as a period of dependence in both legal and biological terms, it becomes easy to disregard children as social actors. Children are thus seen mainly as passive, and their cultural presence is rarely recognized. The foremost novelist in Turkey, Yaşar Kemal (1923–2015), was in this respect incredibly ahead of his time—as with so many other issues. He made a series of journalistic interviews with street children, working children, migrant children, and poor children in 1975: "I don't treat children like kids. If I have a friendship, a relationship with a child, then he or she is my friend, not a child. I don't see them as kids, I don't treat them like a *different human species*. Why? I never believed that it is right to treat children as kids. They are *fully fledged human beings*."[29]

In parallel with the attempt to reformulate and expand the subject, scope, and actors of history writing, there is a growing body of literature on the history of children and youth in the war.[30] Based on the assumption that children's experiences and witnessing made a significant contribution to our historical knowledge, my research aspires to add new dimensions to the historiography of the First World War. This book delineates the variegated experiences and involvement of Ottoman children and youth in the war effort with an empowering approach that recognizes their agency. Ottoman children were engaged in every facet of total war. I argue that children were legitimate partakers of, actors in, and witnesses to Ottoman political action and experience in the war. They became active agents as soldiers, wage earners, farmers, and artisans. They were not simply passive victims or casualties. Ottoman children acquired new identities during the war years and discovered new forms of agency. Rebelling against their orphanage directors or trade masters, marching and singing proudly with their scouting companies, and making long-distance journeys to find their families made them increasingly visible in the public space.

They also played a part in constituting the meaning of the war through their own responses and reinterpretations. They directly contributed to the propaganda and mobilization efforts as symbolic heroes and orphans of martyrs. Ottoman children from different ethnic and religious identities embodied and reproduced internal political crises and rivalries as actors in and targets of nationalist politics. The imagination of childhood and the experience of children differed in the Ottoman Empire from other combatant states. The multiethnic and multireligious structure of the Ottoman Empire and the contested meaning of "nation" complicated the definitions of what Ottoman children represented and stood for. "The child" was not a universal category throughout the Ottoman Empire, one that transcended the particularism and ethnoreligious differentiation that characterized the polity. The CUP government more strongly established the Muslim and Turkic identity of the state, leading to the extermination of the non-Muslim population. In that sense, I emphasize the necessity of situating the Armenian genocide within First World War studies.

Children were also the primary witnesses of the war experience as survivors and veterans in the aftermath of the war. Focusing on the experience of the war in the Ottoman lands and especially on how total mobilization altered the "lives behind the lines" through the testimony of children brings to light such major issues as (lack of) education, workforce shortages, economic dire straits, ethnic hatred, and genocide. I aspire to delineate not only the impact of these phenomena on children's lives, but also how these dynamics were interpreted and shaped by the children themselves. In a sense, the extent of children's agency throughout the war years created "precocious adults" from underage children.

Chapter 1, "The Great War and State Orphanages (*Darüleytams*)," describes what exactly the state did in the field of philanthropy for children and how children responded to these activities. Welfare policies toward children's services such as orphanages, clinics, and children's programs significantly increased owing to and despite the emergencies of the war. A large network of state orphanages (*darüleytams*) was established from early 1915 onward under the newly formed Directorate of Orphanages. Although the directorate kept underlining that they prioritized the children of martyrs, veterans (fathers killed or wounded during combat), and soldiers, the *darüleytams* were also crucial in the context of the Armenian genocide, as innumerable Armenian boys and girls were given to the authority of the Directorate of Orphanages, to be raised as Muslim Turks. As opposed to the official and institutional views on the "progress" of the orphanages in the four-year span of the war, this chapter elaborates more on the personal experiences of children. I concentrate on their deprivations and suffering, along with their resistance and revolt.

Chapter 2, "Ottoman Orphan Apprentices in Germany," provides a history of a large-scale and long-distance Ottoman child-displacement project from the perspective of refugee children, whose lives were changed forever because of that journey. About a thousand orphan boys were sent in 1917 and 1918 to Germany to be apprenticed in handicrafts, mines, and farms. In an attempt to bring forward the voices and experiences of the orphan boys themselves, this chapter describes the details of their long but also hopeful journeys to Germany and their lives in German masters' households or in workplaces. The attempt to reconstruct the personal experiences of the boys also delineates the motives, engagement, and expectations of the Ottoman and German sides.

Chapter 3, "Children as Agents and Targets of Nationalist Politics," puts forward how the Turkish nationalist policies of the CUP exacerbated tensions between children of different ethnic and religious origins. With a short overview of the militarization of the civilian realm, I discuss the paramilitary educational schemes for youth and the emergence and suppression of non-Muslim boy-scouting organizations. Nationalistic socialization motivated children and youth in urban centers to play out nationalist and religious rivalries at the street level by playing "war games," building up gangs, and attacking rivals in real acts of violence. Although interethnic and interreligious conflicts preceded the war, World War I led all communities to fight different battles and dream of different futures. Ottoman children were agents and targets of this nationalist politics. They were not only functional in representing certain nationalist ideals and future dreams, but they were themselves active in assuming new roles. Children absorbed the social and political realities of their time and had no difficulty in replicating them in their games, fights, friendships, and enmities.

Chapter 4, "Survival of Children during the Armenian Genocide," provides a detailed account of the survival strategies of Armenian children during the genocide and its aftermath with a perspective that resists victimizing them. Available literature on the Armenian genocide is denser on issues of death and suffering than on survival and resilience. Recent research on the conversion to Islam, forced "adoption," and abduction of women and children is more interested in survivors and survival but does not necessarily take into account Armenian actors' agency. Constructing the history from children's point of view, one notes that Armenian children were not completely passive in this picture. They had strategies of endurance and resistance. In their struggle to resist death, Armenian children took the initiative, made personal decisions, and manipulated their circumstances, thus becoming active agents. Survivor testimonies in different forms bring into light the "talent" and resilience, together with the self-confidence, of children trying to stay alive. Through playing games, getting into different sorts of adventures, and building friendships, children tried to cope with the death and loss of loved ones, along with holding on to life. Heroic adventure narratives determined how they made sense of their survival.

As these short summaries suggest, the book focuses on four different groups of children: thousands of orphans in state orphanages (*darüleytams*), apprentice boys who were sent to Germany, children and youth in urban centers who reproduced rival nationalist ideologies, and finally Armenian children who survived the genocide. These four groups were chosen for a number of reasons. First, they are the ones who have the potential to write and revise the social history of the war from a different angle. The history of children and youth is relevant as much as it adds to our understanding of already studied phenomena. Following the analogy of *Rashômon*, a new witness is welcome only when she or he offers a paradigmatic shift. Chapter 1, for instance, by listening to the voices of children in orphanages, instead of repeating institutional discourses, puts forward the nonnegligible role of state orphanages in the aftermath of the Armenian genocide. Second, looking specifically for children in the archives has the potential to bring into light thus far dark episodes of the period in question. The protagonists of chapter 2, in that respect, easily found their way into the book as an unexplored affair and "original" contribution to the scholarship on the Ottoman experience of World War I. Third, and most important, from a historiographical point of view, my book views children as capable of social action, with the potential to be at the center of the narrative. These four groups are in the same constellation because it was possible to follow and document their agency in several forms of sources.

Speaking of documentation, in chapter 1, I work with material from the Prime Ministry's Ottoman Archives (Istanbul), parliamentary discussions from 1919, and autobiographical accounts of orphan children themselves. In chapter 2, the main sources are the Prime Ministry's Ottoman Archives and the Politisches Archiv des Auswärtigen Amtes (Berlin), together with contemporary press and personal narratives. In chapter 3, I use Ottoman records, memoirs, contemporary press, and the papers of youth organizations. In chapter 4, I mainly rely on survival narratives in different forms (diaries, memoirs, oral histories) and also reports of the humanitarian agencies and personnel working for the relief and rescue of Armenian children. Still, the book does not promise a complete picture of all different childhoods. It is true that urban children appear more than rural ones, and some chapters inevitably focus more on boys—and not so much on girls.

As I discuss in the conclusion, the lives of the last Ottoman child generation were connected to the lives of the first postwar generation, while the demise of the empire was connected to new nation-states. Those individuals who founded the nation-states of the post-Ottoman era were the children and youth of the First World War.

I

The Great War and State Orphanages (*Darüleytams*)

İsmail Mahir Efendi, the first director of orphanages, recounted the moment that he decided to establish state orphanages in the following manner. A soldier came to İsmail Mahir Efendi in dire straits. He had previously lost his wife, would soon go to the Gallipoli front, and was in a difficult situation regarding his two children, with no one to whom he could entrust them. İsmail Mahir Efendi told the soldier to bring the children to him, that the children would be in good hands and that he should feel at ease. In justifying the necessity of the institution to the CUP state cadres, he claimed that when the father did not worry about those children left behind, he would fight with his heart and soul in the war. Either genuinely made up by İsmail Mahir Efendi or formulated by more prominent Unionists, this discourse succinctly projected the perception and representation of children in wartime Ottoman propaganda, along with the fact that wartime institutions and policies were legitimized solely by war and mobilization, leaving other relevant factors in the dark.[1]

Darüleytam in the Ottoman language is a general term used for "orphanage"; however, in the institutional context, it refers to a large network of state orphanages, which were opened in the course of the First World War and remained open until 1922–23.[2] In other words, it is of utmost importance to note that these institutions were direct products of the Ottoman war effort and total mobilization. The General Directorate of Orphanages (Darüleytam Müdüriyet-i Umumiyesi) explained its "reason for establishment" with direct reference to the care and education of the "orphans of martyrs."[3] Yet the Ottoman institutions for children were not defined by rigid boundaries, and many half-orphans and nonorphans were sheltered in these establishments. In practice, the inmates of the institution were beyond children whose fathers died in the war effort. There were children of serving soldiers, children of invalid veterans (*malul gazi*), orphans of nonmilitary families, and even children with living parents, though in extreme poverty. Moreover, the large network of *darüleytams* was opened not only because of the circumstances of the war but also thanks to the confiscation of educational and philanthropic institutions of the Entente Powers. Despite the obvious silence of the archival documentation and the historiography on the subject, the *darüleytams* were also crucial in the context of the Armenian genocide, as innumerable Armenian orphans in the provinces were entrusted to the authority of the Directorate of Orphanages.

In this chapter, I will first provide a brief history of the Ottoman state's relief mechanisms for the orphans, where I also delve into the history of (or failure in) opening orphanages to compete with the missionaries, especially regarding their success among Armenians. Based on Ottoman archival material, official regulations, parliamentary discussions, ongoing inspections, press reports, and petitions and complaints written by children and their guardians, the main part discusses the primary characteristics of *darüleytams*. I will then provide a discussion of the important role of *darüleytams* in "recycling" Armenian orphans in the context of the Armenian genocide. The next section focuses on several experimental projects of the Unionist government concerning orphan children. Both in the form of orphanages in the pillaged properties of Armenians or Ottoman Greeks (Rum) and in the form of orphan colonies in their emptied villages and towns, the government attempted to raise these children forcefully as Muslims and Turks. The chapter concludes with the closing of the institutions at the end of the war.

Ottoman Institutions for the Orphans

The Ottoman state did not traditionally have centralized and institutional care mechanisms for needy children. In accordance with

Islamic rulings, the state Treasury financially supported both individual households and religious endowments that agreed to provide for orphan, poor, and destitute children. This customary noninvolvement policy of the state changed substantially throughout the nineteenth century, namely, during the Ottoman modernization era (generally called the Tanzimat era, 1839–76), which ushered in a range of reforms in the penal code, property and personal rights, the tax structure, and education.[4] In this period, the state introduced a wide range of new institutions targeting the welfare and education of orphans and destitute children. These new organizations included a large and imperial network of orphanages (*ıslahhane*) providing serious vocational education, a foundling asylum (*ırzahane*), a children's hospital (Hamidiye Etfal Hastanesi), and a poorhouse (Darülaceze) with special children's wards.[5] Despite all these promising and new undertakings, Ottoman state welfare could accommodate only a few thousand destitute children—in other words, a sheer minority.

The usage of the term *darüleytam* with reference to a planned state institution occurred in the late 1890s, in the context of the Armenian massacres of 1894–96 and the competition Abdülhamid II perceived vis-à-vis the missionaries. In 1899 the ministers of foreign affairs and education claimed that "foreigners would have no legitimate right to interfere" if the orphans in the provinces were educated in prospective state orphanages.[6] In May 1899, a small commission, made up of those same ministers, Tevfik Pasha and Zühdü Pasha, legal adviser of the Sublime Porte Hakkı Beyefendi, and the head of secondary schools, Celal Bey, convened to work on the establishment of "special houses of education for orphans" (*eytama mahsus darütterbiyeler*) in the eastern provinces "for the Ottoman children of all creeds" so that the pernicious work of the missionaries could be stopped.[7] The curriculum would respond to the needs of all religious faiths in order to have a "mixed and united" (*muhteliten ve müttehiden*) body of children, in this way saving children from "foreign indoctrination" (*telkinat-ı hariciyye*).[8] Despite a long series of orders and plans from the Porte to enter into the field of orphan relief in order to compete with the missionaries, the scheme of instituting orphanages in the provinces was soon reduced to opening "just one orphanage" at a central place. In August 1899, the Ministries of Education and Foreign Affairs proposed the establishment of an orphanage for boys in the capital. Given the impossibility of bringing the entire provincial orphan population to Istanbul, an urban center already having problems caring for destitute children, two categories of orphan boys were privileged: those boys who were "in the hands of the missionaries" and the ones who had no family or relatives to care for them.[9]

The *darüleytam* was then supposed to be opened in Üsküdar. Land belonging to the heirs of Ahmed Eyüb Pasha in Acıbadem was considered appropriate. The expropriation of 125 acres of vineyards and arable land was agreed upon in return for 2,500 Ottoman liras. The orphanage would admit orphan and destitute boys only from the provinces, ages six to ten. The reference to "provinces" was a direct reference to the Armenian massacres in the eastern *vilayet*s. The number of children to be brought was thought to be as large as twenty-five hundred. The plan was to construct five separate buildings, housing four to five hundred orphans each. According to the budget prepared, the construction of the building would require 90,000 liras, and annual education and training expenditures were calculated at 50,000 liras.[10] The Ministry of Education had a chronic budgetary deficit, owing to its excess of employees and expenses. The necessary amount could not possibly be met by the ministry. Nevertheless, the project was especially crucial for the Ministry of Foreign Affairs and the sultan himself. The Treasury assumed the purchase of the land and also the construction costs, for which it would provide 750 liras on a weekly basis.[11] In the *Yearbook of Education* (*Maarif Salnamesi*) for 1319/1901, it was noted that the *darüleytam* was almost ready to open its doors to its charges.[12] Despite all this documentation on the progress of the project, the orphanage in Acıbadem did not open in the following years. This failure might be related either to financial problems or to the realization of the utmost difficulty of the original plan (of bringing Armenian orphans from the provinces to the capital). What we know for certain is that Abdülhamid II finally sponsored and opened with fanfare a much smaller-scale orphanage. Darülhayr-ı Ali was opened in 1903 in Zeynep Hanım Mansion in Vezneciler (Istanbul).[13] The idea to have a religiously mixed group of children was abandoned, and the institution had a predominantly Muslim character. Some non-Muslim children were converted before entering the orphanage.[14] After the dethronement of Abdülhamid II and heated debates in the parliament, the CUP government closed the orphanage on 14 September 1909.[15]

Opening of State Orphanages

Either unschooled or employed, either from the city or from the country, either rich or poor, innumerable children shared the experience of orphanhood, losing one or both parents. War's devastating impact on children was to create a huge mass of orphans, as hundreds of thousands of children lost their fathers and providers to the war. On their monographs of different aspects of Ottoman home-front suffering, Akın and Mahir Metinsoy note that tens of thousands of unprotected children were starving and wandering the streets, doing anything for food.[16] The number of Armenian orphans of the genocide alone reached into the hundreds of thousands, probably around four hundred thousand. Based on a report prepared by the Children's Protection Society (Himaye-i Etfal Cemiyeti) after the war, there were two hundred thousand orphans in the country.[17]

The organization of *darüleytams* was devised and prepared by Minister of Education Ahmet Şükrü Bey. Enver and Talat Pashas had supported the implementation of the idea. The issues regarding the administration of the orphanages, the preparation of their programs, and the establishment of their principles and purposes had been delegated to the deputy of Kastamonu and the director of the Girls Teacher Seminary (Darülmuallimat), İsmail Mahir Efendi.[18] Kara Kemal from the CUP's central committee was also active in the initial period of opening orphanages, especially in Istanbul.[19] In other words, the establishment and administration of these institutions for the orphans were under the patronage of the CUP and, thus, reflected the Unionist preferences and priorities as a party activity.[20] This point explains the essentially Turkish and Muslim character of the *darüleytams*. It represented a departure from their Tanzimat equivalents, *ıslahhane*s, stressing the multiethnic, multireligious, and multilingual character of the empire, yet a continuity with Darülhayr-ı Ali.

A Network of Confiscated Properties

In both legal documentation and propaganda material, the discourse on orphans of martyrs or soldiers leaving their children before going to the front was very strong. Almost all the regulations relating to the orphanages made reference to the orphans of martyrs in their first article. The provisional regulations of the orphanages dated 1917 stated as the first article that these institutions would educate and train "children of martyrs and orphans" and raise them as useful members of the country.[21] The propaganda articles of the CUP that appeared in the press, also without exception, praised the sacred duty of the institution for the children of martyrs.[22] It is true that these institutions were primarily opened because the Unionists were facing an unprecedented pressing need. However, the orphanages also owed their existence to the confiscation of educational institutions of the Entente Powers, which had been appropriated as a result of the unilateral abolition of the capitulations.[23] The abolition resulted in the confiscation of consular buildings of warring states such as Britain, France, Russia, and Serbia, together with commercial (train and tram companies), financial (banks), and educational enterprises of the citizens of these countries. Educational structures, including buildings, inventories, and staff, had been taken over from foreign relief agencies—mostly missionaries.[24] These schools included, among others, (French) St. Joseph and Notre Dame de Sion in Kadıköy, the Dominican School in Yedikule,[25] Jesuit and Sœurs de la Charité schools, the Russian Monastery, several Russian schools in Beyoğlu and Galata,[26] and a number of schools and buildings belonging to the British.[27] Foreign (Entente) schools were assigned "directors-in-charge" (*mesul müdür*). Numerous schools and institutions opposed this practice, but they were given the excuse that these practices were "required by law," or, rather, the repeal of law.[28] The CUP government also defended itself, claiming that they were used for a philanthropic cause—though generosity was not always the case.

In addition to Entente buildings, many Armenian schools, churches, and monasteries were occupied and used as orphanages, as they had to be abandoned with the expulsion and massacres of Ottoman Armenians.[29] Based on the official report of the Political Council of the Patriarchate sent to the government in July 1919, around twenty-five hundred churches, four hundred monasteries, two thousand schools, and land and rental properties belonging to the patriarchate were confiscated during the war.[30] The American-Hellenic Society argued that "the forced sale" of the Greek orphanage on Prinkipo (Büyükada) for £3,000 instead of £30,000 proved the tendency of the "German-Turkish alliance" to confiscate the property of Ottoman Greeks. The forcible seizure of yet another trade school in Halki Island also supported that claim.[31] More important was the decision the Ministerial Council made in 1916.[32] According to this judgment, the rights of ownership of the monasteries were recognized only as covering the ground enclosed within the walls. All the property outside of the walls, whether forest or land or other, was regarded as public property owned by the state. The application of the decision stripped the patriarchates, communities, and monasteries of their property.

State Orphanages in Istanbul

The first orphanages were opened in Kadıköy in January 1915 within the occupied premises of the famous French Collège de St. Joseph and Notre Dame de Sion.[33] Both of the buildings had been confiscated from the French Catholic missionaries.[34] The orphanages gave precedence to boys older than seven and girls of diverse age groups who had no living parents. Kadıköy Orphanage for boys had only twenty-six orphans when it was opened.[35] In time, it became one of the largest orphanages, providing industrial training to seven hundred to one thousand boys. The girls orphanage in Notre Dame de Sion also had an ambitious program, including a nursery and a kindergarten. Based on the plan of the directorate, the girls orphanage would have four different sections. The first branch would be a child-care department (nursery) of two hundred boys and girls who were two to three years old. The second branch was a kindergarten of one hundred girls and boys between the ages of four and six. The third branch was a primary school for girls over seven. The teaching period was six years, and three hundred girls would be admitted. The fourth branch was a vocational school for girls. It would accept one hundred girls, and the duration of the education was three years.[36] By December 1915, twenty orphanages were already operating and admitting orphans.

After the establishment of the first orphanages in Kadıköy, announcements appeared in the newspapers in May 1915 to "attract" needy children. Despite the official declarations that the institution would target the orphans of martyrs, the announcements welcomed a wider group of children. In addition to children whose fathers were "martyred" in the Balkan Wars or the ongoing war, children who lost their mothers and whose fathers joined the army as well as poor girls and boys were invited to apply to the headquarters of the directorate in Kadıköy.[37] The question of "priority" was actually the biggest debate in the operations of the directorate. The minutes of the Ottoman parliament (Meclis-i Mebusan) prove that many serious (operational and financial) problems of the institution were left aside, and the discussion of the "acceptance criteria" or rather hierarchy never ceased. Based on the resolution reached in the beginning of 1916, the hierarchy would be as follows: orphans of martyrs, children of invalid veterans, children without mothers (and relatives) whose fathers were conscripted, and children with a single living parent who did not have the means to look after them.[38] In 1917 the acceptance criteria were further altered with the enactment of the law on the foundation of the Directorate of Orphanages. Based on the new regulations, the priority would be given to the children of martyrs and invalids and to the children of "refugees" (*muhacir ve mülteci*) in dire straits. Orphans (of nonmartyrs) and other poor and destitute children would come after them.[39] Still, based on the detailed list of children in the state orphanages presented during the budget discussions of 1918, only 2,158 of the 10,850 children were "orphans of martyrs" (almost 20 percent).[40]

Several new orphanages were opened in Istanbul in the course of 1916. Especially after the Gallipoli campaign, which left behind thousands of orphans, these "emergency orphanages" were incapable

TABLE 1: State orphanages in Istanbul (1917)

Name	*Personnel*	*Administrative personnel*	*Teachers*	*Students*
Kadıköy Boys	109	11	26	1,000
Galata/Beyoğlu Industrial Boys	37	7	10	220
Yedikule Boys	61	5	8	140
Haydarpaşa Industrial Boys		7	6	100
Kadıköy Kindergarten (mixed)	70	9	9	400
Kadıköy Shoemaking Department (Boys)		3	1	50
Büyükdere Boys	19	8	4	140
Hoca İsmail Mahir Efendi Girls	13	17	28	800
Bebek Industrial Girls	16	5	15	200
Total	325	72	107	3,050
Total Girls	29	22	43	1,000
Total Boys	296	50	64	2,050

Source: BOA, MF.EYT., 7/51, 5/L/1335 (25.07.1917).

of dealing with the ever-increasing number of orphans. The Bebek Girls Orphanage was opened in the waterfront residence of Said Halim Pasha (1863–1921) and therefore was called "Prens Halim Paşa Darüleytamı."[41] The girls there were taught sock making, sewing, knitting, and lace making.[42] The Galata/Beyoğlu Industrial Orphanage for boys (*sanayi şubesi*), with workshops in shoe making, carpentry, blacksmithing, and turnery (*tornacılık*), was also opened during this time. Boys in this branch were also sent to the imperial shipyards (Tersane-i Amire) and the state printing house (Matbaa-i Amire) to work as apprentices.[43] The Yedikule Industrial Boys Orphanage was opened in the building of a Dominican school in August 1916. The 700 boys living there were sent to work in the neighboring tanneries (*tabakhane*) and also for Chemins de fer Orientaux (Şark Şimendiferleri Şirketi).[44] The Haydarpaşa Orphanage was opened at the end of 1916. The Büyükdere Boys Orphanage was established in the beginning of 1917 to train bricklayers and tilers.

State Orphanages in the Provinces

State orphanages were also established in the provinces, and their numbers were not negligible. The finances for orphanages came from both central and provincial treasuries. In addition, a special "tax for the children of the martyrs" (*evlad-ı şüheda vergisi*) was introduced to meet the increasing expenditures of orphanages. According to a table prepared by the Directorate of Orphanages in May 1915, there were twenty orphanages in the provinces of Kayseri, Hüdavendigar, Adana, Edirne, Urfa, Kastamonu, Konya, Ankara, Diyarbekir, and Niğde. Four of them (in Samsun, Teke, Aydın, and Bolu) were not yet operating, but "in progress."[45]

At the beginning of 1917, there were already sixty-eight orphanages with more than 10,000 orphans.[46] However, the financial burden of opening new branches could not be accurately calculated. The allocation in the budget for their first year (1915) was so limited that it could cover only the expenses of orphanages opened in Istanbul and Bursa.[47] In order to "solve" the problem of allocations, the provinces were ordered to meet the expenses of their local orphanages from their own state budgets. The demands of the provinces from the Treasury were not accepted.[48] In that respect, the orphanages in the provinces were mostly founded with local sources—either in the form of "donations" from certain locals[49] or by organizing fund-raisers.[50]

Orphanages established in the provinces were not limited to the ones mentioned above. The directorate kept taking over new buildings and opening additional orphanages. As of June 1917, forty-nine of them were in the provinces, providing for 5,575 children. The number of children in Istanbul and Ermişe were in total 3,275.[51] Toward the end of the war, the number of orphanages further increased to eighty.[52] In 1917, based on data coming from each institution, the Ministry of

TABLE 2: **State orphanages in the provinces (1915)**

Province	*Name*	*Number of children*	*Children's identity*
Kayseri	Efkere Boys	187	92 orphans of martyrs 95 orphans
	Kayseri Boys	140	70 orphans of martyrs 70 orphans
Hüdavendigar	Söğüt Boys	100	
	Tirilye Girls	60	
Kudüs		?	
Adana		1,350	300 orphans of martyrs 1,050 orphans
Edirne	Center	93	All orphans of martyrs
Urfa		103	All Armenians
Kastamonu		102	64 orphans of martyrs 20 orphans 18 father under arms
Konya		75	35 orphans of martyrs 40 orphans
Ankara		75	14 orphans of martyrs 61 orphans
Samsun		100	
Teke		100	
Aydın		?	
Bolu		40	
Diyarbekir	Diyarbekir	144	49 orphans of martyrs 95 orphans
	Mardin	100	9 orphans of martyrs 91 orphans
	Bitlis	?	
Niğde		50	
Total		2,819	

Source: BOA, MF.EYT., 6/110, 23/Ca/1333 (08.05.1915).

TABLE 3: State orphanages in the provinces (1917)

Name	*Personnel*	*Administrative personnel*	*Teachers*	*Students*
Totals of page 1[a]	114	115	132	4,350
Samsun Boys	11	3	3	100
Jerusalem Boys	15	4	5	200
Jerusalem Girls	19	2	6	250
Kastamonu Boys	13	7	2	150
Kastamonu Girls	13	1	3	150
Kayseri Boys	14	3	4	150
Kayseri Girls	13	1	4	150
Efkere Boys	24	5	6	300
Adana Boys	23	6	7	200
Şeyhli Boys	30	3	5	150
Kozan Boys	13	4	3	150
Tarsus Girls	11	5	3	100
Dörtyol Boys	9	2	3	100
Adana Girls	23	6	6	200
Adana Enver Paşa Boys	8	5	4	100
Ekbaz Boys	8	2	2	50
Muş Boys	11	4	3	100
Kars Boys	7	2	2	50
Balıkesir Boys	13	4	4	150
İzmit CUP Orphanage Administration	20	6		
İzmit Reşadiye	52	6	4	200
İzmit Çiftlik	35	6	0	0
İzmit Talatiye	34	4	3	100
İzmit Saidiye	27	5	2	100
Bahçecik Boys	18	5	3	150
Teke Boys	14	3	3	100
Total	592	213	222	7,800

Source: BOA, MF.EYT., 7/51, 5/L/1335 (25.07.1917).

[a] This document unfortunately has a missing page. The contents of the first page, the names of the orphanages, and figures relating to personnel and children are not in the file. We have only the totals of this page—the first line in the table. Orphanages in Edirne Orphanages (Asım Bey, Edirne Girls, CUP orphanage), Kırklareli (Ömer Naci Bey Darüleytamı), Tekirdağ (Tekfurdağı Gazi Fazıl Darüleytamı), Ankara, Yozgat, Aydın (Aydın center, Alaçatı), Manisa, Kilis, Bursa, Tirilye, Söğüt, Diyarbakır, Mardin, Sivas, Amasya, Merzifon, Konya, Niğde, Canik, Kala-yı Sultaniye, Bolu, Antalya, Maraş, Ayntab, Balıkesir, Urfa, Karahisar-ı Sahip, and other orphanages are, therefore, not listed in the table.

Education declared that they were providing for more than 11,000 orphans in the country.[53] The table prepared by the Directorate of Orphanages in mid-1917 gave the total number of orphans as 10,850.[54] However, at least 10,000 children were waitlisted.[55] In 1918 some institutions were either closed or united with neighboring ones owing to difficulties and in order to decrease the costs and ease the organizational woes. The detailed report prepared for the 1334 budget of *darüleytams* by Faik, the general manager of the directorate (Darüleytamlar Müdür-i Umumisi), also the deputy of Edirne, underlined that the directorate had sixty-five institutions with 8,850 children.[56]

Looking at the available figures relating to the orphanages, one obvious point is the discrepancy between the scope of the "orphan problem" and the sheer capacity of the *darüleytams*. These institutions housed only a fraction of all war orphans. What happened to the rest and how they survived the war are relevant questions that should be addressed. There are a number of different trajectories about the experiences of children (mainly in the cities) that are discernible from memoirs and literary sources.[57] Even very young children were employed in all sorts of businesses, from shoe making to weaving, from cigarette factories to restaurants and hotels.[58] Many children survived solely by relying on begging and stealing.[59] Homeless orphan children sometimes formed into gangs, and they managed to attack shops or sometimes even towns and villages for booty.[60] It is also underlined that very young girls were sold into prostitution.[61]

Gender Dimension

During the war, nine orphanages were opened in Istanbul, only two of them for girls: Kadıköy (Hoca İsmail Mahir Efendi) Girls Orphanage and Bebek Orphanage.[62] By mid-1917 there were 1,000 girls and 2,050 boys in Istanbul orphanages (see table 1). In five different orphanages in Jerusalem, Kastamonu, Kayseri, Tarsus, and Adana, there were more than 850 orphan girls.[63] Presumably, orphan girls were more easily taken into homes and adopted or fostered as domestic labor or wives (or both). Chapter 4 discusses the details of forced or voluntary fosterage of Armenian girls during the war years. Private mechanisms of care were more readily offered to girls regardless of their age, while boys above twelve or so were not so easily accepted into families, as they were seen as either harder to "tame" or even dangerous. In fact, the opening of state orphanages was directly related to the concern that unattended young boys (unlike girls) would become involved in crime.[64]

The admittance of orphan girls and the enumeration of girls orphanages were further complicated with the virginity examination requirement of the Directorate of Orphanages. After the application in mid-1915 of a certain Safinaz for the admittance of her nieces, six-year-old Makbule (a full orphan) and seven-year-old Saniye (no mother, father conscripted), to the Kadıköy Girls Orphanage, the paternal aunt was promised that the girls would be received in November.[65] On the specified date the girls were examined by "a midwife with a diploma" (*diplomalı kabile*), and Saniye was refused. Safinaz then took the little girl to the doctor of Üsküdar municipality, Şakir Bey, and attained a report attesting that the girl was not "deflowered" (*lekedar*) and that she did not have any "malady or disease" (*illet ve emraz*). Even with the new report, she was not able to turn Saniye over to the institution and thus applied to the Ministry of Education with a petition dated 17 January 1916. The ministry immediately asked the Directorate of Health (Sıhhiye Müdüriyeti) to intervene and take the responsibility of virginity examinations of orphans in such cases. This step was necessary to avoid discord between orphanage doctors and other doctors and also to prevent girls from being under a cloud of suspicion (*bir takım etfalin taht-ı zan ve şüphede kalmasına meydan bırakmamak üzere*).[66] The Forensic Medicine Branch (Tababet-i Adli Şubesi) of the Directorate of Health responded that they could intervene in such cases. However, they also warned the Ministry of Education that the initial virginity examinations in the orphanages "must be personally performed by the doctor" (*mutlaka bizzat tabib tarafından*) and not the midwife, owing to the fact that these women had no authority to carry out such examinations (*bu gibi muayenatda sahib-i salahiyet taşımamakta olmaları hasebiyle*).[67]

It is hard to know the frequency and uniformity of the practice in other orphanages in Istanbul and in other localities. Still, it is apparent that orphanage administrators, doctors, and families were aware of and in accordance with the virginity requirement. The outrageousness of virginity tests of girls as young as six was not raised as an issue.

Relative Autonomy and Frequent Corruption

Orphanages were opened in Istanbul and in many provincial cities from 1915 onward. Yet it was decided only in mid-1916 to prepare the necessary documentation (regulations and instructions) on matters related to the admission of orphans to orphanages, their education, training, and so on. It was likewise decided to prepare a new law to establish a new institution, Darüleytam Müdüriyet-i Umumiyesi, to unite all the orphanages in Istanbul and the provinces under a single roof. The directorate had a separate budget, but it was affiliated with the Ministry of Education.[68] The "foundation law" of the Directorate of Orphanages (Darüleytamlar Müdüriyet-i Umumiyesinin Teşkili), penned ex post facto in 1917,[69] defined it as an independent legal entity (*şahsiyet-i hukukiye*).[70] It was discussed in the press that the institution had to continue its existence as a private enterprise with the support of its own organization.[71]

The relative autonomy of the institution left the administrators some leeway for corruption and abuse. In April 1917, the director and the accountant of İzmit CUP Orphanage Saidiye Department were accused of corruption and disorderliness in education and training.[72] It was also very frequent for orphanage staff to steal supplies from institutions to support their own families in the face of wartime scarcities. An accountant of the Kadıköy Boys Orphanage, Hacı Zühdü Efendi, was accused of sending food items to his own household.[73] In the following months, the Ministry of Education ordered a monthly inspection of supplies in the orphanages and strict control over inventories.[74] In a bigger corruption case, the general manager of the directorate, Faik Bey, and the director of orphanage factories (*darüleytam fabrikaları müdürü*), Yusuf Ziya Bey, were accused of fraud and embezzlement.[75]

The Limits of Care and Protection

The development and "prospering" of the orphanages in the four-year span of the war looked promising from a quantitative perspective.

However, the sheer increase in numbers did not necessarily mean "progress." State orphanages were incredibly poor and lacked even the basic requirements of child care. There is a need to underline both the difficulty of sheltering, feeding, and educating so many orphaned children and youth as well as the organizational and financial problems of these institutions.

The orphanages were overfilled. Some housed as many as a thousand children, even though the capacity of these former school buildings was limited to a few hundred. Already in 1916, it was announced in the newspapers that Istanbul orphanages were above their capacity and could no longer admit new applicants.[76] In mid-1916 the Ministry of Education had to warn the Ministry of Internal Affairs, and also other ministries concerned, not to send any more children to orphanages.[77] The directors of orphanages were also advised to refuse new applications. They were already overcrowded, and these high numbers were impeding children's health.[78] The Ottoman Archives are full of petitions from district officials or relatives for the admission of children to an orphanage, whose administrators repeatedly declined for not having any vacancies.[79] The Antalya Boys Orphanage declared that it would not agree to new admissions under any circumstances.[80] Still, based on the detailed report of the directorate, it is obvious that every single orphanage had to accept children above their initial quota.[81]

The institutions were so crowded that children were in fact sitting on top of each other in very small rooms. If they were lucky enough, three to six children were sleeping in the same bed with no sheet or pillow.[82] Usually, they were lying on the floor, holding onto each other for warmth, as their sleeping quarters were far from bcing warm and comfortable.[83] Dense living quarters often provoked fights among the children.[84]

Hunger was the other great problem of the orphans (like the rest of the country). They were constantly fed with low-nutrition soups with very few ingredients. Orphan memoirs are full of nothing but sad descriptions of never-ending hunger.[85] The budgets allocated to the orphanage administration constantly proved to be inadequate to cover the expenditures.[86] The petition of the director of the Mersin

Orphanage describes the financial limits of these institutions, especially in the face of ever-increasing costs. Their storehouse was practically empty, as the state assistance in the form of food products had been interrupted over the previous few months. The ministry was sending only 5 *kuruş* for each orphan as their daily food cost. After a detailed discussion of the prices of food items, he underlined that the institution needed at least 8 *kuruş* as the daily food allowance per person.[87] His demands were left unanswered, and he had to send a telegraph this time, begging because the children were hungry and saying that he had to close the orphanage in eight days.[88] The director of the Yozgat Orphanage also applied with a common demand in 1917. He complained to the Ministry of Education that the monthly 100 *kuruş* was not sufficient for the subsistence of children. He even sent the ministry a detailed table of food costs, comparing the prices of February and May 1917.[89] For the provinces far from Istanbul that had several orphanages, such as Sivas (twenty orphanages with twenty-six hundred children) and Diyarbekir (four orphanages with nine hundred children), feeding the children had been especially difficult, given the excessive prices of food products.[90]

During the Allied occupation of the city, almost all of the Istanbul orphanages were subjected to health screenings in August 1920, most probably with the demand of the Allied forces. According to these medical examinations, undernourishment was the biggest problem of orphanages. The children in several different institutions were all either "meager" (*zayıf*) or "skinny" (*çok zayıf*).[91] Registers of height and weight, prepared by some orphanage directors, point to the "failure to thrive" among orphanage children. The Büyükdere Orphanage made such an investigation and noted that food deficiencies translated into very low progress in height and weight in children.[92] Because of ongoing hunger and starvation, petty theft was a common crime in the orphanages. Children would usually make up teams in order to break into the storeroom and eat a little more to appease their hunger.[93] The boys in the Urfa Orphanage were accused of "stealing orphanage property."[94] In fact, they had to steal food from the kitchen not to starve in the orphanage.

Health, hygiene, and disease were constantly serious problems in the orphanages. Sporadic documentation on hygiene inspections usually left proof of unpleasant conditions. During an inspection, the dining hall of the Galata Industrial Orphanage was found "neither sanitary nor clean" (*sıhhi ve temiz bulunmayan*).[95] There is also documentation on the health screenings and vaccinations of children in Istanbul orphanages, but it is hard to argue that they were done in each and every orphanage.[96] Diseases spread quickly, since the wards were not large enough to separate the sick from the healthy.[97] Most of the buildings did not have their own water sources, toilets were in despicable condition, children had to wear the same dirty underwear for a long time, and they could touch water and soap only when taken to the public bath in the closest city or town center.[98] These problems regarding cleanliness easily translated into widespread cases of scabies and rashes.[99] In 1916 some measures were taken to prevent scabies (*uyuz*), which was very common in Istanbul at the time, from spreading to orphans. Staff coming from outside would take off their clothes, take a bath in *hamam*, and wear clean clothes.[100] Apparently, these "measures" were applicable only when the building actually had a bath.

The epidemic of purulent meningitis (*lekeli humma*) in the Mersin Orphanage, for instance, was directly related to the issue of hygiene. The public baths in the city were reserved for the soldiers, and the orphans were deprived of the means to get clean. In order to solve the problem of hygiene and cleanliness, the director of the Mersin Orphanage applied to the Ministry of Education for the purchase of a "fumigation machine" (steam disinfector) for sterilization purposes.[101] From another correspondence with the orphanage in Bebek (Istanbul), it is possible to argue that fumigation was a standard procedure. Owing to several contagious diseases in the orphanage of more than eight hundred children, the Ministry of Education demanded the Ottoman Red Crescent (Osmanlı Hilal-i Ahmer Cemiyeti) lend their fumigation machine.[102]

Inadequacies in shelter, nutrition, and clothing also led to other serious diseases. In the crowded orphanage of Diyarbekir, more than

117 children out of its 1,000 boys and girls died of tuberculosis within only five months.[103] According to the report, the physical condition of the building of the orphanage, which was an old Armenian monastery, was inadequate. Moreover, speaking of the negligence of the personnel, the director argued that sick children were admitted to the orphanage. He promised to separate the sick from the healthy and also organize separate wards for boys and girls.[104]

There were also innumerable cases of malaria and pneumonia. There were serious cases of malaria among the boys in the Maraş Orphanage, and the director asked the Ministry of Education to intervene in the procurement of quinine.[105] It was reported that 20 percent of the children in the Edirne Orphanage had pneumonia.[106] More than 1,000 had trachoma, and 300 lost their sight for lack of treatment.[107] Many children in the orphanage of Söğüt were also reported to be sick. One had been hospitalized in Istanbul, and the operator found in an unhealed wound in his head ten to fifteen worms as thick as one centimeter.[108] The report of the Directorate of Orphanages to the parliament during budget discussions claimed that in total eighty children died in all the orphanages in 1917 and that this figure was about 1 percent of the total population.[109] Given mortality rates at the time and in war, this number is rather low. It is possible that the directorate was painting a false picture to secure funds for the coming year.

In order to deal with health issues more effectively, the orphanage in Haydarpaşa was transformed into a hospital in early 1918 for the sick children in orphanages.[110] The hospital, with its location close to the main train station, also served as a temporary abode, if not quarantine, for the orphans who were transferred from Anatolia to Istanbul after the end of the war.[111] Starting in June 1918, the hospital prepared reports on its activities, providing information on patients and treatments. Especially in 1919 and 1920, as the hospital scrutinized the number of sick and dead children in all Istanbul orphanages, the chief physician gave advice to orphanage directors.[112]

Despite these difficult conditions and ongoing problems, the 1919 report of the Directorate of Orphanages claimed that children were generally happy and showing promising signs of being sensible and responsible individuals in the future.[113] State officials were exaggerating the happiness and the good character of the orphans in an official report, while inner correspondence brought forward cases of "undisciplined behavior," "rebellious acts," serious diseases, mistreatment, and escapes.

The Limits of Education

The extent of children's activity in these institutions, how they were educated and spent their time, was another issue.[114] The methods of discipline had mostly been primitive, taking the form of physical punishment. It was uncovered by one of the inspectors of the provincial orphanages that the director of the Söğüt Orphanage (Hüdavendigar) was heavily beating the boys.[115]

The curricula were vague in terms of the scope of training. The provisional regulations of the orphanages (1917) and several official declarations underlined the importance of industrial training for children older than twelve (Articles 13 and 14). The second article of the regulation explained that the educational purpose of the institution was to enhance the Islamic and national feelings of the children and to provide them a vocational training by taking into consideration their abilities and the needs of the country.[116] Ideally, the orphanages would concentrate on industrial training so that in time, they generated their own revenues and decreased their needs from the state budget.[117] Most of the orphanages mainly aimed to provide training in arts and crafts. The Kadıköy Boys Orphanage operated as a small-scale shoe-manufacturing factory.[118] The artifacts produced by orphaned girls were exhibited on special occasions and sold, so as to contribute to the budget of the institutions.[119] Girls orphanages in Çağlayan and Validebağ were said to be particularly skilled in sewing, such that they would work on orders from private customers.[120]

Even though there was a discussion of providing agricultural education, the practice remained limited to a few orphanages. Agricultural land was arranged for the Efkere Orphanage, but they were waiting for the barley seeds to be provided by the Ministry of Trade and Agriculture.[121] The Bahçecik Orphanage in İzmit trained its two hundred boys in sericulture (*ipek böçekçiliği*), while six hundred boys in the Ermişe Orphanage specialized in mechanized agriculture.[122] Forty boys from orphanages in the environs (Tekirdağ, Kırklareli, and Edirne) were brought to Lüleburgaz to receive training with new agricultural machinery imported from Europe and used there.[123]

However, not all the buildings were arranged based on the vocational training children would receive. In order to teach girls and boys various things like weaving, ironworking, carpentry, painting (*nakkaşlık*), telegraphy, and so on, workshops were supposed to be built within the buildings.[124] However, most of the orphanages lacked this infrastructure. Moreover, the question of necessary raw materials, depending on the trades trained, had never been resolved, and the orphanages were not supplied in terms of materials. It can be seen from the archival records that in most of the cases, the orphanages were able to provide only formal education and theoretical vocational training. In order to progress in their trades, boys had to be transferred either to other orphanages or to private workshops and factories to practice their trades. For instance, five boys from the Bebek Orphanage were sent to the Validebağ Orphanage to be trained in masonry. Two others were also sent to the Yedikule Orphanage, one to become a tailor and the other a horologist.[125] After receiving a health report from the doctor of the orphanage, boys older than twelve were also sent to factories to practice their theoretical knowledge.[126] For instance, Mehmet Efendi, born in 1906 in Diyarbekir, was sent from the Yedikule Orphanage to work first in a cutlery manufacturer in Davutpaşa İskelesi. Later he worked as an apprentice with Yorgi Usta (master) in a foundry workshop. Then he worked with Nikola Efendi, also in foundry work.[127] While some of the boys in the Galata Industrial Orphanage were taught trades within the orphanage, some were sent to work in the "Bread Factory" in Şişli.[128] Another group of boys from Galata was sent to Matbaa-i Amire, the official state printing house, to be trained in printing. However, there were a number of complaints regarding their late arrival or else absence. The printing house refused to train those misbehaving children and demanded their replacement.[129]

The directorate prepared detailed registers on the industrial training of each child, called "Industrial Life of Students in the Industrial Departments of the Orphanages" ("Darüleytam Sanayi Şuabatında Bulunan Talebeye Ait Hayat-ı Sanaiye"). These reports included basic information on the children involved, such as name, place and date of birth, the name of their orphanage, and their height and weight. Most important, these registers had a section on the observations of their masters and inspector officers.[130] Their masters noted the success and failure of children at their trades and their absences at the workplace. They were also invited to provide their personal opinion about the children. For instance, the opinion of the inspector on Tahsin Efendi, born in 1905 in Vize, was quite negative. This boy was transferred from one master to another several times, owing to problems of disobedience and disrespect. In the end, during his apprenticeship in Zeytinburnu Imperial Factory (Zeytinburnu Fabrika-i Hümayunu), he was accused of not abiding by the rules of the institution and more especially of acting in a rebellious manner (*serkeşane tavırlar*), which led to his removal from the orphanage.[131]

For concerns of morality and chastity, girls were in principle not sent to private workshops or factories. The Islamic Society for the Employment of Women (Kadınları Çalıştırma Cemiyet-i İslamiyesi), established by the CUP, was an exceptional outlet for the training of (mostly Armenian) girls in trades.[132] Moreover, girls older than fifteen were taught how to care for children and trained as kindergarten teachers. In 1916 eighteen girls, who were older than eighteen, were sent to the "kindergarten teaching" section of the Girls Teacher Seminary (Darülmuallimat). In 1917 twelve of them were appointed to different orphanages after completing their training.[133] Also in 1917, ten girls were sent to the "teacher" section of the Darülmuallimat.[134]

The quality of education in the orphanages was hampered by the large numbers of children, coupled with insufficient numbers of teachers and masters. For instance, the boys orphanage in Yedikule had only three teachers for 100 children. The table prepared by the Directorate of Orphanages in 1917 gave the total number of orphans as 10,850 and teachers as 329.[135] In other words, each teacher/master was supposed to teach 33 children. Moreover, in most of the institutions, the capacities of the buildings were not fit to establish workshops and provide vocational training. Children were sent from one orphanage to another for further training or else were apprenticed in factories and in the workshops of master craftsmen. These circumstances were serious setbacks, limiting the effectiveness of education.

Armenian Orphans and the *Darüleytam*s

The emphasis on the "orphans of martyrs" remained very strong in the laws and regulations relating to the *darüleytam*s, along with the propaganda material that appeared in the press and elsewhere. The available literature on the *darüleytam*s does not challenge this official view and so is silent about the extent of Armenian orphans in these institutions.[136] However, the opening of orphanages especially in the provinces was directly related to the Armenian genocide and the incredible number of unattended children it left behind across the empire. As Üngör also underlines, "Rather than roaming the streets and begging for food or money, most orphans were taken by the Young Turk government."[137] Sarafian also notes the use of Ottoman state orphanages as a direct means of assimilating Armenian children.[138] I will discuss the life courses of Armenian orphans in detail in chapter 4, but it is necessary to discuss the role of state orphanages in this section.

There is a significant amount of evidence that many Armenian children were taken into state orphanages.[139] All these Armenian orphans in state orphanages were converted to Islam and given Turkish names; the boys were circumcised and so were raised as Muslim Turks.[140] The CUP leaders supported the conversion, assimilation, and Islamicization of Armenian children.[141] The imposition of a Muslim Turkish identity was an important aspect of the Armenian genocide. The nationalist population politics of the Young Turks transformed children into precious national property. Armenian children were also valuable, as a Muslim Turkish identity could be imposed and they could be instilled with nationalist ideas.[142] Not only was their religion violently and systematically suppressed, but the use of the Armenian language was also forbidden. The names and family names of children, whether in private homes or orphanages, were changed.[143] Children ended up being pure bodies and quantities to be Turkified.

The government sent ciphered telegrams to the provinces and *mutasarrıflık*s in June 1915, requesting them to support the opening of orphanages and collecting Armenian orphans below the age of ten in these institutions.[144] On 12 July 1915, the Directorate for the Settlement of Refugees and Tribes (İskan-ı Aşair ve Muhacirin Müdüriyeti) issued a similar decree to the provinces of Adana, Erzurum, Van, Trabzon, Sivas, and Edirne and the *mutasarrıflık*s of Canik, İzmit, Kayseri, and Der Zor, ordering the placement of Armenian children in state orphanages.[145]

In the middle of 1916, Enver Pasha ordered the Ministry of Education to take in destitute Armenian girls and boys to "our orphanages" (*bizim darüleytamlara*)—in other words, Muslim Turkish orphanages. He demanded the allocation of funds for Armenian children in the budget of the Ministry of Internal Affairs. Otherwise, the necessary amount would be met by the budget of the War Ministry.[146] While Armenian children were usually accepted into existing state orphanages, there is also evidence that some new institutions were established primarily for Armenian children. It was openly mentioned in a report of the Directorate of Orphanages that the orphanage in Urfa was populated primarily by Armenian children.[147] In January 1916 a new orphanage with a capacity of 1,000 children was established in Diyarbekir. The staff immediately began collecting Armenian orphans.[148] In another example from mid-1916, it was underlined that there were uncountable Armenian orphans in Mardin who were destitute and left alone in the streets. As a result, Enver ordered the urgent opening of an orphanage in Mardin, so that Armenian orphans would be "taken under state control." The children would be collected from the streets, and then they could be possibly sent to other orphanages.[149] Based on the statistics of the directorate, there were only nine "children of martyrs" in this orphanage; the other 91 children were defined simply as "orphans."[150] The *vali* of Syria, Tahsin Bey, underlined the necessity of "benefitting from" Armenian deportees' labor power. He opened an orphanage in Damascus for Armenian orphans, along with a shelter for widows in which the women did embroidery and wove carpets.[151] The CUP government also wanted to open an orphanage for Armenian orphans in Kayseri in 1916.[152] Based on a discussion from 1919, the reason for the opening of Kayseri Orphanage was the mistreatment of Armenian orphans in the households of the "notables of the city."[153] Armenian children were usually transported to various different localities in order to disconnect them from their neighborhoods, relatives, and acquaintances. Armenian orphans were transferred from Aleppo to Sivas in 1916, to İzmit in 1917, and to Istanbul and probably several other places.[154]

The commissioners of the League of Nations in postwar Istanbul, Emma D. Cushman and Dr. W. A. Kennedy, had access to Ottoman state orphanage registries and noted that Christian names were crossed out and overwritten with Muslim names.[155] They underlined that about half of all the orphans in the city (5,000) should be of Armenian origin. According to the personal registers of Talat Pasha, of the 10,314 Armenian orphans who had been reported by different provinces, 6,858 had been distributed to Muslim families, while 3,456 were in state orphanages.[156] *Talat Pasha's Report on the Armenian Genocide* is the closest official Ottoman view of the Armenian genocide.[157]

The Ministry of Interior reported in 1917 that the CUP orphanage in Ermişe (Armash) received several hundred Armenian orphans from Aleppo and Syria.[158] After 1918, when orphanages in the provinces and the orphans in them were transferred to Istanbul, the Directorate of Orphanages decided to do nothing about the children in Armash and just left them there.[159] The conscious abandonment of children in the CUP orphanage suggests that the state was aware that under the new political environment of the armistice, the Armenian orphans would be reclaimed. An orphan from the orphanage, Atıf, recounted that Armenian priests identified all the Armenian children in the orphanage by controlling the records.[160] Based on the 1919–20 report of the Armenian National Relief Mission (Azkayin Khnamadarutiun), the "agricultural orphanage in Armash" was transferred to Khnamadarutiun in its entirety, and it was now populated solely by Armenian children.[161]

The War Ministry considerably supported the opening of orphanages both in Istanbul and in the provinces. The ministry also had its own orphanages. The Rum (Ottoman Greek) Orphanage in Büyükada (Prinkipo) was "rented" by the ministry and used as an orphanage.[162] While numerous orphanages were closed or discontinued toward the end of the war, the War Ministry was still opening new orphanages or operating the existent ones. For instance, the high school (*mekteb-i sultani*) in Sivas was transformed in 1919 into a girls orphanage of 500 children to provide for "children of refugees and martyrs gathered in the center" (*merkez-i vilayette toplanan muhacir ve şüheda evladı*).[163] Here, the term "refugee" can be a reference to Armenians, since Sivas had been a main center for Armenian survivors.[164] In addition to the Diyarbekir (Cevat Pasha) Orphanage, the orphanages in Kilis and Aintab (Nuri Bey Darüleytamı), in the *vilayet* of Aleppo, were also not closed after the war and still had 170 children.[165]

A considerable number of orphan boys had also been enrolled in military schools. Based on the regulations of the military high schools (*mekatib-i idadiye-i askeriye*), Kuleli Military School in Istanbul would give precedence to orphans.[166] Although it is hard to provide an exact number of Armenian boys in this institution, it is an interesting coincidence that the school was used as the largest Armenian boys orphanage during the Allied period, with an orphan body of more than 1,000 children.[167] The interest of the military officials and CUP leaders with the conversion, assimilation, and Turkification of Armenian orphans has not been limited to the war years. Several hundred children were brought from "eastern Anatolia" to Istanbul in the aftermath of the war to be enrolled in military schools. However, 300 boys out of the 700 who were transported did not prove healthy enough to pass the military school medical examination.[168] As it would be impossible (even cruel) to send them back to the difficult circumstances in "eastern Anatolia," the War Ministry looked for places in the *darüleytam*, and then Darülaceze. Both philanthropic institutions refused the boys for health reasons. They also needed healthy children to provide them with industrial training. The story of "eastern Anatolian" children sent to Istanbul to be educated in military schools is very similar and emblematic of the CUP's "uncalculated grand projects."[169]

Late nineteenth- and early twentieth-century nationalists were obsessed with demography and "the quantity and quality of the nation's children."[170] Based on this understanding, the CUP leadership used the *darüleytam* structure for the transformation of Armenian children into new Turkish Muslim generations.

State Violence and Experimental Projects

Wartime propaganda frequently portrayed children as victims, but it was also common to depict them as the bearers of a better future. In periods of exceptional change, chaos, and disorder, it is not rare that states rely on children in realizing entirely new, experimental, or questionable projects. In some cases, children were asked to assume such responsibilities that the line between adulthood and childhood became blurred. Ethnic cleansing of non-Muslims and the pillaging of their property by the Ottoman authorities (and civilians) during the war inspired many experimental projects of the Unionist government concerning children, with the assumption that they held a "special promise." It was easier to try out things on this utterly disadvantaged group of children, since they had no one to protect or defend them and for that reason no one could hinder or resist state-imposed conversion or Turkification. Children, as a consequence, served as open grounds to essay pilot projects in a climate of uncertainty. In this part, I discuss a number of ambitious projects of the Unionists targeting orphans and imbued with initiatives of change.

In the forcefully emptied former Ottoman Greek town of Burhaniye, "orphans of martyrs" were mobilized for nationalist and propaganda purposes.[171] In a very curious project, the local governorship arranged the settlement of orphans into two different neighborhoods, one for boys and one for girls.[172] Each of them would carry an identity disc indicating their age and where and how their fathers were martyred. They would live and be observed as the living remains of their fathers, of martyred heroes. Moreover, in their own quarters, orphan children would live together as a collectivity and would be exposed to a different sort of socialization and political acculturation. The report of the governor envisaged a model child colony, in which nationalist and religious patriotism was built in early on.

The İzmit CUP Orphanage, in the town of Ermişe (Armash), which occupied the premises of the Armenian monastery of Armash, was also planned as an ambitious agricultural orphan colony. Based on the original project, each and every town from the Ottoman provinces would send ten orphans to the colony. After finishing their theoretical and practical education on agriculture, they would go back to their villages.[173] In the end, the town would be inhabited almost entirely by eight to ten thousand orphans over the age of thirteen. These rural children would be equipped with both theoretical and practical agricultural training. After completing their studies, some of them would form and live in pilot villages, while others would go back to their own villages in order to modernize agricultural production. Based on the initial project, an Austrian company would establish nine different factories in the colony. In other words, Armash would not only be an agricultural colony but also become an organized industrial zone.[174] Moreover, orphan girls and boys of the colony would be married to each other, and thus "the town of orphans" would become "the village of felicity" (*saadet köyü*).[175]

As can be imagined, none of these grand plans—such as training ten thousand children, establishing nine different factories, or bringing in orphan girls as the prospective wives of orphan boys—could be realized. The Armash agricultural orphanage was opened in early 1917. It was relatively big, with about six hundred, mostly Armenian, orphans, learning and practicing mechanized agriculture in four separate departments honoring the key rulers of the empire: Reşadiye, Saidiye, Talatiye, and Enveriye.[176]

Closing of Orphanages in the Provinces and the Exodus to Istanbul

Already in mid-1918, there were efforts to downsize the network of orphanages, and orders were sent to provinces for the transfer of provincial orphanages to Istanbul.[177] Based on the regulation prepared by the Ministry of Interior in May 1918, about forty orphanages in the provinces were to be closed and partially moved to Istanbul.[178] The directors of some of the provincial orphanages, such as the ones in Edirne, Bursa, and Adana, insisted on keeping their institutions open in their localities.[179] In the end, some provincial orphanages were united into a single unit and remained in their localities but with the number of students decreased, and some children were still sent to Istanbul.

With the victory of the Entente and after the resulting occupation of parts of the Ottoman territories, the Allied countries demanded the immediate evacuation of the confiscated buildings, together with an investigation regarding the damage.[180] The Unionists were no longer in power after October 1918, and the CUP's impact, especially at the capital, was pretty limited. The state orphanages in occupied Entente, Armenian, and Greek buildings had to be discontinued, since the Allied forces ordered the immediate evacuation of buildings.[181] This requirement was the main reason why most state orphanages had to be discontinued; it led to the final decision to close the orphanages in the provinces.

"Regulations for the Transfer of Provincial Orphanages to Istanbul" ("Taşra Darüleytamlarının Dersaadete Suret-i Naklini Mübeyyin Talimatname") explained in detail what the inspectors should do. They would first go to the orphanages in the regions they were in charge of, and they would begin their operations in accordance with the instructions in hand.[182] The inspectors would first go over the financial situation of the institution and then examine the condition of the children. This pronouncement was based on the decision of the Directorate of Orphanages that children with living parents should be sent to their parents. As the Ministry of Education approved the proposal, some children were repatriated with their families after some investigation.[183] Children in all provincial orphanages were first asked to find family members to take care of them and leave with them. If they had no one to take care of them, the second option was to find a foster family.[184] The directorate had always been supportive of the practice of adoption and fosterage, and especially in the postwar period, when most of the institutions were being closed down, a large number of girls both in the provinces and in Istanbul were given as "foster daughters" (*evlatlık*).[185]

As I have discussed elsewhere, adoption in the legal sense was unknown in the Ottoman society.[186] Formal adoption (*tebenni*), which existed in pre-Islamic Arabic societies, was prohibited after embracing Islam. According to legal experts, adoption was impossible in Islamic law, since it was not in accordance with Islamic understanding of lineage (*neseb*). It would cause confusion of lineage and lead to approval of various forbidden acts, concerning the rights of legal inheritors and borders of intimacy (*mahrem*) in the household. Despite the absence of legal regulation for adoption, it was evidently common to have foster children (*besleme*) in Ottoman society. In other words, it was a fictitious adoption. The real objective was to use foster girls as maidservants for house chores.

At the end of 1920, the Directorate of Orphanages was even thinking of fostering out all the children under its "custody" and in a sense abolishing the institution by "getting rid of" its children. Based on this scheme, the girls should be given to "the honorable and the dignified families" (*erbab-ı namus ve iffetten olan aileler*), and the boys should be given "as apprentices to the tradesmen" (*esnaf nezdine çırak olarak*).[187] The main aim was to keep as many children as possible in their localities.[188] If they had no other recourse, they would then be sent to Istanbul.

Children were transferred to Istanbul or to other orphanages closer to their district mostly by train, and the inspectors were supposed to accompany them to the station. Travel organizations for these little children, who were supposed to make considerably long journeys, were far from perfect. Children had to wait for long periods in the train stations. For example, the 41 children from the Maraş and Aintab Orphanages had to wait for a week in the Fatıma station. Finally, the Ministry of War interfered, and they were transferred to Istanbul.[189] When the Kayseri Orphanage was closed and its 400 boys were supposed to be transferred to Sivas, almost half of the children "died on the journey" (*yollarda telef oldukları*) owing to negligence of the authorities. The Sivas governorship accused the *mutasarrıf* of Kayseri of making a stupid decision in putting the boys on the road in the middle of winter.[190]

In total, probably 10 percent of the orphans from orphanages in the provinces ended up in Istanbul. In Istanbul children were distributed into different orphanages. Before entering into these buildings, they were cleaned and disinfected and also subjected to medical examination.[191] Based on a decision made in 1920, all seven orphanages in the city were to be united into a single campus in Validebağ Pavilion (Adile Sultan Kasrı). The building was quite spacious and had already been in use as a girls orphanage. With some additional buildings, the complex might provide for the entire orphan population in the city.[192] This proposition had not been put into practice. An article published in 1921 suggests that there were 2,810 orphans in nine orphanages (see table 4). As stressed in 1923 parliamentary discussions, the number of children in six state orphanages—in Validebağ (for girls), Çağlayan (for girls), Halıcıoğlu, Yedikule, Balmumcu, and Beykoz—was somewhere around 3,000 to 3,500.[193]

The memoir of Hasan İzzettin Dinamo has a very long section on the closure of their orphanage in Samsun. At first, a group of Armenian religious authorities and American missionaries visited the orphanage to determine and "save" Armenian orphans. Then remaining children were encouraged by the orphanage directors to find family members or "benevolent strangers" in order to leave the orphanage and start a new life in a new household. If they had no one, they were asked to find Muslim households to provide them shelter. In the meantime, Hasan and his fellow orphans (including his two sisters) had to leave the orphanage building. They were transferred a few times to other "abandoned" Armenian mansions. As Armenian survivors were returning to the city, the orphanage had to be moved out of the Armenian quarter.[194] Children under these circumstances were practically left without any provisions. They wandered around the city all day to find a bit of food for themselves. Their favorite spot was the bakery. They would go there either early in the morning or late at night to beg for stale bread.[195] After spending several months mostly on their own,

TABLE 4: State orphanages in Istanbul (1921)

Name	*Personnel*	*Orphans*
Bebek Boys	95	470
Balmumcu Boys	65	300
Ortaköy Boys	90	420
Beykoz Boys	60	400
İmrahor Boys	40	250
Yedikule Boys	20	90
Çağlayan Girls	120	600
Validebağ Girls	60	250
Validebağ Boys Agricultural	?	30
Total	550	2,810

Source: H. Nedim, "Darüleytamlarımız," *Yeni Ziraat Gazetesi* 18 (01.10.1921), 89–90.

those children who insisted in staying in the cold orphanage building and had no one with whom to take refuge were sent to Istanbul in 1919 on a steamer called *Şam* (Damascus).[196]

• • •

A large network of *darüleytams* was established from early 1915 onward owing to the pressing circumstances of the war and thanks to the confiscation of educational and philanthropic institutions of the Entente Powers. Although the directorate kept underlining that they prioritized the children of martyrs and veterans, the *darüleytams* were also crucial in the context of the Armenian genocide in raising Armenian children as the new Turkish Muslim generation. The resistance of Armenian children and their self-empowerment will be discussed in more detail in chapter 4.

2

Ottoman Orphan Apprentices in Germany

AHMED TALIB was born in Istanbul in 1901. His mother passed away when he was three years old. His father married again after a few years, but Ahmed was not at all satisfied with this situation. He constantly complained to his brother about the stepmother. Before the war, the family's economic standing was not bad. The father had a shoeshine shop in Kadıköy, and he was also an ice dealer (*sellac*). The fate of the family changed dramatically with the explosion of the First World War. Ahmed's father was drafted in late 1914 and was killed the next year in Gallipoli. As an "orphan of a martyr," Ahmed Talib had the privilege granted by the Ministry of Education to be admitted to the *darüleytam* in Kadıköy, which was located within the premises of the famous French Collège de Saint Joseph.

In this crowded orphanage, housing about 1,000 boys, Ahmed was registered to the trades department and started his training in shoe making. When he heard in early 1917 that a large number of volunteer boys would be sent by the Orphanage Administration to Germany for further training, he applied immediately. Sixteen-year-old Ahmed was among the first group of 314 "craft apprentices" who arrived in Berlin in late April 1917. He was first transferred to Frankfurt (Oder) and then to Fürstenwalde, where he stayed in the household of Albert Pöthke as an apprentice cobbler. In the following years, he learned and improved his German. Ahmed passed the "journeyman exam" (*Gesellenprüfung*) in shoe making on 30 April 1921 and worked at Pöthke's shop until 10 February 1923. He worked at different workplaces and factories in Berlin until he opened his own shop in late 1927. He married a young German woman and became a father. In 1935 Ahmed Talib was himself certified as a master by the Chamber of Trade in Frankfurt (Oder) and started to have apprentices of his own. He continued living in this little town until the end of his life. Ahmed was a well-known figure in his neighborhood. People called him a "typical shoemaker from Fürstenwalde."[1] He was among the few whose struggle for creating a new life for himself proved successful. After years of homelessness and orphanhood, he had a well-established business and a family.

Ahmed Talib's life story is situated in the context of sending Ottoman orphans to Germany for apprenticeships during the First World War. Yet it differs substantially from most of the almost 1,000 orphan apprentices who were less lucky in terms of earning a livelihood and integrating into German society. As destitute and rootless lads, they were practically uprooted from their home country. Being part of a group of all male orphans may have further exacerbated the isolation of migrant orphans. They were also discontented with their living conditions in Germany. They suffered from poverty as well and felt deceived because of their exclusion and foreignness as migrant workers.

This chapter is about the sending of orphan children from the Ottoman Empire to work as apprentices in all types of crafts, mining, and agriculture in Germany during the First World War.[2] The designed project implied large-scale and long-distance child displacement, offering foster care as a solution to accumulating orphan populations in urban areas. The unilateral apprentice exchange program between the Ottoman and German Empires was curiously initiated in the middle of the war. Sometimes the term "student" (*talebe*) had been used in official correspondence, and actually there was a significant body of Ottoman students in Germany at the same time. Yet this chapter deals only with orphans sent from the state orphanages. Both governments made it clear that the transfer was not designed for formal schooling; instead, these children were to acquire vocational skills and work as apprentices. Although there were negotiations regarding sending girls, they proved not long enough for the fulfillment of this phase of the project. In other words, gender-wise, the displacement comprised only boys. The project was launched swiftly and with considerable enthusiasm—about 1,000 boys were sent throughout 1917 and 1918. Yet the implementation phase had not been as successful, disappointing both the German parties involved and the orphaned apprentices.

The project was initiated by the leading figure of the CUP, Minister of War Enver Pasha. He made it clear to the German military attaché Otto von Lossow in late 1916 that the government was willing to send 5,000 to 10,000 orphan boys to Germany.[3] The German-Turkish Association in Berlin (Deutsch-Türkische Vereinigung [DTV]), the sole party responsible for the handling of the project, decided to begin with several hundred boys—about 300 handicraft apprentices, 200 mining trainees, and 200 agricultural apprentices.

Chapter 1 described the limits of financial and human resources in the hands of the Ottoman government, as the context in which German master craftsmen and mine owners appeared to be an option to provide for the orphans. I have also explained the poor conditions in the orphanages that might have encouraged the inmates to volunteer to be sent away into the unknown. Although they were not properly informed about their country of destination, they somehow assumed that they would live in much better conditions in Germany. It is clear from the reports of the DTV that a serious number of orphans assumed that they would become factory workers and earn a good salary.[4] What awaited them in Germany was quite different, though.

By and large, Ottoman authorities treated orphan boys as state property, over which the state had unrestricted rights of disposal. The opportunities offered to the boys or the trades they were trained in were neither problematized nor scrutinized. The bankrupt Directorate of Orphanages tried to send out as many orphans as possible to relieve itself of the high cost of providing for them. As the entire financial burden of the project was borne by the German master craftsmen and the DTV, the project, curiously enough, was free of cost to the Ottoman government.[5] The hypothetical debt of the Ottoman administration was in fact met by the young apprentices themselves, who were not entitled to any form of financial compensation. The exchange between the two countries looked a lot like a fosterage agreement concluded between two households: a child is transferred to a foreign household (since his natural parents are no longer alive or unable to provide for him), and in exchange he is asked to help with the chores.

Relying on the Prime Ministry's Ottoman Archives and the Political Archive of German Foreign Affairs (Auswärtiges Amt),[6] together with contemporary press and personal narratives, this chapter raises many questions about the implications of this policy of child displacement. First, I discuss the political and diplomatic reasons behind the implementation of the project as a mirror of the relationship between the German and the Ottoman Empires, together with their differing expectations for the displacement policy. The child-displacement effort is also situated within the context of the war, in the sense that specific circumstances and difficulties during the war played a major role in the formulation and realization of the project. It is also not a coincidence that the boys were called back home with the end of the war.

In an attempt to bring forward the voices and experiences of the orphan boys themselves, the main aim of this chapter is to shed light on the experiences of the Ottoman orphan boys in Germany with a critical overview of their otherness and acculturation. I focus on how this long-distance child-displacement policy changed the lives of these children. The main part of the chapter is devoted to the details of their long, painful, but also hopeful journeys to Berlin on military trains and how they were greeted in this foreign country. I shed light on the orphan apprentices' lives in German masters' households. The attempt to reconstruct the personal experiences of the boys will also help to delineate the motives, engagement, and expectations of the Ottomans and Germans involved in this project. Finally, the chapter concludes with the children who returned to the Ottoman Empire and discusses some trajectories that their lives took. This forgotten episode of the Ottoman-German alliance during the First World War brings to light the impact of the war on children's lives.

Educational Collaborations between the German and Ottoman Empires

In 1912 journalist and Turcophile Ernst Jäckh[7] founded the DTV. The goal initially was to bring together financial and industrial corporations with interests in the eastern Mediterranean. These corporations donated significantly to the DTV for its declared aim of cultural rapprochement, including guided tours to Germany for Turkish politicians and businessmen to impress them with the country's achievements, as well as educational initiatives in the Ottoman Empire. More important, the DTV built organic links with the German Foreign Office such that it had serious control over the implementation of foreign policy toward the Ottoman Empire. In particular, the DTV would use the considerable funds at its disposal in coordination with the Foreign Office for expenses exceeding the latter's budget. Hans von Wangenheim, the German ambassador in Istanbul from 1912 onward, pushed for a close alliance under Jäckh's guidance and through his friendship with Enver Pasha, one of the most powerful figures of the Ottoman government and an enthusiastic admirer of Germany.[8] Once the Ottomans had entered the war, the German Military Supreme Command and Foreign Office pursued good relations with the Ottoman government and tried to build channels of German cultural influence.

With the impact of the Germanophiles in the Ottoman administration, the educational and cultural collaboration with Germany was gaining ground. A German official was appointed to a key position in almost every Ottoman ministry. Dr. Franz Schmidt,[9] former inspector of the German schools abroad, became the German adviser of the Ottoman Ministry of Education and worked out a new law on basic education. He devised a large-scale reform program, which included the alteration of the curriculum, appointment of German teachers and professors, and instruction of the German language in schools. Teacher training seminars were organized, and a number of aspiring teachers were sent to seminars in the Reich. German teachers started to teach in certain elite high schools, such as the Lycée Impérial Ottoman de Galata-Sérai, together with vocational schools in Anatolia. Twenty German professors were appointed to Istanbul University both to teach and to contribute to its reform.[10] As part of efforts for educational collaboration and exchange, hundreds of boys were sent to the Reich for education and training. The sending of Ottoman students to Germany had already happened on a minor scale prior to World War I.

With the initiation of Jäckh, an Ottoman delegation of fifteen prominent men, consisting of politicians, businessmen, army officers, administrators, agriculturists, and journalists, was invited to Germany in 1911. Financially, the project was funded by the German Foreign Office through a German consortium of banks. The guests traveling from Istanbul arrived in Berlin on 18 June 1911. They made a twenty-seven-day visit to Germany, through the cities of Preußen, Sachsen, Württemberg, Bayern, Hamburg, and Bremen. They saw the landmarks of German industry, especially the arms industry. When they were finally in Berlin, they were presented with German progress in municipal enterprises, such as hospitals, fire departments, tramways, slaughterhouses, waterworks, and open-air swimming pools.[11] It was Undersecretary of State Edhem Bey, one of the participants of the tour, who decided to send bright graduates of vocational schools to Germany for training.

The choice of Germany as the educational partner of the Ottoman Empire was largely imposed by the changing power constellations before the war. While German military advice had been used extensively starting from the military reforms of Selim III in the late eighteenth century, the number of supporters and idealizers of Germany as a role model—instead of France—was increasing. The German example became an inspiration in other fields, especially after the rise of the CUP to power. Educational journals were filled with articles on German education, economy, and industry.[12] German proficiency in technical education has been frequently underlined, and some technicians, apprentices, and vocational school students had been sent to

Germany already before the war. Before 1914 a total of twenty-four technicians were trained in German factories. In addition, higher-level students were also dispatched to pursue their university studies, again as part of the effort to reinforce German cultural influence in the Ottoman Empire.[13]

As the Ottoman government became a part of the Central Powers, the well-established practice of sending successful students to France was altered as part of the new Ottoman educational rapprochement with Germany.[14] During the war, the policies of sending Ottoman youth to Germany took a new direction and extent. Pupils and apprentices, together with workers and university students, were sent to Germany continuously and in much higher numbers. About 2,000 young people, between the ages of twelve and eighteen, were sent to Germany to be trained at German schools and German companies as engineers.[15] According to the report of Muslihiddin Adil Bey, the head of the inspection committee sent to Europe in May 1918, there were 1,954 students in Europe, most of them sent via the initiatives of "official (state) and private institutions" and some via their own personal arrangements.[16] Of these, 1,488 were in Germany, 329 in Austria, and 137 in Switzerland.[17] The Ministry of Foreign Affairs also reported in December 1918 that there were currently about 10,000 Ottoman subjects, officers, and students (*on bine karib tebaa ve zabit ve talebe-yi Osmani*) in Germany.[18]

Enver Pasha was the mastermind behind the idea of sending Ottoman orphans to be trained as apprentices in Germany. In late 1916, Enver informed the German military attaché in Constantinople, Otto von Lossow, that the government was willing to send a large number of orphan boys (5,000 to 10,000) to Germany. They would be apprentices in all types of crafts (cobblers, tailors, carpenters, locksmiths, blacksmiths, and so forth), in mining, and in mechanized agriculture—including forestry and dairy farming.[19] The project would be handled as a mutual activity of both countries. During negotiations, as well as in organizing and carrying out the plan, the officially supported German association the DTV played a leading role. The

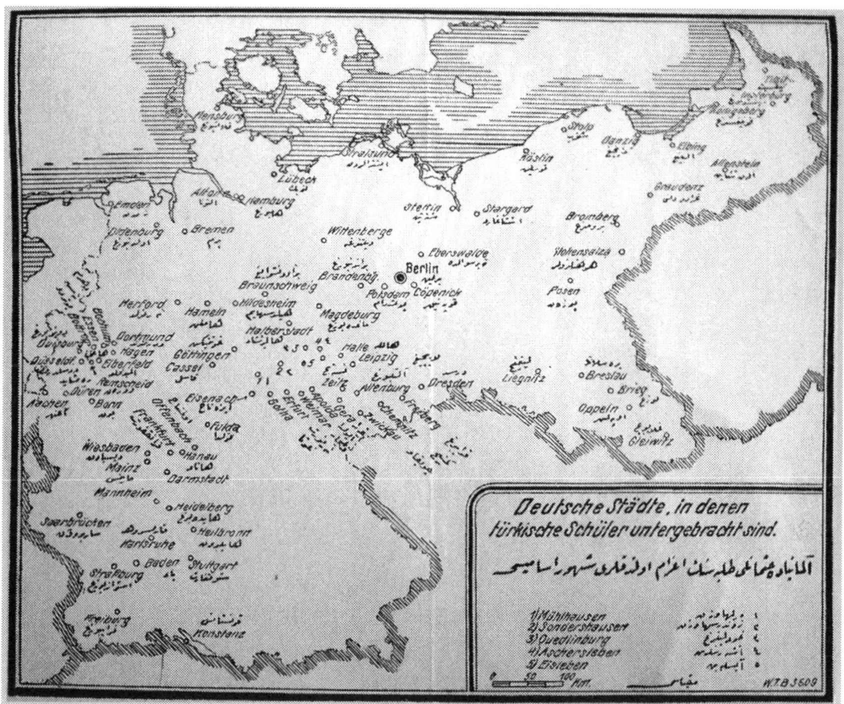

1. German cities where Turkish students have been accommodated (1917). *Source*: "Karte, die die deutschen Städte veranschaulicht, in denen bisher türkische Schüler untergebracht sind. 29. Januar 1917," PA AA, R63062.

German side was personified by Ernst Jäckh, Dr. Franz Schmidt, Paul Rohrbach,[20] Hjalmar Schacht,[21] Dr. Hans Hermann Russack,[22] and Dr. Gerhard Ryll.[23] On the Turkish side, represented by the Turkish-German Association in Istanbul (Türkisch-Deutsche Vereinigung [TDV]) in Istanbul, CUP central committee members such as Enver Pasha, Talat Pasha, and Dr. Nazım[24] were in charge.[25] The selection of children was to be done by the general board of the TDV; funding, in the form of tuition-free placement, was to be provided by German Chambers of Commerce and municipal governments. Acting as an information bureau on education in Germany and giving exams to those students who applied for scholarships, the TDV office in

Istanbul also established a German-Turkish Friendship House (Türk-Alman Dostluk Yurdu) in Istanbul, founded literary committees, and organized numerous public events.[26]

War Orphans on Military Trains

In February 1917, after the German Chambers of Trade and Industry had agreed to arrange accommodation and work for apprentices, the project could finally be started with a few hundred boys—about 300 handicraft apprentices and 200 mining trainees. The selection committee, made up of Jäckh, representatives of the Ottoman Ministry of Education, and the Orphanage Administration, quickly decided on the first group of craft apprentices. In line with the most frequent wartime representation of children, they were all declared to be "orphans of martyrs." They were chosen from Istanbul orphanages on the basis of voluntary application. They were between fourteen and sixteen years old—one among them, Ibrahim, was only seven.[27] The Orphanage Administration prepared special passports for orphans going to Germany (see figure 1). In addition to detailed personal information relating to age, family background, and physical description, these passports also had comment pages to be filled in by the masters every third month. In a sense, passports made it possible to track orphans' vocational and educational development in Germany.[28]

The first group of 314 boys departed from Sirkeci Train Station (Istanbul) in April 1917. The Balkanzug, the luxury passenger train, which took three days to cover the distance between Istanbul and Berlin, was discarded as an option in order to keep the expenses at a minimum.[29] Owing to the inconsiderate and coldhearted decision of the CUP leaders, the boys had to spend ten days in a military freight train (*zehntägige Fahrt mit Sonderzug*) without warm clothes or shoes.[30] This partially explains why so many of them were sent back after a few months. They had lung diseases.

Before departing for different workplaces, the orphans were housed in one of the City Council's Quarters in Sophienstraße 34. Soon after their arrival, they were gathered in the courtyard of the public primary

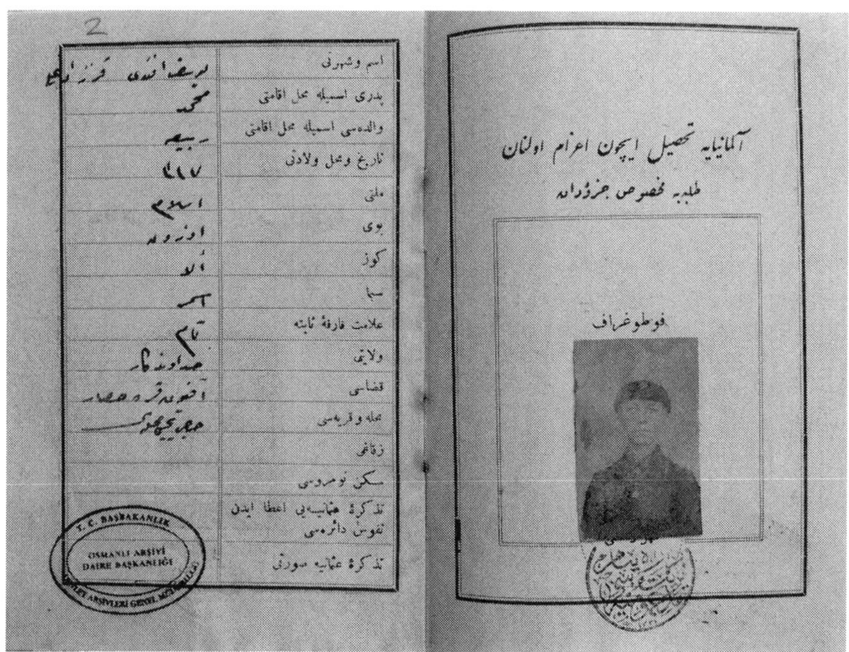

1. The passport of Yusuf Efendi, the son of Mehmed (deceased) and Rabia, born in 317 (1899), Muslim. The document gives information on his physical characteristics as well (tall, hazel eyes, dark skin). In the first page of the document, it reads: "General Directorate of *Darüleytams*, Special passport for students sent to Germany for training" (Darüleytam Müdüriyet-i Umumiyesi, *Almanya'ya tahsil için izam olunan talebeye mahsus cüzdan*). *Source*: BOA, MF.EYT, 2/117, 29/Ş/1334 (01.07.1916).

school (*Grundschule*) at Koppenplatz and were greeted by Major Ramsen from the Ministry of War, the Privy Councilors (*Geheimrat*) Cleff and Göhmann from the Ministry of Commerce, Dr. Glock from the Ministry of Agriculture, and Vice Consul Tahir Bey from the Ottoman Embassy. They were all clothed with "shirts and trousers in the European style," with a "blue pelerine as a coat and a blue fez-like cap on the head" (see figure 2). Each apprentice had his own identity card, which listed his profession, workplace, assignment number, and the Chamber of Trade to which they were attached. Administrators also intended to add a photograph of each boy to their cards.[31]

2. Ottoman orphan apprentices in Berlin (1917). The reporter argued that the boys came "from various ethnic groups" (*Völkerstämme*) and that "one can see both the white faces of the Armenians and Jews, Anatolian types and also Arabs and negroes among them." *Source*: "Türkische Jugend in Berlin," *Berliner Tageblatt* 216, 6 May 1917.

From Berlin, the boys were sent to their posts in Augsburg, Breslau, Bromberg, Düsseldorf, Frankfurt (Oder), Mannheim, Oldenburg, Schwerin, Weimar, and Ulm. The master craftsmen and the Chambers of Trade and Industry committed to paying for the boarding expenses but not for their return journey, which should be paid either by the Ottoman authorities or by the boys themselves.

In June 1917, a second group of 200 Ottoman boys arrived to be apprenticed in mining areas.[32] In contrast to the first group, who came from orphanages in Istanbul, these boys had been chosen from orphanages in the provinces—from Maraş, Aintab, Kilis, Ankara, Söğüt, Niğde, Konya, Bursa, Manisa, Karahisar, and the CUP orphanage in Edirne. The journey of the boys from the eastern provinces lasted thirty days: twenty days on the Anatolian railway and ten days on the military train from Istanbul to Berlin. In Berlin they were housed in the rooms of Gustavo's Inn (Gastwirt Gustavo) at Hasenheide 52/53. As in the case of the first transport, a greeting ceremony was planned, and Dr. Söhring of the Foreign Office was invited by Dr. Russack of the DTV to visit the boys on the occasion of their distribution to various mines.[33] Yet there is no evidence that he actually visited the boys. Based on the plan prepared by the Ministry of Trade and Industry, representatives of the various mine administrations took them from Berlin to their mining districts. They were about equally divided between the Rhenish-Westphalian mines in the area of Dortmund and Bonn as well as Saarbrücken and the central German mining areas in the districts of Halle and Clausthal. A small group went to Upper Silesia (Wroclaw Mining Administration). Most of the boys worked in metal-ore mining (iron, zinc, lead, copper) and the coal industry, and a small number were employed in lignite (*Braunkohle*) and cement manufacturing.[34]

Sending the last group of agricultural apprentices took much longer than expected. Already in May 1917 approximately 500 agricultural positions were made available for Ottoman boys via a memorandum sent by the DTV to the German Chamber of Agriculture. The boys were to be dispatched from two different centers: those to be placed in the Southwest were to arrive at Karlsruhe, and the boys heading to the Northeast were to arrive in Berlin. However, state affairs were moving slower in the Ottoman Empire. A large number of boys were brought to Istanbul from the provinces to become agricultural apprentices in Germany. Yet they had to wait in crowded Istanbul orphanages for the details to be finalized.[35] For one thing, travel permits for boys born in 1899 and 1900 could not be received from the Ministry of War until October.[36] As they were waiting in Istanbul, the behavior of the boys from the provinces was criticized by the directors as inappropriate and spoiled. The administrators raised concerns that the Istanbul orphans might be negatively influenced by these village boys. They insisted that the boys from the provinces would be immediately transferred to Germany.[37]

TABLE 5: **Locations and specialization of handicraft apprentices in Germany (1918)**

Profession	*Total*	*Augsburg*	*Berlin*	*Breslau*	*Bromberg*
Metalwork					
Smithery	27	3	2	4	5
Blacksmith	1	1	—	—	—
Coppersmith	1	1	—	—	—
Locksmith	5	1	—	1	—
Engine fitter	3	—	—	—	—
Mechanic	7	2	—	—	—
Machine building	4	2	—	—	—
Machine technicians	2	—	—	—	—
Electrical technician	5	1	—	1	—
Plumber	3	—	2	—	—
File cutter	1	—	—	—	—
Iron molder	1	1	—	—	—
Iron lathe operator	2	—	—	—	—
Metalworker	2	—	—	2	—
Total	64				
Woodwork					
Carpenter (Tischler)	24	2	3	3	5
Cabinet maker	1	—	—	—	—
Modeler	2	—	—	2	—
Wagon maker	13	1	1	—	3
Carpenter (Zimmerer)	3	—	—	2	—
Woodturner	1	—	—	—	—
Total	44				
Clothing works					
Tailor	18	1	—	—	1
Shoemaker	9	—	—	—	—
Total	27				
Foodstuff works					
Baker	1	—	—	—	—
Miller	10	—	—	1	—
Total	11				

Düsseldorf	Frankfurt	Hannover	Mannheim	Oldenburg	Schwerin	Ulm	Weimar
2	2	3	—	2	—	4	—
—	—	—	—	—	—	—	—
—	—	—	—	—	—	—	—
—	—	—	—	2	—	1	—
—	—	—	—	—	—	3	—
1	—	—	—	—	—	4	—
—	1	—	—	—	—	1	—
—	—	—	—	—	—	2	—
—	—	—	—	1	—	2	—
1	—	—	—	—	—	—	—
—	—	—	—	—	—	1	—
—	—	—	—	—	—	—	—
—	—	—	—	—	—	2	—
—	—	—	—	—	—	—	—
—	3	3	—	1	1	3	—
—	—	—	—	—	1	—	—
—	—	—	—	—	—	—	—
2	—	3	—	1	2	—	—
—	—	—	1	—	—	—	—
—	—	—	—	1	—	—	—
5	3	4	—	—	2	—	2
1	5	1	1	1	—	—	—
—	—	—	—	—	1	—	—
—	—	6	1	—	1	1	—

Table 5: **Locations and specialization of handicraft apprentices in Germany (1918) (*Cont.*)**

Profession	*Total*	*Augsburg*	*Berlin*	*Breslau*	*Bromberg*
Miscellaneous					
Optician	4	—	—	—	—
Watchmaker	1	—	—	—	—
Painter	6	1	1	1	—
Mason	1	—	—	—	—
Basket maker	4	—	—	4	—
Glass polisher	4	—	—	4	—
Glazier	1	1	—	—	—
Saddler	6	1	—	—	—
Furrier	1	—	—	—	—
Bookbinder	2	—	—	—	—
Printer	3	—	—	—	—
Hairdresser	1	—	—	—	—
Gardener	2	—	—	1	1
Total	36				
Overall	182	19	9	26	15

Source: Hans Hermann Russack, "Die türkischen Lehrlinge," in *Türkische Jugend in Deutschland: Jahresbericht der Schülerabteilung der Deutsch-Türkischen Vereinigung* (Berlin: Deutsch-Türkische Vereinigung e.V., 1918), 52–53.

In the autumn of 1917, the Ottoman Ministry of Education, again in collaboration with the Orphanage Administration, compiled a list of boys and sent it to Germany. However, the DTV officers in Berlin objected to the selection, underlining that only about 100 boys out of 500 had a rural background.[38] Following the demands of the DTV administrators, Dr. Nazım promised to organize a new selection and send a large number of agricultural apprentices consisting of Anatolian "farmers' sons" (*Bauernsöhne*) and "not orphans from the city" (*Waisenkinder aus der Stadt*).[39] As the preparations for their departure continued through the winter, the transfer was postponed until spring. In the end, fewer than 150 agricultural apprentices arrived in two different convoys in June and July 1918.[40] The boys were mainly

Düsseldorf	*Frankfurt*	*Hannover*	*Mannheim*	*Oldenburg*	*Schwerin*	*Ulm*	*Weimar*
—	—	—	—	—	—	4	—
—	—	—	—	—	1	—	—
—	1	—	—	—	—	2	—
—	—	—	—	—	—	—	1
—	—	—	—	—	—	—	—
—	—	—	—	—	—	—	—
—	—	—	—	—	—	—	—
2	1	—	1	—	—	—	1
1	—	—	—	—	—	—	—
—	1	—	1	—	—	—	—
—	—	—	3	—	—	—	—
1	—	—	—	—	—	—	—
—	—	—	—	—	—	—	—
16	17	20	8	9	9	30	4

sent to the North and East of the country to be trained in mechanized agriculture. There were only a few of them in central Germany and in the Rhineland.

Foreign Boys in Foreign Homes

Based on the training contract signed by the Chambers of Trade and Industry and a representative of the Ottoman Embassy, the apprentices agreed to a nonpaid three-year apprenticeship and also to work for a year as a journeyman in the same place for a journeyman's wage. In return, the master craftsmen would provide shelter, board, and in time some clothing (excluding underwear and shoes). The DTV considered it desirable to have the apprentices study German. Some attended part-time or night classes in order to improve their language skills.[41] Those boys who completed their apprenticeships were given certificates. A few examples are preserved in the Ottoman Archives, submitted by the apprentices themselves for translation and accreditation purposes.[42]

The DTV chose the master craftsmen after thorough examination of their households and family structures. An apprentice was entrusted only when the DTV was convinced that the boy would be treated as a child of the house.[43] In its informative leaflet for German households accepting Ottoman boys, the DTV underlined the program's two separate goals.[44] The boys should become accustomed to German morals, ethics, honesty, thoroughness, and industriousness. In order to facilitate this kind of cultural transfer, the mining apprentices were lodged with experienced miners' families, so that they not only worked but also lived in a mining environment. But their religious and national character was not to be threatened. Religious influence should be avoided, and the boys should be given the opportunity to perform their daily prayers and observe Islamic religious holidays. The masters were also told not to offer them pork and alcoholic beverages, both prohibited by Islam.[45] On paper, the rules and responsibilities of both sides were well defined and consistent with standard procedures. However, the experiences on both sides were far from perfect.

The most recurrent conflict in the first months after the arrival of craft apprentices was the "insufficient preparation" (*ungenügende Vorbereitung*) of the Ottoman side for the transfer of the boys. German masters repeatedly complained that they were providing for the boys beyond the original agreements owing to insufficient clothing of the boys. The Chambers of Trade and Industry underlined that Professor Jäckh had prepared the contract, which stated that the boys would bring two outfits, underwear, and shoes so that their masters did not have any clothing costs for at least a couple of months until the boys became productive to compensate for their own expenses. However, the clothing they had when they first arrived "could not be poorer" (*denkbar dürftig*); they had nothing to wear but only blue caps and pelerines provided by the DTV. This description is not hard to believe knowing the circumstances in Istanbul orphanages. Some masters claimed that they had to spend around 100 Mk. to clothe their apprentices since they were ashamed to let the boys—parts of their household—be seen on the street with the clothes they had brought with them.[46] There is, in fact, evidence that the Ottoman Ministry of Education ordered one of the army tailors—Haim, son of Rafael—to produce outfits for the orphan boys to be sent to Germany.[47] However, this was in mid-April, and it is probable that he could not finish the task before the boys' departure date.

The same complaints regarding the boys' "lack of equipment" (*mangelhafte Ausstattung*, particularly shoes and underwear) reappeared when the two hundred mining apprentices arrived. There was a long-lasting "shoe controversy" between the masters and the DTV, on the one side, and the Ottoman representatives, on the other. Apparently, many of the orphan boys arrived in Berlin without shoes. The ones who had some sort of footwear were not sufficiently protected against German winters. Several institutions and masters were forced to provide shoes for their apprentices out of their own pocket and later applied to the Foreign Office for compensation.[48] The DTV demanded in turn that all the expenditures caused by the Ottoman Ministry of Education's "blunders" (*Missgriffe*) should be covered by them.[49]

For the orphan boys themselves, insufficient clothing was a very serious issue. Three mine apprentices from Frankleben, Necdet, Hüseyin, and Süleyman, turned to the office of the DTV with the complaint that their clothes were not warm enough and that they were constantly cold.[50] The work in the mines, coupled with uncongenial temperatures, proved to be health hazards. An apprentice died at the Charité Hospital (Berlin) as a result of a lung disease, and another died in Wittenberge (northern Germany) from appendicitis and peritonitis. Another orphan apprentice was put in the Municipal Insane Asylum in Berlin-Dalldorf,[51] for reasons that were kept unmentioned in the minutes.[52]

The plan and preparations for the transfer of children were so hastily made that there was frequent criticism regarding the selection of children from several levels (masters, Chambers of Trade, the supervisors of the DTV). German masters reported the "wrong selection" (*schlechte Auswahl*) to voice their discontent with the orphan apprentices. It is obvious that the Ottoman authorities had made the selection on purely numerical terms—to reach certain numbers, be it three hundred, two hundred, or whatever. This process did not result in a group of appropriate candidates with skills appropriate to the vacant positions. The DTV also claimed that the Ottomans sent essentially all who volunteered, without a detailed medical examination or testing their intellectual or moral qualities. The masters complained of poor health and unsuitable age—some were too young or too weak, especially for mine work. As a result, during the first two months, 25 percent were sent back in order to "clean up thoroughly the unsuitable elements" (*den ungeeigneten Elementen gründlich aufzuräumen*).[53]

Moreover, the selection committee in Istanbul was accused of disregarding both the boys' previous training and the list of vacant apprenticeship positions, prepared by the German Chamber Trade and Industry. A large number of apprentices (about 50 percent) were in professions other than their previous training. Mining apprentices frequently applied to the DTV with the grievance that their previous training was something else and that they did not want to perform the work they were assigned. When possible, boys were assigned to another but related trade. If not, they had to remain at their assigned positions. This mismatch is why many were unhappy at their workplaces and applied for either relocation or definite return to the country; it is also why several of them escaped or showed signs of disobedience. For instance, a mine apprentice, Mazhar, and a trade apprentice, Mustafa Osman, escaped from their posts in Fürstenwalde because they were not content with their jobs. Previously trained for two years as lathe operators, they found their present apprenticeships not compatible with their vocational qualifications. The German Chamber of Trade and Industry responded that it was not possible at the moment to accommodate them as lathe operators.[54] The Chamber was also unhappy about the arrival dates and job reassignments of the boys. The starting date for German apprentices was traditionally Easter, but the transfer of the Ottoman boys to their posts was delayed until the middle or end of May. Consequently, the change in their choice of training caused further hardship for the Chamber.[55] Months after their arrival, many trade apprentices had to be accommodated in hotels in Berlin, since the authorities were considering whether they should return home or be assigned to another apprenticeship.[56]

The Ottoman administrators, on the other hand, were inclined to put the blame on the boys in "making mistakes in their career choices." Muslihiddin Adil Bey, director general of Ottoman secondary education and later head of the inspection committee sent to Europe in May 1918, prepared a report of his visit to Germany in May 1333 (1917), in the form of a travelogue. He claimed that most of the boys went to Germany without having any idea of the curriculum of their future studies. Most of them chose their trades by mere chance, and others were placed in trades that were not in accordance with their skills and aspirations. Actually, very few apprentices were informed of the trade they would be apprentices in, the length of their training, or the city or school they were going to.[57] As they arrived in Germany lacking accurate knowledge, it was normal that many of them had problems with their workplaces and the nature of the work they were asked to perform.

In accordance with the demands of the Ottoman government, most of the boys were assigned to workshops in small and medium-size towns to facilitate their integration into a foreign society and to enable the boys to meet intermittently. This way it was also easier to monitor them. At the same time, the integration of Ottoman orphans remained an unaccomplished goal, even though the DTV was convinced that better-integrated Turks would be better envoys of German culture and ethics. Language deficiency was an obstacle that made everyday life difficult for the boys. Apprentices were not offered a period of language training, so all of them arrived at their posts with literally no knowledge of German. Some tried to attend courses, but the reports of the Chambers of Trade and Mining Administrations indicate that the progress of most of the boys was next to nothing. In order to facilitate the communication between masters and apprentices, a seven-hundred-word dictionary was prepared at the initiative of the Chamber of Trade.[58] However, it was not useful at all for the Ottoman boys. All sections, explanations, and words were from German to Turkish and not the other way around. Moreover, it was written in the Latin alphabet, whereas these boys, even if they were literate, knew how to read and write only in Arabic script.

Apprentices could have learned the language in the exact same way that they acquired knowledge and skill, by observing, imitating, practicing, and interacting with experienced workers and masters. However, relations have not always been smooth between Ottoman apprentices and their German colleagues and masters. As a pilot integration project, Ottoman apprentices in the ore mines near Eisleben stayed in the same dorm with German apprentices. The administration assumed this setup would facilitate the linguistic progress and mutual interaction of the boys. However, there were serious problems and difficulties, from verbal harassment to physical disturbance and fights. Later the boys were not only accommodated in separate dorms, but also separated during work hours.[59]

Another source of discontent in the everyday life of the apprentice boys in German homes and workplaces was food. Many of them acknowledged that the bread was much better in Germany. Yet they were never sure whether the meals contained pork or not. What they were constantly served were dark-colored soups that tasted unfamiliar to them.[60] In other cases, boys complained that they were provided with only one meal each day and nothing else.[61] Four mine apprentices from Altenberg and Eschbach escaped, complaining that the food was bad.[62]

Critics of the project argued that Ottoman students were usually settled with poor soldier families in order to make sure that these people were provided with some means of assistance. Student boys' pocket money (either sent by their guardians or state scholarships) was to become family's income, since the residents paid for food and board. When the boys complained, as they frequently did, of the scarcity or distastefulness of food, they were told in a hostile manner "to write to home for better food,"[63] or else when they applied to the DTV, they were threatened with being sent back to become a soldier.[64] German school directors, pension holders, and craft masters were in a difficult position about the food costs of the Ottoman boys. They claimed that catering their preferred food under war conditions was extremely costly. They consumed rice, mutton, a lot of bread and sugar, and other things, which could be procured only with great difficulty. Moreover, they did not eat pork and refused sausage, which were cheaper and easier to provide.[65]

Disobedience and Escape as Empowerment

The accounts of boys running away and other such stories have been documented only sporadically. However, we know for certain that by November 1918, there were only 140 mine apprentices left in Germany of the 200 initially sent and only 182 trade apprentices from the original 314.[66] In other words, almost 40 percent of the boys were either unsuitable for the designated project or dissatisfied and discontented at their posts.

These numbers suggest that the conditions the Ottoman boys encountered abroad were far from idyllic. It was a paradise lost. Orphan boys definitely dreamed of a better training and work environment with more opportunities. They were hoping to earn some money, if

TABLE **6: Ottoman apprentices in Germany (1917–1919)**

	June 1917	*November 1918*	*December 1919*
Trade apprentices	314	182	140
Mine apprentices	200	140	40
Agricultural apprentices	140 (delayed)	90	70
Total	654	412	250

Sources: "Türkische Jugend in Berlin," *Berliner Tageblatt* 216, 06.05.1917; "From die DTV to Dr. Söhring, Auswärtiges Amt, 13.Juni.1917, Berlin," PA AA, R63063; "Jahresbericht des Schülerheims, 1.Nov.1918," PA AA, R 63065; "Jahresbericht der DTV für 1918 [–1919], 11.Dezember.1919," PA AA, R63443.

not get rich, and benefit from the promises of European prosperity. When these dreams shattered owing to poor living and working conditions, orphans started to resist, even revolt. The Chamber of Trade and Industry was worried that only a few masters gave positive feedback of their well-behaved and modest apprentices, who fitted well with German standards. Many masters regretted that they had agreed to have Ottoman boys, who were demanding monetary compensation and free time.[67] Both were considered incompatible with the rights and responsibilities of an apprentice in Germany.[68] The boys were supposedly acting very arrogantly and confidently. They insisted that they were promised, so entitled to, employment in a factory and a handsome monthly salary.[69] No matter how futile it was, orphan boys kept asking for time and money to remedy their situation, to empower themselves, and possibly to move elsewhere.

The main problem was the children's misinformation or overestimation. Most of the boys came assuming that they would be employed by their trade masters in accordance with their previous training. They had no idea that they would end up in mine work. In the coal mines of Breslau, the boys were openly resistant. They were rude toward their coworkers and frequently refused to perform the tasks they were ordered to do. The boys said they were being exploited with very hard work, and they quit the work premises.[70] Four mine apprentices from Altenberg and Eschbach escaped because they had no pocket money and were treated badly.[71] It is perfectly understandable, given the difficulty of coal mining. Orphan boys in the Rammelsberg mine administration reportedly escaped their duties and clearly had no interest in the work operation itself.[72] Apprentices, on the other hand, were complaining that they were not learning anything apart from transporting stones from here to there.[73]

There was a serious uprising in the Royal Oberharzer mining and metallurgical works (Oberharzer Berg- und Hüttenwerke). Fourteen Ottoman boys, supposedly under the leadership of a certain "negro Mehmed Tevfik," refused to perform their tasks and disturbed the work discipline. Mehmed Tevfik was accused of discouraging his countrymen from working with "threats and ill-treatment" (*Drohungen und Misshandlungen*).[74] What turned minor cases of resistance into an open revolt was the employment of several boys in the same workplace. Group feeling strengthened the boys and encouraged them to take action. A common form of collective resistance was to escape to urban centers and allegedly get involved with "various vices of the cities." For instance, eight of the total ten apprentices in the Royal Mining Inspection at Rüdersdorf escaped the mines shortly after their arrival and did not come back. A few weeks later, five of those eight escapees were found at the Friedrichstraße train station and sent back to their posts at Rüdersdorf by the DTV. However, the whereabouts of three others were unknown.[75]

The source material for this research, that is, the reports of the DTV (prepared by either local administrators or central supervisors), is absolutely biased in terms of putting all the blame on the apprenticed boys—they were either ill-prepared for the nature of their training, or they were not accustomed to work discipline, or they were rude, or they incited one another, and so on. The disobedience of the boys was regarded with a more or less manifest "imperial gaze."[76] Dr. Russack argued that the difficulty of teaching them regular work, discipline, and obedience stemmed from the boys' untamed nature. They were "children of nature" (*Naturkinder*), lacking the basic formation of civilized manners to adapt to German standards of hard work.[77]

Social historians, informed with postcolonial theoretical frames, underline the difficulty of hearing the voices of the subaltern as well as the importance of rereading the sources for traces of agency of the disempowered, be they colonial subjects or children. In this section, I focus on children's voices in the complaints they filed and based on their escape stories. Reconfiguring the narrative from the perspectives of the boys themselves, it is possible to give another meaning as to why they were labeled "lazy," "disobedient," or "problematic." These children were deeply disillusioned with the limited opportunities they were offered in Germany. Most of them could not even pursue the vocational training they were promised. Their hopes to lead more prosperous lives were shattered. What the authorities saw as "going out of the way" was their search for a way out of their disappointments.

The Return

The farewell speech of a student, made shortly before the departure of *Gülcemal* in August 1919 from Hamburg, emphasized the Turkish students' "deepest gratitude for the hospitality and helpfulness" of Germany and Germans. He continued by saying that these were "the best years of their lives," which they would always "remember with heartfelt pleasure." More important, he stressed that they were "well aware that [they] owe much to German culture, which helped [them] become competent."[78]

The following speech by General Zeki Pasha, who was the military delegate to the German Headquarters, underlined "the sincere helpfulness of Germany" and expressed the high opinion of the Ottomans regarding the importance of German culture and German hospitality. In other words, despite numerous crises, regrets, and disappointments of both sides, official declarations tended to emphasize the gains and accomplishments. Ottoman orphan boys were definitely not of the same opinion.

The pressure and necessities caused by the war facilitated rather than impeded the policy of child displacement between the two empires. The project was initiated in the middle of the war, and it practically came to a close with the end of the war. The defeat of the Central Powers not only led to the collapse of the German and Ottoman Empires but also made the continuation of educational collaboration projects impossible owing to both financial difficulties and organizational breakdowns.[79] After November 1918, influential Unionists, among them the founders of the TDV, escaped the country, and the CUP was no longer ruling the empire.

In April 1919, the DTV reported that the students and orphan apprentices under its authority were on the whole eight hundred boys. The educational and daily costs of some students were paid by their family members. Others had full or half scholarships from the DTV. As the communication between the two empires was cut off with the conclusion of the armistice, money transfers from Istanbul were interrupted. No longer receiving the monthly payments of the families, the DTV had to pay for the expenses of the entire student body. Their funds, however, were about to be depleted, and so they started to consider the option of repatriation.[80] The Entente agreed on 20 April that the Ottoman ship (*Akdeniz*) that brought German troops back from Constantinople could take on board Ottoman citizens living in Germany on its way back. The departure date was very close (30 April), and so the time to organize and bring the boys scattered all around Germany was very short. Still, with the demand of the Ottoman Embassy, the DTV informed the masters and mine authorities that Ottoman orphan apprentices were supposed to return via the steamers departing from Hamburg.

The steamers *Akdeniz*, *Reşid Paşa*, and *Gülcemal* departed in May, June, and August 1919, carrying back Ottoman soldiers, officials, and students.[81] The DTV was not insistent on sending them back. On the contrary, it was underlined that it was "politically valuable" to help students continue their education without interruption and let them return to their homeland only after graduation or when their parents called them back.[82] It was believed that German-educated youth would sustain and promote Germany's reputation in the East and would also translate into economic gain.[83] Therefore, those students who paid for their own expenses and apprentices whose masters agreed to provide for them were allowed to stay.[84] Ahmed Talib, for instance, had an exemplary master–apprentice relationship with Albert Pöthke and could stay with him, despite the official termination of the political agreement.[85] In late 1919, about half of the students and apprentices (320) were sent back, but the DTV still had 250 orphan apprentices and 230 students as its dependents.[86] In a report sent by the Directorate of Orphanages to the Ministry of Interior in October 1919, it was underlined that the orphans in Germany were "discharged from" (*ilişikleri kesilen*) the jurisdiction (and protection) of the directorate.

They were at the beginning under the supervision of the inspectors of the Ministry of Education. At the end of the war, the Ministry of Education declared that it could no longer meet their needs because of financial problems. Therefore, all the children were "transferred" (*devredilmiş*) to the direction of the military, and they were now "protected" (*himaye*) by military inspectors.[87] Lieutenant Şükrü Bey, who was in charge of the supervision of the children, reported that 139 orphans were still at their posts in Germany. Although they were "deprived of any form of protection and guidance, they were persevering and endeavoring in their training."[88]

Most of the orphan apprentices arrived in Istanbul in the same needy circumstances that they left the city. The most serious problem was to lodge these destitute boys, since many *darüleytam*s had to be discontinued after the Allied occupation of parts of the empire and the repossession of confiscated buildings by their rightful owners. A couple of hundred of orphan boys who came back from Germany could not be easily fit into these already downsized and crowded orphanages. For instance, two boys from the tailoring department of the orphanage in Kadıköy, Mehmed Fikri and İshak Namık, came back from Germany to find their former orphanage closed. Petitioning the Ministry of Education, they asked to be admitted to the Yedikule Orphanage.[89] Almost all of the orphans who came back from Germany were actually put into this orphanage because of its closeness to state-owned factories. Returnees were about five years older than the rest of the boys in the institution, and they were employed in the Zeytinburnu Imperial Factory (*Zeytinburnu Fabrika-i Hümayunu*). Each morning, they walked about three kilometers to their work and came back tired in the evening. A younger inmate of the same orphanage complained in his memoirs that these older boys talked, made naughty jokes, and laughed all night.[90]

Boys who were brought from the orphanages in the provinces were in particularly dire straits. Not only were their orphanages closed, but they were also hundreds of kilometers away from their hometowns and with no means to return there. Some orphans were "temporarily" sheltered in the poorhouse (Darülaceze) and in hospitals. However, this supposedly limited residence lasted longer than expected. They were not sent back until March 1922.[91]

Grands Soirs et Petits Matins

The sending of Ottoman orphans to Germany was one of the boldest and most interesting educational undertakings shared by the two empires. Both sides were hoping to achieve mutual cultural understanding and economic benefits through the direct contact of numerous Ottoman boys with the German language and culture. In sending students and trainees to Germany for vocational training, the Young Turks were hoping to train pioneers for a national bourgeoisie, who would play key roles in creating a national economic policy and, thus, economic independence from Europe.[92] The apprentice scheme would have served well the dreams of the Unionists to establish a "national economy." Benefiting from their unaccountable emergency powers and extreme policies under wartime conditions, the CUP leadership not only worked toward the elimination of the non-Muslim populations of the empire (largely artisans and craftsmen), but also thought of means to remedy the expected shortage of skilled labor.

Side by side with this theoretical and long-term economic imagination and planning, the Ottoman administration also wanted to kill two birds with one stone. By sending hundreds of orphan boys to Germany (which was initially envisioned by Enver to be as many as ten thousand), the CUP would solve a *current* and pressing problem of sheltering, feeding, and educating so many orphaned children and youth, while promising to invest in a better future. Hastily made plans and preparations for the transfer of children (lacking clothing, equipment, and the like) and disregard for selection criteria (former vocation, health, work ethics, and so on) imply that the primary concern of the Ottoman government was the quantity they sent. They wanted to *get rid of* as many orphan boys as possible, regardless of the opportunities offered to them. Orphan boys were sent without any decided return date. The way the *vorzeitig* returnees were treated is also indicative of the fact that they were not really expected to come back, at least not in the near future.

The two goals behind sending orphans to Germany—to get rid of thousands of extra mouths, while training the artisans and workers of the next Ottoman generation to replace the non-Muslims, who were killed during the genocide(s) of Ottoman Christians—both remained largely unaccomplished. Only a few hundred boys could be sent to Germany, and very few of them mastered the trades in which they apprenticed. The malfunctioning of the scheme from the very beginning and its bitter end shared the fate of many other wartime policies, which similarly suffered from corruption, lack of organization, and epic failures. Why the Ottoman government was not able to "utilize" such a large labor force at home can also be understood by looking closely at the logic of foster-care arrangements. Poor households were not able to benefit from their children's labor as much as rich households. Sending a child away helped save scarce resources, even increasing the dispensable income that a household earned. Orphans in the Ottoman Empire were in that situation. The state had a weak organizational structure. There was an ongoing financial crisis, and there was low economic production during the war years, in both agriculture and industry. Therefore, the government was unable to turn this army of boys into a real workforce *at home*.

Economic considerations also played a part in the German context, given growing labor shortages.[93] Millions of men left their jobs in industry to serve in the armed forces—eleven million men were mobilized in Germany.[94] The labor shortages provided new job opportunities for women and for immigrants as well. Moreover, plagued by hunger, hurt by the increased cost of living, and frustrated with the continuing war, hundreds of thousands of long-suffering German workers organized a total of 561 labor strikes in 1917.[95] German trade masters and mining authorities, volunteering to take in Ottoman boys as apprentices into their homes and establishments, probably hoped that these children would be silent, obedient, and hardworking laborers. Still, the reason why Germany accepted the heavy burden of educating and feeding Ottoman orphans lies in what Fuhrmann calls a "semicolonial mentality."[96] The key names at the head of the DTV, such as Rohrbach and Jäckh, were critical of the direction of German foreign policy toward the Ottoman Empire. According to them, this policy was obsessed with the numerically calculable benefits of major investments, such as the Baghdad Railway or technocratic advisers. Instead, they underlined the importance of "moral conquest" of the hearts and minds of the people. In this way, they would build sympathy for Germany among Turks and gain consent for larger political agendas.[97] Starting with the Ottoman entry into the war, the German Military Supreme Command and Foreign Office pursued good relations with the Ottoman government and hoped to build channels of German cultural influence. Educational and cultural collaborative possibilities were gaining ground and growing. German business circles and Turcophiles, among which were Ernst Jäckh and his DTV, were the most prominent, wasting no time in forging ambitious plans for the "economic development of the 'Sultan's lands.'"[98]

The quality—either of the boys or of the training they were offered—was not a big issue for the Young Turk government. There is even evidence to the contrary. The Ottoman Ministry of Education acted as if the German educational outlets were banishment centers for unsatisfactory students, together with burdensome orphans. In October 1917, the ministry ruled that those boys who failed to pass their classes more than once and the ones who did not have any chance of graduating would be sent to Germany to be trained as apprentices in crafts and agriculture.[99] The DTV and the German foreign policy makers, however, accepted the heavy burden of educating and feeding Ottoman orphans only because of the promise that they would receive "the sons and daughters of the best families of the country."[100] Since there were only a few German-educated Ottomans, educating them in Germany was a great opportunity to create a new generation who "are friends of Germany."[101] In that respect, the Germans' educational aspirations had a quasi-colonial quality, driven by a long-term vision and dependent on the boys they were able to mold. Dr. Ryll, the inspector of the DTV for the Ottoman youth in Germany, described the issue in his July 1918 report titled "Quantity or Quality?" with the following words:

> The evidence is growing more and more by supporters and experts of our work—both from the Turkish and German sides—that our success does not depend on whether the number of Turkish youth studying in Germany is increasing every year by several hundreds. It depends more on the arrival of "the best minds of Turkish schools" (as it says in our guidelines) and to educate and train in our country those, who could alone be the bearers of a better Turkish future. Thereby one might at first think of the "best families," i.e. the social elite of Turkish society, who has previously played the leading political role and who is also likely to continue to play that role for the time being.[102]

Squeezed between Ottoman demands for quantity and German demands for quality, orphan boys were expected to accomplish a mission impossible. Orphans themselves felt betrayed on two fronts. On the one hand, their hopes to lead more prosperous lives in Germany were shattered. On the other, they were not welcomed back in their country as qualified workers to help rejuvenate the economy. They were still being treated as needy orphans for whom the state had a hard time providing. Despite the miles they traveled and all the hardships they encountered, they were unable to remedy their situation as destitute children.

3

Children as Agents and Targets of Nationalist Politics

WITH THE FORMATION and espousal of nationalist ideologies during the second half of the nineteenth century, children and youth assumed a significant new role that made them representatives of the "future of the nation." During the First World War, the engagement of children with the nation through propaganda, heroism, and symbolism became all the more prominent. The climate of nationalism and separatism shaped the Ottoman Empire in the nineteenth century. The hypothetically universal category of "children" had difficulty in transcending the particularism and ethnoreligious differentiation that characterized the political landscape. Children were part of nationalist, ethnic, and religious agitation. From schools and media, their families and friends, Ottoman children received distinct messages about whose war they were fighting and whose future they represented. In the case of France, Britain, and Germany, the political and economic centrality of children to the home front has been underlined and their position as workers, peasants, and symbols of the nation and its future has been noted.[1] In all these cases, the nation appears as an indispensable link between children and war. There was only one nation in question and also one war. Children labored and sacrificed for the nation and provided the rejuvenating source for the nation's future. However, the multireligious and multiethnic structure of the Ottoman Empire and the disunity of the idea of the nation complicated what Ottoman children represented and stood for. The

Ottomanist promise of the 1908 revolution was shattering, and the umbrella "Ottoman" identity was put aside, especially following the 1913 coup. Persisting legal inequalities and periodic violence against non-Muslims and non-Turks and culminating Turkist tendencies of the Unionists contributed to children's self-identification as Bulgarians, Armenians, Greeks, and so on.

The first part of the chapter gives a short overview of the militarization of the civilian realm. The second part is on the paramilitary education of youth and boy-scouting activities, which were instrumental for the nationalist and militarized socialization of children and youth. I first summarize the available literature on state-sponsored (Turkist) organizations, which were very active, especially during the war years. More crucially, this part focuses on the emergence and suppression of non-Muslim scouting organizations, which were visible only before and after the war. The third part brings to light how children played out nationalist and religious rivalries at the street level by focusing on "war games" or real acts of violence between boy gangs. Children took initiative for their national interests and attacked their rivals as active agents. The replication of war on a daily basis was at the heart of children's identity formation. The last part discusses adult fights over the possession of orphaned or destitute children whose national belonging was disputable—and thus could be reshaped.

This chapter, based on research in the Ottoman Archives, contemporary press, school books, memoirs, and the papers of youth organizations, focuses on the politicization and socialization of Ottoman children and youth along religious, ethnic, and nationalist lines. The constituting elements of the multinational empire were pulling their members in different directions, as the central government more strongly emphasized the Turkish and Muslim identity of the state.[2]

Militarization of Daily Life

As Cynthia Enloe notes, forms of political violence that we witness or that we simply experience as a constant presence in our lives inevitably have an impact on our private selves and personal relations.[3] She defines militarization as "the step-by-step process by which something becomes controlled by, dependent on, or derives value from the military or militaristic criteria."[4] It is a subtle and pervasive process that recruits gendered and racial sets of social practices and self-understandings and permeates every aspect of life. Anthropological research proves that violence-producing practices of states, militaries, and nationalist movements often translate into everyday violence within the family, against women, or among children.[5] This rather natural process that easily encompassed the entire population in a cycle of violence probably worked much more smoothly during the First World War. It was the first large-scale industrialized military conflict in world history, and it gave birth to the concept of "total war," which implied the systematic erosion of the distinction between the military and civilian spheres.[6]

The year 1913 was a decisive time in transforming the politics of the post-1908 era into a single-party authoritarian regime after the coup of the CUP. The defeat in the Balkan Wars led Ottoman authorities to initiate radical military reforms in order to establish the military as the political ruling group. The government and many state positions were filled with men from a military background. Moreover, the CUP portrayed the new law of conscription (requiring each and every able-bodied Ottoman man to serve in the military) as essential to the survival of the empire. The Ottoman state mobilized its male population on short notice in 1914, building an army of almost three million troops. As touched on in this book's introduction, young boys also became part of the war effort, combat, and fighting. Although it is almost impossible to ascertain the number of underage soldiers in the army, boys as young as sixteen were conscripted to compensate for the large number of casualties and deserters. Hasan İzzettin Dinamo recounts in his autobiographical novel, *Savaş ve Açlar* (*The War and the Hungry*), how his older brother was conscripted at the age of fifteen and killed after only a few months in Sarıkamış.[7]

Under the undeniable impact of Marshal Colmar von der Goltz, the founding father of the concept with his 1883 book, *Das Volk in*

Waffen (*Nation in Arms*), Enver Pasha declared in June 1914 that to become a "nation-in-arms" (*millet-i müsellaha*) was the only option for survival in this era.[8] The term was emblematic of the CUP's militarist culture during the period. The National Defense League (Müdafaa-i Milliye Cemiyeti) aimed to popularize the militarist ideology through public demonstrations, propagating nationalistic ideals and enthusiasm for the war effort.[9] The figures such as Black (Kara) Fatmas[10] or legends such as "120 children"[11] propagated the sacredness of military sacrifice for nonbelligerent segments of the Ottoman society, especially women and children. The mobilization was, therefore, not restricted to the military domain. The entire society was militarized as a result of the mobilization and propaganda campaigns. Atrocity propaganda and boycott movements secured the defining role of military engagements in civil relations.[12]

Paramilitary Training of Children

Children and youth were not exempt from the sweeping militarization of daily life. A major development that drew children into roles as nationalist actors was the formation of the first boy-scouting organizations on the eve of the First World War. In the period immediately following the 1908 Constitutional Revolution, Baden-Powell's new phenomenon, the Boy Scouts, was met with enthusiasm among various ethnic and religious communities of the empire as the perfect combination of patriotism, athleticism, and skill building for children and youth.[13] These societies were pumped and promoted with the utmost enthusiasm and became major centers that called for children's heroism and patriotism.

In the first decade of the twentieth century, physical culture became increasingly militarized, and paramilitary organizations were presented as a source of appeal for youth. Their training programs envisioned military exercise and drill for premilitary-age students.[14] In the early twentieth century, the field of sports was loaded with highly nationalistic symbols that coincided with national strategies based on a "salvation ideology." In this respect, children were used as the paramilitary and nationalist forces of future nation-states that would detach from and transcend the multiethnic, multireligious, multilingual Ottoman past.[15]

Murat C. Yıldız notes an integral link between the spread of gymnastics and national sentiment in the decades prior to the war. Sports clubs, including scouting associations, were established along communal lines and attracted members from a specific ethnoreligious community.[16] The language and symbols used in logos, official documents, and the press projected a distinct ethnoreligious identity. Communal cohesion was brought forward, while divisions and differences between communities were emphasized. Young men established ethnic-based solidarities in these clubs. Educators and writers intentionally emphasized their own ethnoreligious communal affiliations and referred to communal divisions while discussing the sports and scouting activities.[17] They compared the accomplishments of different communities and tried to encourage their own community to invest more in physical education. Yıldız also stresses that despite their largely segregated nature, communities did not live disconnected from one another. They were informed about each other's activities, they interacted, and they shared a common preoccupation in regard to scouting, sports, and community.

Turkish associations were essentially different from non-Muslim clubs from a number of perspectives. In these communally divided civic spaces, non-Muslims often became members of Turkish associations, while the Turks did not join non-Muslim organizations. Membership in Turkish clubs had tangible and intangible benefits for a young non-Muslim man who was interested in having "access to a bourgeois space that oscillated between embracing an Ottoman and Turkish identity."[18] From another perspective, Turkish sport clubs, such as Fenerbahçe and Galatasaray, could easily claim to be both Ottoman and Turkish sports clubs, whereas Maccabi, Hercules, and Artavazt could claim to be only Jewish, Greek, and Armenian clubs.[19] Another major difference between Turkish and non-Muslim sports and scouting organizations was their treatment by the authorities. Even before the war, the Public Security Directorate ordered in July 1914 the closure of all non-Muslim sport clubs in Istanbul, while

Turkish paramilitary organizations were polished, pampered, and thus developing at full speed.

Turkish Paramilitary Youth Organizations

Scouting, as constructed in the late nineteenth century with the examples of Boy Scouts in Britain, Pfadfinder in Germany, and Eclaireur in France, was introduced to the Turkish-speaking public in an article in 1910 using the Ottoman term *keşşaflık* as the translation of "scouting." The CUP government aimed to increase its capacity for social control and penetrate further into society through the establishment of paramilitary youth organizations, which were among the channels used to spread Turkism after the Ottoman defeat during the Balkan Wars.[20] These associations would not only make the mobilization effort permanent, but would also serve as a readily visible propaganda medium to arouse support on the home front. However, as I will discuss below, there is a need to underline the instances of parents' resistance to children's mobilization.

Turkish Muslim scouting activity started with the foundation of the Türk Gücü Cemiyeti (Turkish Strength Association) in 1913.[21] Turkism was the dominant ideology of Türk Gücü, prioritizing "the physical strength of the Turk."[22] In 1914 sporting and scouting clubs were reorganized the under the name "Ottoman Strength Associations" and were institutionalized at schools in a more centralized manner. The new curriculum made membership obligatory for students of state schools and madrassas (Muslim religious schools).[23] It envisioned physical education activities for premilitary-age students involving exclusively military exercise and drill (both with and without arms). The public visibility of Turkish children with arms was considered a successful form of war propaganda. "In order to keep the people's warlike character and keep their love for the army alive," the practices were also open to civilians for a small fee.[24]

Ottoman Strength Associations aimed to integrate military training into the Ottoman school system and make each young boy a perfect soldier by opening branches even in small villages.[25] There was a strong emphasis on masculinity and manliness, because being a

Turkish man was invariably associated with being a soldier. Ottoman Strength Associations would create a new generation of "manly soldiers" who would be "embarrassed to spend their time in coffeehouses like today's weak youth or become women under soft cotton sheets."[26] Those men who were not part of the "soldier cult" were represented as feminine. The "other men," non-Muslims and non-Turks, were also excluded from the "nation-in-arms" and intentionally kept unarmed in labor battalions.

In 1916, as the war's demand for permanent mobilization continued, Colonel von Hoff of Germany took control of the organization to create a more efficient and extensive network of paramilitary training, taking German militarism and youth organizations as its model. The name was further changed to Genç Dernekleri (Youth League). According to the new regulation, "every Ottoman boy" of a certain age had to be a member.[27] In practice, however, the membership excluded non-Muslims, as the declared aim had still been to "improve the health of Turks."

Every provincial and district governor was required to establish a branch of the Youth League.[28] The Inspectorate of the League demanded a list of boys between the ages of twelve and seventeen from all the governors in order to make sure that they were registered.[29] The task of keeping the records of young people who were required to participate in the activities of the Youth League was assigned to headmen (*muhtar*) in the districts, who were to prepare lists of eligible young boys in their administrative units and make sure they attended the activities. These records and lists were also necessary preparation for conscription. Ottoman authorities aimed not only to train young boys for military service, but also to propagate their war cause in rural areas and overcome reluctance toward and resistance to conscription.[30]

Resistance to Paramilitary Education

From the perspective of families, wartime obligations were becoming more and more numerous each day, now even to include young children. Though further research is required, there was a strong antiwar sentiment in all segments of society, even if it did not turn into an organized and associational pacifist movement.[31] Women from different cities of the empire organized resistance against the war, mostly via food riots. In the very first months of the war, women in Erzurum organized an antiwar demonstration that the observers qualified as "extraordinary." Women waited in front of the governor's house for hours; throwing stones at the building, they requested the governor send a telegram to Istanbul defying the war.[32] In March 1916, women broke into railway yards whence troop trains were about to leave, shouting protests against sending the men "to go to their death." They threw themselves on the rails in front of the trains. The authorities refrained from using force to remove them, fearing a mutiny among the soldiers.[33] Although it might be necessary to take these newspaper reports with a grain of salt, Elif Mahir Metinsoy recounts a few other cases of women's demonstration against conscription.[34] She notes that a delegation of Turkish women visited the *Goeben* battleship and protested that their husbands, sons, and brothers had been sent to battle. In another case, peasant women from Bilecik started screaming and protesting during the screening of a propaganda movie, after seeing how their husbands, fathers, and sons were dying. Muslim Turkish women also took an active role in desertion.[35]

As the Youth League targeted rural boys of the provinces and its trainers were drilling boys as if they were soldiers already, many people in rural areas started to believe that the state was forming "an army of children," or that the state would now conscript children even younger than fifteen.[36] These rumors caused open resistance to the Youth League in some areas, and mothers refused to let their young boys attend training sessions.[37] The need for the labor of unschooled peasant boys in agricultural areas was a crucial issue. In a report from Kütahya, it was clearly stated that young boys in villages were busy with agricultural work, and so no branch was established in the villages.[38] In another from Konya, it was emphasized that unschooled young boys had to work in the fields, since their fathers and guardians were under arms already.[39] Despite all these difficulties, in 1918 von Hoff stated that the Youth League had educated about two hundred thousand Turkish boys under the supervision of thirty-five hundred trainers.[40]

Paramilitary Education in State Orphanages

The heightened importance of physical education and military training added a military dimension to education during wartime.[41] Ottoman educators believed that the war might be fruitfully utilized to generate a generation of courageous, bold, outstanding, and, most important, nationalist adults who acted under the spirit of sacrifice. The Ministry of Education decided to include military training in the curriculum of *darüleytams* in 1915.[42] The Directorate of the Orphanages claimed that in order to "raise these children the most profitable way possible both intellectually and physically" (*fikren, bedenen en nafi bir şekilde yetiştirilmeleri*), and also "in order to gather entirely the fruits of the efforts spent day and night" (*geceli gündüzlü sarf edilen mesainin semeratını tamamiyle iktitaf için*), the children should be trained with rifles and guns. Consequently, the War Ministry sent three hundred rifles to the boys orphanage in Kadıköy, and training of children with rifles started immediately. The director of the orphanage noted that the boys very quickly showed obvious signs of "order and nationalist feeling" (*intizam ve hiss-i milli*). As a result, he asked for at least a thousand rifles to be sent to the Directorate of Orphanages, in order to make sure that not only Kadıköy boys but all orphanage students received a uniform military education.[43]

The director also demanded Ottoman flags from the War Ministry as a "monument of victory" (*abide-yi zafer*) in Gallipoli. In addition, he asked for "enemy flags" (*düşman bayrağı*) and "enemy uniforms and military equipment" (*düşman elbise ve alat-ı harbiyesi*) that were captured from the front, along with four hundred portable tents that remained locked in the inventories of the Maçka barracks. The director explained that all these items would be used for the new organization of boy-scout training in the orphanages. The boys would *play war* in the orphanage yard by using these real artifacts from the front. The educators aimed to use both military equipment and the symbolic representations of enemy soldiers in order to set up the scene for a war game within the walls of the orphanage, to create a patriotic generation, and to make sure that the "orphans of martyrs professed talent in their training with guns" (*evlad-ı şühedanın silah taliminde iktisab-ı mümarese etmeleri için*). The choice of Gallipoli as the front to replicate in a game is telling. The boys would be instilled with nationalistic and militaristic feelings with reference to both their fathers' martyrdom and their fatherland's victory.

It is also not a coincidence that the Ministry of War sent Colonel von Hoff, inspector general of the Youth League, to give a talk to all the teachers of the male orphanages (in Istanbul) on the importance of the league and its primary aims. He said that according to the new regulation of the Youth League, all boys above twelve years of age were supposed to be incorporated into the organization. Boys younger than twelve would be subject to a new law on boy scouting.[44]

In 1914 the Ministry of Education declared its decision to open a "Physical Training School" (Terbiye-i Bedeniye Mektebi) in Vefa (Istanbul). The *Tedrisat-ı İbtidaiye Mecmuası* (Journal of Elementary Education) made short news of the decision and the concrete steps that were being taken. The school would offer students theoretical courses in anatomy, physiology, and hygiene; show them proper gymnastics methods; and train physical training instructors.[45] However, the construction of the school was interrupted in 1916 because of financial difficulties.[46] Following the continuous advice of the government on the importance of physical training, one of the teachers of Maraş Orphanage declared his will to attend and receive "physical training" in this school. He was kindly rejected by the Ministry of Education, since the mentioned institution could not be opened.[47]

The ambitious efforts of Kazım Karabekir after 1920 to train Armenian orphans in Erzurum as "little soldiers" from a very early age onward in his "village of orphans" (*yetimler karyesi*) were also part of the same obsession with paramilitary education in orphanages.[48]

Scouting Organizations of Non-Muslim Communities

Non-Muslim communities of the empire were also interested in boy scouting in the early twentieth century, yet the outbreak of the war and the Turkish tendencies and suspicions of the CUP government suppressed these initiatives. In the case of the Armenians, from the early 1900s forward, the Armenian athletic movement was prospering in Istanbul and the provinces.[49] There were Armenian clubs in larger urban centers, such as Izmir, Salonika, Alexandria, and Cairo, as well as in smaller cities, such as Sivas, Erzurum, Trabzon, and Marsovan.[50] An Armenian student at Robert College, Shavarsh Chrissian,[51] with the help of his periodical, *Marmnamarz* (Physical Training [1911–14]), wanted to bring together Armenian students at school by organizing activities, lectures, and athletics.[52] Robert College was also an important meeting point for other Armenian physical culture enthusiasts, such as Chrissian, Vahram Papazian, and Levon Hagopian, where they internalized a common sympathy for physical education and sports. *Marmnamarz* dedicated large discussions to scouting. One suggestion of the journal was to unite all athletic groups under one scouting organization.[53]

In the case of the Greeks, there was a serious group of physical culture enthusiasts who created more than a dozen voluntary athletic associations and regularly organized athletic competitions. Selim Sırrı and Vahram Papazian, one speaking to the Turkish, the other to the Armenian public, both praised the sporting activities of the Greeks in order to motivate their own communities.[54]

Non-Muslim sporting and scouting activities were already under strict state scrutiny before the war. The gymnastics clubs of the Greeks were followed closely, with the suspicion that they were providing military exercises (*askeri talim*) to their members. This suspicious attitude led to the inspection or even closure of a few clubs in Lesbos (Midilli).[55] It was also noted that these clubs organized parades in the form of military march and roamed around the villages.[56] A larger concern was caused by the fear of possible demands by the Greeks in the islands to join Greece. Within this context, sports clubs were accused of spreading this idea through a nationalist discourse and armed drills.[57] In another case, the gymnastics teacher of the Greek school in Korçë (Görice) was accused of training boys with an arms drill (*silah talimi*).[58] The Jewish Gymnastics Society Maccabi (Société

Juive de Gymnastique, known as Maccabi) in Istanbul was also suspected of making Zionist propaganda.[59]

In late June 1914, the boy-scouting team of the Armenian youth club in Kadıköy was accused of training children with "military exercise and drills" (*askeri eğitim ve talimler*), which was "against the Regulation of the Ottoman Strength Associations" (*Osmanlı Güç Dernekleri Nizamnamesine aykırı*).[60] Arguing that boy scouting was only a pretext and that these were essentially "political activities" (*siyasi faaliyetler*), the Ministry of Interior ordered the disbandment of boy-scouting teams.[61] A few days after the trouble with the Kadıköy club, the Public Security Directorate (Emniyet-i Umumiye Müdüriyeti) ordered the abolishment of all non-Muslim sport clubs in Istanbul.[62]

In other words, the Legal Department of the ministry, together with the Public Security Directorate, openly distorted the content of the regulation, which defined boy-scouting organizations' duty as being to "prepare the youth for the army" through military training and drill.[63] However, it is obvious from the application of the regulation that "youth" was equal to Muslim Turks for the government. Youths belonging to Armenian, Greek, Jewish, and other communities were not trusted and thus were not granted the same opportunity to become "manly soldiers," despite the Ottomanist promises of the 1908 Revolution and the presence of non-Muslim deputies in the parliament. In some provinces, all the associations of Armenians and Greeks were disbanded after the declaration of total mobilization. Karesi was one such example, where non-Muslim voluntary organizations were all closed.[64]

Postwar Scouting Activities of Non-Muslims

Boy-scouting organizations of the non-Muslim communities were only reactivated during the Allied occupation period (1918–22), as they were disbanded by the Ottoman authorities and had to postpone their activities to the postwar period. Shortly after the signing of the cease-fire, the Ottoman authorities were alarmed by the visibility of Greek boy scouts' activities. In July 1919, the police forces were panicked that Greek soldier uniforms were being distributed to Greek boys in Istanbul.[65] Soon after, the authorities concluded that Greek boys were being prepared to take part in an uprising against the state, since Greek soldiers were assigned as teachers to boys schools.[66] Greek boy scouts were very active in this period. Dozens of them were reported coming to Maltepe and setting up tents in the Taşocakları area.[67] In May 1919, *mutasarrıf* of Çatalca reported to the Ministry of Interior Public Security Directorate that Greek soldiers took out around forty students from the Greek school for boys in Çatalca. The students were put in line in a military manner and received military training for about an hour around the town.[68] When they returned, they marched in the streets, singing "vulgar and obscene songs" (*galiz ve şeni şarkılar*) that would "very much disturb the Ottoman and Muslim sentiments" (*hissiyat-i Osmaniye ve İslamiyeyi pek ziyade rencide edecek*). One of the songs went as follows:

> We, the Çatalca folks, will take out our crosses for trouble's sake
> We are going to destroy the mosques of the Turks,
> Let's tear them down, let's tear them down
> Let's wipe out these Muslim dogs with bombs
> We, the Çatalca folks, we are children of Greeks
> We should train and learn the Greek military training
> Because Çatalca and its environs is Greek now and it belongs to
> Greece.[69]

Apart from the Ottoman state sources, it is hard to provide evidence from other sources on this event and this particular song. Yet the originality of the lyrics makes the document "credible." Moreover, other sources confirm the culmination of ethnic hatred and conflict in these years between Muslims and Greeks.[70]

On 27 June 1920, there was a massive celebration at the gardens of Taksim to honor the victories of the Greek army and to celebrate the presence of Greek diplomatic and military authorities.[71] There were Greek and Allied flags everywhere, pictures and busts of Venizelos were exhibited and sold, young people dressed in traditional costumes sang and danced, and boy scouts bearing torches paraded in the gardens. The manifest use of Greek national symbols in the celebrations verified that the Rums (Ottoman Greeks) had severed their bonds with their Ottoman past and chosen to become Greeks. For them, victory belonged not to the Allies but to Hellenism.

Armenians also had active boy-scouting organizations in the immediate postwar period. In November 1918 Armenian athletic groups were reunited under the name of Homenetmen (Armenian Athletic General Union and Scouts).[72] In 1919 the number of boy scouts in Istanbul were as high as 5,000.[73] An Armenian Boy Scout Association was formed in Izmir in May 1919, and in the course of three months they enrolled more than 450 scouts. The association also declared that "hundreds of boys" were "continually joining" them, and "their exemplary character" was rousing sympathy among all Armenians.[74] There was also a reinstated scout group in the Robert College (Istanbul) and a large scouting company in the Kelekian Orphanage of the Armenian General Beneficiary Union in Dörtyol (see figure 3).[75]

Toomas Avedisian's memoirs also describe in detail the organization of boy scouts in the Armenian orphanage in Yedikule (of the Surp Prgiç Hospital) in 1919.[76] General Mesrop, whom Toomas learned fought "Turkish and Kurdish guerillas" together with General Antranig, was coming to the orphanage "to organize the first boy scouts of Armenia."[77] He put together 200 boys between the ages of twelve and fifteen. The boys chosen for the scouting program wore white caps and were distinguished from the rest of the boys. Their emblem bore the inscription of a sunrise behind Mount Ararat. Over the rays of sun were the words "Rise Raise." It meant you rise first, then raise others after you. The general took the boys frequently out, and they went to all-day maneuvers in the nearby hills, with a snare drum leading the group. The boy scouts of the orphanage had a parade in December 1919 on the shores of Kumkapı and Yenikapı, during which they were singing military songs that got the attention of Ottoman authorities.[78] As time passed, the general divided the group into smaller units of ten and selected a leader for each. A significant part of the scouting training was "skillful gymnastics," such as a pyramid formation. Gymnastics were performed,

3. Scouts of the Dörtyol Kelekian Orphanage during a visit by Catholicos Sahag II (ca. 1920). *Source*: AGBU Nubar Library, Paris.

along with military drills and exercises for audiences traveling by boat or train on Sundays or on holidays.[79]

The presence and visibility of non-Muslim paramilitary organizations definitely increased in this period. The governorship of Istanbul, police department, Ministry of Interior, and Ministry of Foreign Affairs were all worried about these activities. Prepared consecutively in 1919 and in 1921, two different security investigations collected hundreds of pages of documentation relating to the scouting activities of Ottoman Greeks and Armenians.[80] Although the fleeing of the CUP leaders in the aftermath of the war changed the political dynamics, it is interesting that the postarmistice Ottoman authorities were not so different from the CUP governments of prewar and war years in their perception of the voluntary activities of non-Muslim communities. Especially with the strengthening of Turkish nationalist, in Kévorkian's terms the "Kemalist-Unionist," movement in Anatolia, the treatment of non-Muslims did not really differ from CUP-era policies.[81]

War among Children

This part, providing an introductory discussion on the increased visibility of "idle children" on city streets and the concerns over juvenile delinquency, discusses how children, mostly boys, played out nationalist and religious rivalries at the street level by focusing on "war games" and real acts of violence between boy gangs. Even at the height of the popularity of Ottomanism, the category of "Ottoman children" was necessarily divided into ethnic, linguistic, and religious subgroups.[82] Their separate schools, their distinct media, their parents, and their peers, together with state-imposed discrimination and violence, socialized children into utterly different identities, teaching them the insurmountable borders of "us" and "them." These children expected different results from the war; their ideal future scenarios were completely dissimilar. The replication of war on a daily basis was at the heart of children's identity formation. Children took initiative for their national interests and attacked their rivals as active agents.

The CUP propaganda of "enemies within," namely, Armenians and Rums, led to the emergence of segregated child spaces. Increasing emphasis on the Turkish and Muslim identity of the state and violent acts of ethnic cleansing and genocide, before and during the war, entirely estranged the non-Muslims. Given their experiences of genocide, forced migration, massacre, conversion, and abduction, it is not surprising that the non-Muslims of the empire welcomed Entente forces after the armistice.

"Idle Youth" and Juvenile Delinquency

In the academic year 1913–14, schooling was far from universal. The number of public primary schools throughout the empire was quite low, with a total of 4,486.[83] The war turned weakness into absence. The consequences of mass mobilization were severe for public education in primary and secondary schools. There are no equivalent statistics for the war years, but the archival records show that as schoolteachers were conscripted, many schools were suspended.[84] Narrative accounts refer to the closing or simple absence of schools, especially in less urban areas.[85]

The government closed foreign schools belonging or connected to the Entente. Teachers having French, British, or other Entente nationalities were dismissed.[86] German schools, along with some American and Alliance Israelite schools, could remain open.[87] In 1915 the remaining foreign educational institutions came under the control of the Ministry of Education.[88] Many private schools were also discontinued, as the War Ministry refused to postpone private schoolteachers' induction into military service. Schooling was also disrupted for the Armenians. Several orders from the Ministry of Interior, signed by Talat Pasha himself, prohibited the continuation of educational activities of the Armenian community.[89] Almost all of the educational (and religious) buildings of the Armenians were occupied by the army, by the Directorate of Orphanages, or by local governorships. The ruination of the Ottoman Armenian educational system was part of the genocidal process.[90]

Lack of schooling led to the middle-class concern, which made itself visible in the daily newspapers and magazines, that children were oversocialized with street life and developing delinquent behaviors. Delinquency in the urban context had been on the agenda of Ottoman social reformers before the outbreak of the war, and the war came to be perceived as a catalyst.[91] In response, Ottoman authorities developed a critical discourse on unschooled city boys. Minister of Education Ahmet Şükrü Bey (1875–1926) claimed that the opening of state kindergartens for the first time in 1915 was to rescue thousands of children from "socialization on the streets" (*sokak terbiyesi*).[92] The opening of orphanages was also directly related to the same concern regarding the effects of living on the streets on the morals of children.

After the establishment of the first state orphanages in Kadıköy in 1915, police officers were asked to send begging children or those who wandered idly in the streets to these institutions.[93] However, there were so many begging children in the streets that the measures taken were not enough. As a temporary solution, children were gathered and put into public baths in various Istanbul neighborhoods. Throughout the war years and also in the postwar period, street children were sporadically admitted into the orphanages.[94] Later it was argued that street children and beggars could not adapt to life in orphanages. A report prepared by the Directorate of Orphanages notes the impossibility of erasing the "traces of street life" (*sokak hayatının bıraktığı izler*), "the obscenest words repeated for years" (*senelerin öğrettiği en müstehcen sözler*), and "the past memories of dark streets" (*şehrin köşelerine ait hatırat*). Even though it was necessary to take care of street children and beggars, the director assumed that their presence was risking the morals of remaining hundreds of children.[95] These children collected from the streets also frequently escaped from the orphanages to return to the streets, since they could not adapt to the order and discipline in these institutions.[96]

Playing War

The 1959 autobiography of Şevket Süreyya Aydemir, the famous journalist and author of early Republican Turkey, depicts in a graphic way how children belonging to different communities embraced and imitated the discourses, and sometimes even the actions, of the war front and reproduced them on the home front. The following quote is a rare example of a first-person Turkish account of how wartime developments and propaganda influenced the everyday lives of children:

> In the streets of our neighbourhood . . . our games were fighting, raiding, and war. . . . The games that we played the most were the bandit (çeteci) and the komitadji (underground revolutionary). First we chose our captains and voivodes (*hospodar*). These were the names given to the chiefs of the Rum or Bulgarian brigands. We chose our captains from among the strongest and the most daredevil. They divided us into [rival] teams. . . . Then the armament would begin. We would put sticks and pieces of wood to our belts that would look like knives or guns. We would fill our pockets and waistbands with stones in place of grenades. Sometimes we put a stick in between our legs and jumped as if we were riding a horse. . . .

We waited for the sign of the captain, then we were supposed to attack the enemy çete with a lot of noise and shouts, have a corps fight, until we won a victory. . . .

The *war* which started at one end of the neighbourhood might spread to the next. Then, new forces would join the game from both sides. Some would act as dead, wounded, or captives. Sometimes captives were rescued with a raid. . . .

The most interesting of these çete games were the ones between the [Muslim] boys of our district versus the neighbouring non-Muslim boys. These were like the conflicts between actual brigands. . . . This was *no longer a game.* This was a real fight between bordering neighbourhoods. *These fights between children, who were the citizens of the same state, but who were also descendants of races that remained segregated for centuries, were small-scale replicas of a soon to be bloody revenge.*

These fights would erupt when a Muslim child was stoned passing by the Rum or Bulgarian neighbourhood or when a Christian child was badly beaten as he entered the Muslim neighbourhood. Both sides had well-known ringleaders, daredevil warriors. They would assemble the boys of their neighbourhood, who almost had a [military] training, around them in teams. They would drive them to the edges of the city, drive them to *war.* There were large Muslim and Christian cemeteries in the outskirts of the city. . . .

We piled up stones, prepared barricades and dug trenches. Watchmen and pioneers took their positions. We sent out exploration teams. Occasional stone fights started. . . . Some lay down long and round tombstones over the trenches and toward the enemy as if they were canons and pretended to explode them by shouting "Boom! Boom!"

While we used to imitate the Rum and Bulgarian language and shout at each other with incomprehensible words in our local bandit raid (çete baskını) games, in *national fights* between neighborhoods we spoke nothing but Turkish. We continuously shouted, "Allah, Allah, attack!" . . .

At one time, [parents] who came to end the fight jumped all of a sudden on each other's throats. Knives were taken out; heads were

> cut open. . . . It was as if both sides already commenced the last and definite showdown that they sooner or later would engage in as a result of an unexpected spark of fire.[97]

Şevket Süreyya was born in 1897 and spent his childhood years in Edirne. His memoir depicts the impact of the independence movements in the Balkans over the children of both sides, while also providing a forecast of the coming Balkan Wars and the First World War. There is reason to be skeptical about the memoirist's ability to capture "the reality" of an earlier time period. Still, he graphically describes how children absorbed the social and political realities of their times and had no difficulty in replicating them in their games, fights, friendships, and enmities.

First World War propaganda not only targeted adults but was also directed at children.[98] Propaganda posters, picture books, and pamphlets made the war part of the childhood experience. Children wore soldier uniforms, carried weapons, and "played war" with their friends or foes.[99] In these war games, the main "learning outcome" and fun came from hating the enemy. State propaganda often glorified violence against the enemy and generously employed stereotypes to dehumanize it as a monster.[100]

As Aydemir's quote demonstrates, teaching children to hate and defile those of a different nationality prepared the grounds for interethnic boy gang fights in numerous multiethnic cities of the empire.[101] When simply "playing war" was not enough for these mobilized children, they engaged in real physical violence. While writing about the Rums and Jews in Salonika, Mazower underlines that although communal leadership on both sides formed cordial relations, gangs of Rum and Jewish boys held weekly stone-throwing "battles."[102] Elli Kohen's family history also gives numerous examples of typical Jewish versus Rum children's fights in Istanbul during his childhood (1906–15). Based on this account, "there were all kinds of rows and showdowns between Jewish and Greek youths," but they would never get into fights with Muslim Turks.[103] Antranig Dzarugyan's autobiographical book, *Men Deprived of Their Childhood*, recounts several instances of boy gang fights between Armenian and Arab children in Aleppo.[104] Such conflicts multiplied during the war years, as children were more prone to initiate the fight when the side they were identifying themselves with was stronger in the ongoing conflict.

In the postwar period, street fights were taking place mostly between Muslim and Rum children in major cities. Melek Sevgin (born in 1908 in Istanbul) writes that she spent her entire childhood in Bakırköy with many Rum friends and that she even spoke their language. Yet right after the war and during the occupation of the city, there was a grim period (*tatsızlık*) when the Rums were looking down on them.[105] The Istanbul Police Department reported in May 1919, in other words after the Greek occupation of western Anatolia, that there were recurring cases of Ottoman Greek children throwing stones at Muslim children and using derogatory language (*tezyif ve tahkir*) toward them.[106] The report of the Meclis-i Vala-yı Ahkam-ı Adliye (Supreme Council of Judicial Ordinances) noted that this act of "stoning" (*taşa tutmak*) had been going on for a while, and for that reason the police department was asked to take action. Furthermore, the Ministry of Justice and Sects would warn the Greek Orthodox patriarch in an appropriate manner.[107]

The CUP War Propaganda and "Enemies Within"

Ottoman atrocity propaganda, mostly a product of the Balkan Wars, is contextualized by Çetinkaya within the framework of the "total war." It had a large impact on the noncombatants on the home front and played a vital role in the Ottoman society in the demonization of the so-called fifth columns and, thus, in legitimizing the elimination of non-Muslim communities.[108] In the CUP's state propaganda, about 1.8 million Ottoman Greeks, the oldest inhabitants of western and central Anatolia, together with the entire Armenian population of the empire were presented as "enemies within." The ethnic Turkist tendencies of the Ottoman ruling party, the CUP, led to the prewar expulsion of hundreds of thousands of Ottoman Greeks in the summer of 1914 from the Aegean coast.[109] The alliance of the independent Kingdom of

Greece with the Allies—though as late as 1917—also meant ongoing threats, harassment, and assaults against Rums. They were scapegoated as a traitor community that already had an independent nation-state of their own. The government fed the hostility toward them by constantly questioning their loyalty to the Ottoman nation.

Children were also vital parts of this nationalist rivalry in the appropriation of a geographic area. For Turkish children, the ultimate enemy was either the Rum or the Armenian. It was as if the empire was not at war with Britain or France; the war was within former or current Ottoman territories. As a striking example of this bitter war, newspapers in Greece reported that many Ottoman Greek children from Ayvalık and its environs arrived at the mainland of Greece with their hands amputated.[110] It was argued that these children were active in resisting the order of deportation by throwing stones with slingshots at the gendarmes and at other Muslims. This stone throwing is why their hands were cut off by Muslim boys or by gendarmes as a punishment. The Ottoman authorities approached the story with suspicion and purportedly started an investigation to find out whether these children had some sort of "accident" in Ayvalık. Despite the authorities' "nominal suspicion," amputation appears to have been a common punishment for resistant boys, as the same theme appears in a Greek short story. In Elias Venezis's short story "Lios," Petros is a young man from a fishing family in Ayvalık.[111] During the war, at the age of fifteen, he is recruited by the British to secretly land on the bare islet Gymnos, just outside the bay of Ayvalık, to survey the coast and prevent the Ottoman soldiers from landing there. Yet one winter's day, Ottoman soldiers land on the islet and kill the entire group, except Petros, whose hand is amputated as punishment and as a demonstration of "Turkish rule." He never stops telling his story to each and every person in the community.[112]

◆ ◆ ◆

In early-twentieth-century Ottoman cities, boys formed nationally defined collectivities and engaged in acts of violence against their defined others based on "nationalistic sensitivities." The war facilitated children's identity formation and made them active agents. Children took initiative for their national interests and attacked the enemy. War was replicated on the street level in their everyday lives.

Nationalist Population Politics and Adult Rivalries over Children

The streets also became a central stage for adult nationalists who initiated a rivalry of their own over hundreds of unattended children on the streets whose national belonging was in dispute. The ability of children to learn new languages, religions, and identities inspired the Unionist cadres to "rescue" non-Muslim children and raise them as Muslim Turks. Non-Muslim communities were constantly on a knife edge with the threat of losing their underage members to "Muslim kidnappers." The following accounts from 1917 provide the basic tropes for such fights over orphaned and destitute children.

"An important personality" from the Istanbul Greek community reported to the press agency of Salonika in 1917 that almost a hundred thousand Rum refugees from Anatolia came to Istanbul and that one came across the unbearable sight of beggars all around the city, increasing day by day. He reported that, for the previous few years, the situation had become critical for the Rum population of the city: "In the streets of Pera, we saw even middle-class women and children begging for some food."[113] A few philanthropic organizations were founded to help the poor with soup kitchens. More important, charitable organizations were preoccupied with saving "thousands of orphans" who had lost their parents during the war or the massacres in Asia Minor and who arrived at Istanbul in a half-naked, hungry, lamentable condition. At night they were sleeping on the cobbled streets of Pera and Galata without blankets. One night the Ottoman authorities collected some of these orphans and, "under the pretext of saving them," put them into the dormitories of the Ottoman imperial military academy in Harbiye, Nişantaşı. According to this prominent figure from the Istanbul Greek community, the boys were then forcefully converted to Islam.[114] The American-Hellenic Society also argued that the streets of the large cities were full of begging Ottoman Greek orphans and that the authorities were gathering them in

Turkish schools in order to make them Muslims.[115] The *mutasarrıf* of Beyoğlu district, Saadettin Bey, was swearing on his honor that beggar children who were collected from the streets were given to their own religious authorities.[116]

Ottoman officials fiercely resisted this interpretation and claimed that the policy of incorporation proved that the state was benevolent toward all religious groups and ethnicities. Rather than an act of kidnapping, they insisted that the collection of non-Muslim orphans should be seen as a humanitarian effort. Turkish newspapers also mentioned a very similar event with a very different tone. According to a news article that appeared on 14 July 1917, in the daily *Sabah* (Morning), five hundred orphan and destitute children were collected from the streets and put into the Ottoman imperial military academy in Harbiye. The ministry would cooperate with the Children's Protection Society (Himaye-i Etfal Cemiyeti) for the education of these children and in order to open workshops for their vocational training.[117]

The American-Hellenic Society claimed that non-Muslim children were collected as part of the CUP Turkification policies, which had started already in 1913. The plan to eradicate the "Hellenic element" was carried out methodically through the mixed settlements of Rums and Turks, always with a predominance of Muslim males and Rum females in order to compel mixed marriages. Moreover, consular reports from 1915 to 1917 speak extensively of forcible abductions of young girls and conversion to Islam.[118] The society argued that what was done to the orphans during the Great War was reminiscent of the infamous Janissary system:

> These orphan institutions have in appearance a charitable object, but if one considers that their inmates are Greek boys who became orphans because their parents were murdered, or who were snatched away from their mothers, or left in the streets for want of nourishment, (of which they were deprived by the Turks), and that these Greek children receive there a purely Turkish education, it will be at once seen that under the cloak of charity, there lurks the "child

collecting" system instituted in the past by the Turkish conquerors and a new effort to revive the janissary system.[119]

Documents and controversies from the aftermath of the war also prove that significant numbers of Ottoman Greek children were taken into state orphanages and Muslim households and converted to Islam. In an order sent by the Ministry of Internal Affairs to the province of Canik, the province was asked to take care of 486 Rum children already in Samsun, together with another 150 who would arrive soon.[120] The Greek Orthodox patriarchate of Istanbul was busy trying to retrieve Islamized Rum Orthodox orphans after 1918.[121] The Istanbul government, under the strong influence of British occupation forces, sent many orders to local governors for the "release" of non-Muslim children from Muslim households.[122]

In another similar account, the prime minister of the Kingdom of Serbia, Nikola P. Pašić, declared in London that the Austro-Germans and Turks had deported 8,000 young Serbian girls, aged ten to fourteen, and shut them up in the "harems of Constantinople." The declaration of Pašić was published in several British newspapers.[123] It was also broadcast by the radio program *Eiffel Tower* on 4 August 1917, under the title of "Serbian Deportations." The National League of Serbian Women wrote a little booklet (of twelve pages) on the issue and appealed to "all Societies of women in the Allied and neutral countries to raise their voice against the attacks on the honor of Serbian women and young girls."[124] The Ottoman Ministry of Foreign Affairs immediately took the necessary steps to disavow the accusations in the foreign press.[125]

The similarity in both cases is that children, both boys and girls, especially when they were unattended or orphaned, were considered to be under greater threat in wartime conditions. Not only were their lives in danger owing to war circumstances, poverty, and starvation, but they were also under the moral threat of losing their religion, nationality, and, in the case of the girls, their chastity. Unprotected children were being adopted or abducted, even bought, sold, or married. Intervening parties from different sides of the conflict conducted a war on their behalf. Based on the interpretation of the interested party, children were either kidnapped or rescued.[126] It is also necessary to note the extent of nationalist agitation, therefore exaggeration, regarding the claims.[127] As I will discuss in detail in the following chapter, the nationalist fight over the *possession* of orphaned children became even more crystallized in the case of Armenian orphans.

◆ ◆ ◆

Children embraced—or were forced to embrace—overtly ethnic, religious, and national identities during the war. The Ottoman Empire was not much different from other multiethnic, multireligious empires, such as the Habsburg and the Russian Empires, in the sense that the conglomerate of ethnic and religious communities was discernibly breaking apart from one another. The Ottoman state, however, was radically different from other empires. Wartime state propaganda and mobilization stressed the identity of the empire as Muslim and Turk. The state, therefore, not only attempted to eliminate its non-Muslim population (Rums, Armenians, Assyrians, and others), but also claimed the target groups' children as its own.

4

Survival of Children during the Armenian Genocide

THE WORDS "genocide" and "children" next to one another inevitably reminds one of a number of saddening visions. We see starving, crying, dying children, lying on a barren land with their skinny, sick, skeleton-like bodies. These images are all memorable visions of a cruel historical reality. That is what happened to many children during the years of genocide. Little babies were killed outright or perished during their long marches without food or water. Many children were tied to one another and drowned in rivers. They were thrown down from the cliffs; thousands were even burned after pouring gas over them. In light of overwhelming evidence, children were murdered systematically during the Armenian genocide. This chapter on the Armenian children who survived the genocide, however, is written from a perspective that resists victimizing them.

In a very strong survivor memoir, Avedis Albert Abrahamian contemplates how it was possible to survive the conditions that killed so many, how he was able to "sustain life," and how he could "come through hell alive." He concludes that they were "trying to struggle against an enemy who was trying to exterminate" them. In this battle, "people exerted superhuman efforts to survive," which was their one and only weapon "to frustrate their goal."[1] No matter how easy it was to kill a child, it was harder to kill his or her will to survive.[2]

Survivors were not simply miserable children who deserved pity. This chapter, dwelling on survivor testimonies in different forms (oral histories, memoirs, and diaries), points to the fact that many of the surviving children were more than passive victims. They not only survived but, as we shall see, played games, made friends, and took part in adventurous journeys. Their will and rationale of survival were stronger than anything. It provided children with resilience, "talents," and the strength to fight for their life.

In the beginning, I will provide a general summary of the suffering of Armenian children during the genocide and focus on the question of Turkification. Approaching the issue of "abduction" and "rescue" of children from a different angle, I reconfigure the story from the children's point of view. In the second part of the chapter, I will discuss several ways in which Armenian children exercised agency. The available historiography victimizes Armenian children as dependent, vulnerable, and passive beings. My work, as part of a new historiography on children and youth, recognizes the historical identity of children, along with their agency.[3] I hope to construct a different historical narrative that not only considers children as part of history, but also puts them at the very center of it. Armenian children managed to become active agents and manipulated the circumstances for their own benefit. They used their intelligence, talents, charms, and beauty, basically whatever they had, to stay alive. Armenian children's survival narratives are not only tragic stories of loss, but also sagas of courage and resilience.

The last part of the chapter focuses on various children's activities as part of their survival. In the literature of the genocide, there is more work on death and suffering than there is on survival and resilience. In this part I will try to highlight how everyday life activities, having both mundane and dramatic moments, helped the survivors handle the burden of existence. Children, in particular, tried to focus their attention toward their games, adventures, friendship, and fun to cope with the terror all around them. Survival testimonies are undeniably tragic stories, but they do not exclude all these children's activities, like sports, separating into rival teams and fighting with adversaries, escaping from school or orphanage, going to distant places alone, climbing up fruit trees and running away with a full tummy, collecting stuff, riding on and off trains, petty theft, looking for treasures, and more. Many stories recounted by Armenian survivor children were actually many children's dreams and the subject of the most beloved children's books. These accounts portray happy moments of these children, full of laughter and playfulness. Despite the manifest stress on the "loss" (of families, loved ones, homes, and the like), these stories were told in a proud and self-confident manner. These stories turn memories into adventures and the narrator into a hero.

A Note on Sources

The Armenian sources of testimony and representation of the genocide are very rich. In fact, there is an immense body of literature that extends over the entire century and includes different genres (like diaries, memoirs, oral histories, and novels). Survivors were also the witnesses of the genocide, and they have started to tell their stories from the moment they were experiencing the genocide and then did not stop telling them. Narration had already started as a form of oral transmission by 1915. As people were reunited in convoys or in camps, people from the same town or lost-and-found family members started to tell their own experiences to each other. When children in Muslim households found out that the other servant in the same house, or next door, or in the next village was also a converted Armenian, they immediately met and asked and told each other their stories.

In written form, publications were already numerous even in 1919. The first generation of educated survivors gave accounts of their experience in the form of memoirs, longer or shorter reports, or narratives written almost immediately upon return to Istanbul. They made a permanent impact regarding the necessity of testifying, conserving the memory of the events, and telling the story of their ordeal to pay homage to the dead.[4] There was an uninterrupted growth of Armenian literature and testimony over the course of the century. Nichanian emphasizes that this "memorial fervor" had a collective dimension in the years after the Armistice of Mudros, and it continued to be an uninterrupted effort in the following decades.[5] These memoirs were written in Armenian, in Turkish, and in the languages survivors acquired in their respective diaspora communities. A large number of them were published in Lebanon, Syria, the United States, and Soviet Armenia. Although those accounts published in English and French reached a certain number of readers, many of the ones penned in Armenian and Turkish remained either unpublished or unexplored. In some cases, little notebooks of the survivors remained hidden in a drawer and were discovered only following their death by their children or grandchildren and were then published.[6] Many of these testimonies were in a way rediscovered in the 2000s, and there was an ongoing translation effort. The year 2015, the one-hundred-year commemoration of the genocide, was especially important for those rare accounts that could not, over the past hundred years, reach the readership they deserved.[7]

Apart from a few intellectuals who survived the genocide and wrote their experiences, most of these testimonies came from people who had never written anything before. Their only concern was to tell their own story. Many testimonies were also collected by philanthropists, missionaries, and Armenian intellectuals. Aram Andonian, a journalist who was deported in April but survived the genocide in hiding, started collecting testimonies in Aleppo in 1918. He writes in his *Medz Vochiri* (*The Great Crime*) the following:

> When the British entered Aleppo, I profited from the situation in order to save history and I began to interrogate those among the survivors who were capable of recalling the unspeakable terror and atrocities of the past five years. Thousands of women, young girls, and men came to see me. They spoke and they wrote. Each one of them had their own story to tell and not one of the tortures they had to endure was similar to the others. And they were more than a hundred thousand who had a volume of things to tell.[8]

Different genres of testimonies were used as primary sources for this chapter. As summarized above, some were written immediately after the war or in the early 1920s. Others were written by then middle-aged survivors in the 1950s. There is also a great repertoire of oral histories conducted mostly in the 1970s and 1980s. Most of these

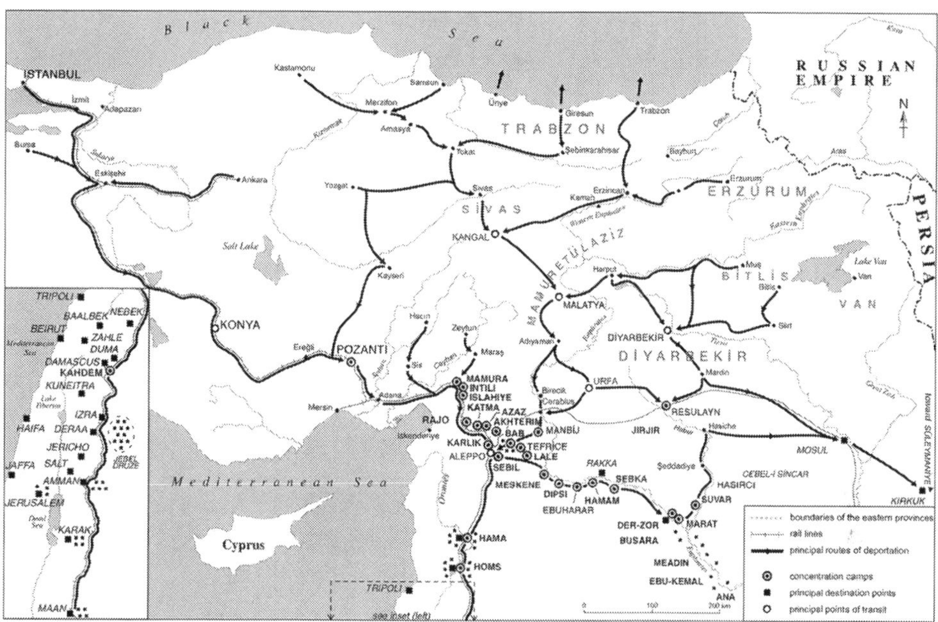

2. Map of Armenian deportations. *Source*: Raymond Kévorkian, "Carte générale des axes de déportation," in *Le Génocide des Arméniens* (Paris: Odile Jacob, 2006).

memoirs or testimonies were written a long time after the event. This time gap and the new political and cultural conditions the authors found themselves in, while sitting down to write or tell these stories, must also have affected the tone and content of their narratives. However, all different genres of testimonies almost equally stress Armenian orphans' agency under extraordinarily difficult circumstances.

The Armenian Genocide and Violence against Children

As the concept genocide refers to the extermination of a religious, ethnic, or other group in its entirety, the "victims" were also often treated as a monolithic category. With the progress of research on the Armenian genocide, there is now a more nuanced analysis of violence targeting different groups of victims within the same category of Armenians. The literature on Armenian women's differing experiences during (and also after) the years of genocide became very rich in the past two decades thanks to works by Matthias Bjørnlund, Vahé Tachjian, Katharine Derderian, Ara Sarafian, and others.[9] These scholars, examining the sexual violence against women, which took the shape of rape or abduction, focused on gender-specific aspects of the genocide. The genocidal fate of Armenian children was also for a long time subsumed within the story of the entire victim population and was not generally treated as a separate and distinct subject of study.

In recent decades, genocide studies have paid closer attention to certain patterns that define the treatment of children during these periods of mass violence. Within this perspective, children are reinterpreted as a distinct group of victims.[10] Miller and Touryan Miller's valuable work of oral history on the Armenian genocide is one of the earlier examples treating children (and women) as separate categories of people who were affected differently in the course of the genocide.[11] Vahakn N. Dadrian's earlier research on violence against children provides the extent of children's suffering.[12] He argues that unlike previous Armenian massacres in the Ottoman Empire, which mostly spared women and children, "the World War I genocide" was planned as a "thorough job," exempting no Armenian.[13] His work specifically focuses on children's victimhood, speaking of "bloodthirsty murderers" (*kanlı katil*), listing a variety of "ferocious and sadistic methods" with which thousands of Armenian children were murdered. In addition to unending series of dislocations and deportations to the deserts of Mesopotamia, exposure, exhaustion, starvation, disease, and epidemics aggravated the death toll. A significant number of children fell victim to massacres carried out in different parts of the empire. Dadrian argues that there were three principal methods for killing children: drowning, burning alive,[14] and wholesale rapes to precede killing.[15] Other sources also point to the prevalence of throwing children off cliffs.[16]

It is impossible to determine the number or the percentage of children who lost their lives in these atrocious massacres. Still, a significant number of Armenian children had the chance to escape death, as the Ottoman society needed them as labor, as slaves, and as concubines. Armenian children, along with numerous women, were forcefully abducted, bought and sold, kidnapped and stolen by Turkish, Kurdish, and Arab households.[17]

In addition to the private acts of seizing, adopting, or selling children, the Ottoman state also gave orders for the collection and redistribution of Armenian orphans. Already in July 1915, the Ministry of Interior sent orders to the provinces authorizing them to distribute Armenian orphans to wealthy families, for the purposes of "care and education" (*bakım ve terbiye*), and also to households of modest means who would receive a stipend for the child.[18] Based on the order of the Ministry of Interior (30 April 1916), Muslim households and state orphanages were ordered by the CUP government itself to take in Armenian children and Islamize and Turkify them:

> (1) The distribution of families without male guardians (who are either deported or in the army) in a dispersed manner *to villages and towns where there are no Armenians and foreigners* . . . and assuring that they become familiar with local customs; (2) marrying off young and widowed women; (3) the distribution of children up to twelve years old to local orphanages and boarding schools; (4) if the number of the orphanages is not sufficient, children should be given to Muslim notables for their upbringing and assimilation (*terbiye ve temsil*) in accordance with local customs (*adab-ı mahalliye*). The rest could be distributed to poor families in villages with a thirty *kuruş* stipend (*nafaka*) for the expense of their maintenance.[19]

The Prime Ministry's Ottoman Archives is filled with documents attesting to the "adoption" of Armenian girls by administrative and military officials.[20] The Directorate of Public Security openly announced that the state had no objection to those state officials who adopted Armenian girls into their households.[21] Probably tens of thousands of male and female children were absorbed by Muslim households and, following conversion to Islam, became servants, concubines, or wives.[22] The Ministry of Interior also transferred hundreds of orphaned Armenian children from Anatolia to Istanbul through the Islamic Society for the Employment of Women (Kadınları Çalıştırma Cemiyet-i İslamiyesi). Girls were distributed to Muslim households selected by the ministry, and boys were given away to workshops and small businesses.[23]

As discussed in chapter 1, many Armenian orphans were taken into Ottoman state orphanages and other state institutions such as the Red Crescent to be raised as Muslim Turks. Talat Pasha personally ordered that "young women and girls be married off to Muslims, so that they will be raised according to Islamic principles."[24] At the end of the war, Armenian relief committees and other European and American aid workers estimated that there were at least sixty thousand Armenian children in Muslim households and state orphanages.[25] As Sarafian noted, survival through marriage, conversion, and suppression of identity was an essential part of the genocidal process.[26]

Children definitely had a greater chance of survival thanks to their importance as a demographic resource. Unlike Nazi racial policies during the Holocaust, the CUP policy toward Armenian children pointed to more of a tabula rasa understanding of human resources. These children born of Christian Armenian parents could still be raised as Muslim Turks. Apparently, the ability of children to learn new languages, religions, and identities saved many lives during the Armenian genocide (and later during the Second World War).[27] Armenian orphans were assumed to have a potential for "recycling," as much as they forgot or suppressed their family origins and embraced a new identity. The population was a decaying resource during the war and also the highest measure of national power and prestige in its aftermath. Nationalist population politics (coupled with Wilson's "right to self-determination") increased the importance of "numbers." Within this configuration, orphans and destitute children were treated as a profitable form of investment, as a commodity to be possessed, kidnapped, or reshaped.[28]

The "Rescue" of Armenian Orphans

The issue of "continuity and change" between the World War I years and the postwar period is worth noting. Obviously, socioeconomic problems originating in the war years continued all the way to the postwar era. Certainly, the political and cultural dynamics changed once the war ended. With the escape of the CUP leaders on 1 November 1918, the post-genocide politics also took a different shape. Mabel Evelyn Elliott noted that "English officers walked the streets of Constantinople with that air of rulers of earth," such that the "Turks moved quickly aside to let them pass." "The English had said that Christian girls must be released; they were released. When there was a rumor that a Christian girl was in a Turkish house, Allied soldiers walked through the ancient sanctities of the harem as though Turkish customs were tissue paper."[29]

The new government, actually following the orders of the Allied forces, sent a series of orders to the provinces for the release of Armenian slaves, political prisoners, orphan girls, and women starting in November 1918.[30] These telegraphs by the Ministry of Interior ordered that all "Christian girls and children that had been kept by force (*cebren*) in Muslim households be freed and returned to their relatives,"[31] or they should be handed over to the local Armenian religious authorities.[32] Where there was no Armenian community organization, they would be handed over to the commissions formed by the Armenians.[33] In the absence of any Armenian body, they would be handed over to the state orphanages or civil administrators, while creating a registry with their names.[34] Those who kept Armenians in their homes had to surrender them to the authorities immediately; otherwise, they would be punished severely.[35]

The Istanbul press was also visibly interested in the subject. The Armenian newspaper *Nor Geank* (New Life) published a letter addressing the representatives of the Allied states and demanded the "rescue" of Armenian orphans held in Turkish households.[36] The Turkish newspaper *Sabah* (Morning) also wrote on 9 January 1919 that Christian women and children were forcefully kept in Turkish homes.[37] Another Turkish newspaper, *Yeni İstanbul* (*New Istanbul*), claimed that Armenian girls had formerly been distributed to the houses of Unionist leaders; seven of them were with Reşid Bey, the governor of Diyarbekir, and three were with Halil Pasha.[38]

In late 1918 Armenian patriarchal authorities launched a full-fledged campaign to find, liberate, and reintegrate children and women who had spent the past few years in Muslim households and orphanages. The recovery of lost children was considered especially crucial for the national regeneration of the Armenian community, decimated by genocide, war, and displacement. The *vorpahavak* (որբահավաք) campaign, which meant "the gathering (or reclamation) of orphans," was the most crucial activity of the Armenian community in post-genocide Istanbul. Many Armenian children were repatriated to their families in this period.[39] There were both national and international efforts at repatriation and rehabilitation of these "enslaved" Armenian women and children. The League of Nations closely followed these efforts in Aleppo, Mesopotamia, and Istanbul.

As part of the efforts of the Armenian patriarchate and priests, clergymen toured the provinces and visited numerous orphanages and households to repatriate Armenian children. He himself also a war orphan, and later a novelist, Hasan İzzettin Dinamo gives numerous examples in his autobiographical novel, *Öksüz Musa* (*Orphan Musa*). He recounts that Armenian priests came to the Samsun Orphanage and checked the registry records (*künye defterleri*) in order to identify Armenian orphans. Numerous girls in the Samsun Orphanage were actually Armenians. Most of them immediately escaped when they heard that the Armenian authorities were in the city. Dinamo writes that after the departure of Armenian girls, the girls' section of the orphanage, which previously housed 800, became very small.[40] The story of Fatma/Arşaluys is interesting. When the priests wanted to take Fatma away from the orphanage, the little girl resisted, saying that she was a Turk. An older girl was trying to remind her that she was Armenian and that her name was not Fatma, but Arşaluys (*Kız, sen Haysın, senin adın Fatma değil, Arşaluys'tur*).[41] In the case of older girls, there was no question about their identity. For instance, both Musa and her sisters knew that their friend Lütfiye was Armenian.[42] Considered with the general efforts of orphan gathering, the control based on registry records was a general procedure.

Emma D. Cushman, who worked in Istanbul from 1919 onward for the recovery of Armenian children, reported that the work was at the beginning comparatively easy. "The Turks were frightened, and children were produced more readily—in fact, decent self-respecting Turks brought the children to us themselves."[43] According to the Armenian patriarch Der Yeghiayan, innumerable Turkish families feared the British so much that they immediately handed over the Armenian children that they had kept throughout the war.[44] The British High Commission definitely played a key role in the search for Armenian orphans and young women. Based on the report of the Istanbul Police Department (28 April 1919), a mixed delegation was formed under the supervision of the British, consisting of an American, a Turk, and an Armenian, to recover the orphan Armenian children in Ottoman institutions and the Turkish families and to determine the nationality of the suspected children.[45]

British high commissioner Sir Horace Rumbold documented 2,300 cases of women and children who had been taken from Muslim homes and institutions. These were in addition to undocumented others voluntarily released and freed. According to the American Committee for Relief in the Near East (or Near East Relief), 10,000 Armenian women were recovered from Muslim households by late 1919. Of the total number reclaimed, many were recovered from state orphanages in the area.[46] The nominal rolls of Ottoman orphanages that have been seized by the Allied authorities and handed over to the Armenian patriarchate showed that the names of Christian children have been struck out and Muslim names were superimposed. Based on these registers, the Armenian authorities estimated that nearly 50 percent of the children in state orphanages were Armenian.[47] As for children in private households, the Armenian authorities claimed that there were about 6,000 such children in Istanbul and its environs (İzmit, Bursa, and Eskişehir) and some 67,000 in Anatolia and the adjoining territories.[48]

Arakel Çakıryan, a former chemistry professor at Istanbul University, was promised help by one of the functionaries at the British Embassy, Commander Smith, in liberating Armenian orphans. He claimed that he started the work all alone and prepared a report in April 1919.[49] Upon receiving his report, a Vorpahavak Marmin (Orphan Collection Agency) was constituted with four orphan-collection officers, with Çakıryan acting as their chief.[50] He personally went to the general headquarters of the Islamic Society for the Employment of Women and took the four registers kept by the society of the children distributed to Muslim households.[51] Registers, which then came into the possession of the patriarchal authorities, listed the original names, places of origin, and new identities of the Armenian children who had been entrusted to Muslim families.[52] The patriarchate used these records to reclaim Armenian orphans in households. Although Ottoman officials partially obstructed the work of *vorpahavak*, Parliamentary Commission member Nerses Ohanian declared to the Armenian National Assembly in December 1922 that 3,000 of the estimated 4,000–5,000 captive Armenian orphans in Istanbul had been "rescued."[53] The League of Nations' "Commission of Enquiry with Regard to Deportation of Women and Children" put the number of Armenian orphans reclaimed from Muslim households and institutions at 90,819, whereas 73,350 more were still in these places.[54]

The new government's supportive attitude toward repatriation was a short-lived peace for Armenians. As the Turkish nationalist movement took shape, public sentiment became increasingly anti-Armenian. The Ottoman authorities increasingly denied charges that Armenians were being held against their will. They even countercharged that many of the children recovered by Armenians and Allied personnel were actually Turks.[55] Many of these household heads were either military or administrative officers of the state, and so they filed numerous complaints that their adoptive children were taken away with the "false presumption" that they were Armenians.[56] The Ottoman officials also changed their subdued attitude, denied the charges that Armenians were being held against their will, and started to challenge the work of *vorpahavak*. The Armenian or Allied authorities were no longer allowed to go to Muslim households on their own. In other words, postarmistice Ottoman authorities, albeit for a short and exceptional parenthesis of barely eight to nine months, were not so different from the CUP government in their perception and treatment of the issue of Armenian orphans.

Humanitarian "Rehabilitation" and the Violence of Rescuing

As the countercharges and complaints of the Ottoman officials and household heads became very frequent, the British High Commission instructed the setting up of a "neutral house." This was a "clearing house" in which the children involved in doubtful cases would be temporarily lodged, pending the results of investigations into their origins.[57] The Armenian patriarchate rented the building, but the institution was supported by the League of Nations and the Near East Relief and was under the protection and supervision of the British High Commission and the British police. Many of the children who ended up in the Neutral House, which was opened first in Şişli and later moved to Bebek, had no documentation attesting to their identity. They were also unable to provide other details such as their birthplaces, parents' names, if they had siblings, and more. These "disputed" cases were observed by the representatives of the Armenian and Rum communities[58] (either secular officials or patriarchal authorities), a representative from the Ottoman Red Crescent Society (Osmanlı Hilal-i Ahmer Cemiyeti), and advisers from the British High Commission and League of Nations.[59] Then community representatives voted for each child.

Very few of the disputed children were determined to be Muslims. Accusing the Neutral House committee of bias, the Turkish representative Nezihe Hanım resigned, after the case of eleven-year-old Hatun Şayan (Zabel). This girl insisted so strongly that she was a Muslim and that she wanted to go back to her Turkish family that Nezihe Hanım found the act of keeping her at the Neutral House to be "cruel and Godless."[60] Later her successor, Nakiye Hanım, also resigned. After their resignation, the work in the Neutral House was continued entirely by the Armenian authorities until the institution was shut down in August 1922, following the orders of the British High Commission.

Memoirs and reports by the relief workers, who worked for the repatriation of Armenian children, and especially the ones in the Neutral House, underlined the reluctance of children to reclaim their Armenian identity. The Armenian patriarch, as a result, described the duty of the Armenian representative as "awakening in the child's mind memories of her youth, an association of facts or incidents." This "hard and delicate" task could be accomplished only by reminding the child her mother tongue, religion, customs and manners, legends and tales, nursery rhymes, and folk songs to help them remember their origin.[61] The patriarch also added that "no one else but an Armenian born on the same native land, brought up under the same pedagogic circumstances, could possibly address himself to that infinitely intricate task of freeing the child from the heinous effects of Turkish breeding both mentally and spiritually."[62]

Cushman underlined that a change of environment was necessary to bring about "a mental change" in these children and to help them "discover themselves."[63] Armenian boys and girls, who had spent the past three to four years in Muslim households, had actually become Muslims as well as Kurdish, Arab, or Turkish speakers. Their Armenian identity was questionable. In other words, the Neutral House (and other institutions receiving reclaimed women and children) was interested in not only rescuing women and children from households, but also unearthing their hidden, latent, even lost identities. The community leaders, along with international humanitarian agencies, contemplated how they could "resurrect" this Armenian identity and "rehabilitate" the children as the bearers of the future "Armenian nation." Rehabilitation, through resocialization, reconversion, and relearning a language, was crucial to "revive the nation."

> The *most pathetic scenes* are described by eye-witnesses in this [Neutral] House. Children who were known almost certainly to be Armenian Christians *would continue for weeks to say Moslem prayers, until in a hidden corner, or under stress of a sudden emotion, they would begin repeating prayers in Armenian, in which the name of Christ constantly*

> *recurred. Even then it was difficult to reassure and pacify them when they realized that they had been overheard* [emphasis added].[64]

Cushman attributed children's resistance to the carrot and stick used by their former Muslim foster families. Some children were blindfolded with gifts and the promise of a better life in an affluent household. They did not want to "leave a comfortable Turkish home to go to an Armenian institution where no luxury existed." In other cases, they feared the consequences of repudiating their new name and religion.[65] It needs to be acknowledged that these were very young children, who were raised by Muslim families for the past four to five years. They learned the rules of Islam and became practicing Muslims. They were sincerely afraid of the possibility of redemption and hell in the case of renouncing their religion.[66]

Moreover, what the observers interpreted as *reluctance* could also have been their own prejudice that all these children must have been Armenians. The reports consistently used the verb "confess" with regard to children in the Neutral House who admitted to their Armenian origin. There are many stories in an "Index of Children Brought to the Neutral House" in which children were pressured for days until they provided the *confession* that was expected of them.[67]

Sixteen-year-old Nesmiye (Verjine) first assured the committee that she was a Turk, but later on she "*confessed*" that she was an Armenian.[68] Another, Zarife (Gülyan), "after insisting 15 days obstinately" that she was a Turk, "confessed."[69] Lütfiye, an eight- to nine-year-old girl, brought to the Neutral House on 12 May 1919, after a week of questioning and observation, "on May 20th at last *confessed*" that she was an Armenian from Erzurum and that her name was Nvart.[70] About another nine-year-old boy, Reşat (Garabed), who said he was a Turk, the committee thought "they had better keep him for one or two days in the Neutral House, because he was too young to remember all particulars at once." But he was kept in the house for fifteen days, after which he confessed to being Armenian.[71] In spite of her insisting that she was a Turk, Gülşan (Armenuhi) was also kept in the house. Armenian and American relief workers in the house wrote, "On our visits we *made her confess with great difficulty* that she is Armenian."[72] There were only a few cases who did not *confess*. Thirteen-year-old Vicdan, who was brought on 1 May 1919 from Dr. İrfan Bey's house in Kadıköy, for instance, was allowed to leave with the doctor "because she insisted she was a Turk *to the end*."[73]

In mid-1921, after the resignation of Turkish members one after the other, a serious controversy arose between the Armenian members of the commission running the Neutral House. Dr. Artinian, Zaruhi Bahri, and Mrs. Daylarian had a dispute concerning the issue of the determination of a certain orphan's identity. Later, Dr. Artinian wrote a newspaper article, criticizing the Neutral House Commission as an "Inquisition court," as he was deeply disturbed and offended by these "confession rituals."[74] The Armenian patriarch openly underlined that their job in the Neutral House was to *convert* Armenian children "back" to Christianity. "We find it difficult enough to *convert* the terrorized Armenian child fed up for four years with all that is Turkish, how could we possibly convert the real Turk in a fortnight's time?"[75]

• • •

The available literature approaches the issue of the "rescue" of Armenian orphans from Muslim households from the perspective of religious communities and imagined nations, while the experiences and needs of the children are considered marginal. It is without doubt that Armenian children were wrongfully possessed by Muslim households, CUP officials, or prominent families close to the ruling elite. Armenian women and children were forcibly abducted and forcefully converted to Islam. However, children involved in these "rescue" efforts were not asked either for their opinion or for their consent while being taken away from the households that they had spent the past few years. They were simply treated as the rightful possession and property of the Armenian community. As will become clearer in the next section, children themselves were actively involved in making decisions. Some of them chose to stay in Muslim households, based on their experiences and expectations. Others, on the other hand, managed to escape on their own, without waiting to be "rescued." Those children who were too young at the time of their "adoption" sincerely believed that they were Muslim Turks, and it must have been painful for them to depart from the location of their earliest memories. Humanitarian "rehabilitation" of children brings into view the violence of rescuing, which involved a rather tough period of (re-)conversion to a national and religious identity.

Survival of Children and Empowerment

Stanley E. Kerr, a relief worker of the Near East Relief, who had photographed nearly two thousand orphans in Aintab and Maraş and transcribed the survival narrative of each, later wrote that he found some of the stories simply "*fantastic*" and in a way "unbelievable, but one by one they corroborated each other." The extent of the violence and death that these children experienced and normalized as part of life was so great that they were able to speak of their tragic stories as if "*it was happening to someone else*."[76]

Despite the prevalence of the figure of the child *victim*, who is either slain, bought, sold, kidnapped, or rescued in the available historiography, I aim to give voice to those youngest witnesses and survivors of the genocide as "actors," having a say in their own fates. When we focus on how children made sense of their survival, we see a very strong image of the survivor. Their self-representation in these survival stories was not one of victimization but one of resilience. In order to understand how Armenian orphans, displaced and unattended, could survive, there is a need to highlight children's assumed agency and self-empowerment in the period. Armenian children during and after the genocide were not weak and passive creatures, as the middle-class cliché would assume. They were strong and courageous; they were active agents. It was as if the circumstances of the genocide created "underage adults."

Armenians use the word *carbig* (ճարպիկ, talented) to describe someone who is clever and able to manipulate circumstances to his or her benefit. This word *carbig* appears time and again in memoires and testimonies in reference to children who survived.[77] Children who survived were depicted as clever, sharp, and quick in making decisions. It meant taking risks that could easily have led to death and making choices that gave them control over their circumstances. The "talent" that numerous survivors were talking about was nothing but agency.

Antranig Dzarugyan's (1913–89) autobiographical 1955 book, *Men Deprived of Their Childhood* (*Mangutyun çunetsoğ martig*), describes the lives of orphans at the Near East Relief Orphanage in Aleppo in 1918–19.[78] Dzarugyan wrote that there were two types of boys in the orphanage: the talented (*carbigner*) and the untalented (*ancaragner*). The talented were the ones who could secretly sleep during the Bible reading but not get caught by the *Mayrig* (head of the orphanage, called the Mother). The untalented were those children who were punished (brutally beaten) for falling asleep. The talented were the ones who could pretend to be ill to be sent to the hospital—to "the orphans' heaven"—with tenderhearted nurses, abundant food, and soft mattresses. The act of untalented children was easily discovered and so punished.[79] Injarabian also made the same dichotomy between the talented and untalented. When the orphans were left without food in the Near East Relief Orphanage in Urfa during the fight between the French and Turkish nationalist forces in 1920, those "talented" ones were coming up with various strategies. One of them, Abraham, caught and cooked a cat! Another time he stole the lunch of a teacher.[80]

The frequency of the word *carbig* is truly remarkable, such that every survivor narrative revolves around these skills and abilities. These *talented* children charmed their potential saviors with their sweetness, abilities, or intelligence and managed to exploit opportunities for their own advantage. Sometimes they strove to be taken into Muslim households or orphanages. At other times, they escaped from these relatively secure environments to go after other "opportunities." Some of them successfully resisted their masters or orphanage directors. They became thieves if necessary, went into business to make money, or made long-distance train journeys to find family members.

In and Out of Muslim Households

Aram Haigaz was fifteen at the time of his village's deportation. While his family was put on the road, his mother was extremely nervous that her almost grown-up son was in real danger. He quickly realized that conversion was the best option to stay alive. Without further delay, he approached the soldier accompanying the convoy, choosing his words extremely carefully, and made the speech below. The soldier was convinced of his words. He told him to walk right beside him, and then "no one will touch a hair" on his head.

> Today I saw the light, do you know how? God is one for all the civilized nations and people, right? He is the one that created us and the universe? The only difference is that some people recognize Jesus as the prophet . . . some Moses . . . some Muhammad. For centuries my forefathers and I called upon Jesus Christ. But see what has become of us! Today we are homeless, hungry, and thirsty. From now on I am going to call the Lord "Muhammad." Even if I die, I want to die a Muslim.[81]

Focusing specifically on the issue of the abduction versus rescue of children, it might be enlightening to see the picture from the children's point of view. It is true that most of the Armenian children and women were forcefully abducted and taken into households.[82] Yet survivor accounts also tell us that adoption or marriage was also a survival strategy, voluntarily opted for by the children themselves. Many children strove to be accepted into Muslim families. For example, an Armenian boy remembers being disappointed that a group of Kurds did not pick him: "I remember standing by the wall and crying that I did not get to go with them."[83] Another girl noted that "anytime someone came to take me to another place, I went willingly, looking for a better place."[84] She changed several homes, one after the other, until she actually found the best possible place for her. Thus, it is clear that many children saw adoption as a survival strategy and resorted to Muslim households to escape death.

However, sometimes adoption was a temporary solution. Children feeling safe in a household also decided to run away for a variety of reasons. After learning that the Ottoman authority had melted away, they escaped by finding relatives (or simply other Armenians) or entering an orphanage (after Near East Relief started its operations around 1918). In other words, under new circumstances, adoption was no longer the best strategy. They now had other choices. Now that survival was no longer at stake, they had the chance to think about their families, roots, and identity. As Aram Haigaz put it, if he stayed with his Turkish master and "put down roots" by marrying the Muslim girl that he was in love with, he might never go back. He would live "as a Muslim slave serving the Turks forever, licking their boots like a beaten dog."[85] A girl who had been taken in by an Arab family said she was treated like a daughter, but she still had to run away: "No matter what, I was Armenian and they were Arabs. If I remained there, I, too, would become an Arab and lose my Armenian identity. I thought that if I ran away, some Armenians, some place, would take care of me."[86]

Most of the "rescued" children in the post-genocide period were in fact *self-rescuers*. Papken was nine years old when the deportations started in Amasya on 21 June 1915. In less than a few months, he lost his entire family and was left alone.[87] He stayed with a number of Kurdish masters, as their servant, or "as a slave," as he calls it. When he heard in 1918 that Armenian children were gathered in the Near East Relief Orphanage in Urfa, he started dreaming of running away. He felt like he should join other Armenian orphans and maybe find members of his family. He tried to convince a number of other Armenian adopted/slave boys in the neighboring villages, but they were scared and undecided. He himself was also pretending that he was a true Muslim and that he would never run away. When he finally did, he could not reach Urfa. Instead, he settled down with other masters (in total he had nine different masters). In Cimbolat he became friends with another Armenian boy, now called Resho. They planned their escape to Urfa together but had to postpone it a few times. Finally, they reached the orphanage in the summer of 1919. "At last, I had reached the orphanage . . . the heaven . . . the home I had desperately dreamed about. How many troubles and how much misery had I endured to arrive here! I thanked our Lord for his mercy and stepped through the doorway of the orphanage, beaming with joy. Walking through the gates of heaven would not have made me happier!"[88]

Although he describes his entry to the orphanage as entering heaven, he also ran away from there after a short while. Suffering too much from hunger in the orphanage,[89] he decided to find a new master as a better option for survival. He was ready to convert for the third time (he converted once to Islam, then again to Christianity at the orphanage). Luckily, he found an Armenian shopkeeper at the marketplace and stayed with his family. With yet another twist in the story, he left this household as well when he heard that the orphanage would be transferred to Lebanon. He appealed to rejoin the orphanage and go with his friends. The orphanage administration declared that "no escapees would be readmitted." In the end, he paid for his own travel expenses to Aleppo and joined the orphans there. He was then registered to the orphanage list, took the train to Beirut with the other kids, and was admitted to the orphanage of Antelias.[90]

However, this description is in no way meant to suggest that only those children who escaped were agents and the ones who stayed in Muslim households were victims. For instance, Yevkineh, an Armenian girl with two babies from her Kurdish husband, wept bitterly when she heard about the independent Armenia. Yet she decided to stay with her husband, as she could not leave her children.[91] Narrative sources point to the fact that children and youth made their decisions on their own. Some chose to leave, and some chose to stay.

Resistance in State Orphanages

In the case of adoption of children by private households, Armenian children were usually alone in the house, and they were surrounded completely by a foreign environment. Armenian children in institutional settings, on the other hand, were usually numerous and had better chances of solidarity and resistance in the face of Turkification. Escape was a common form of resistance for Armenian orphans. Children escaped from deportation caravans, camps, orphanages, and Muslim households when they had the chance. Despite the imbalance of power between the state and Armenian orphans, it is still possible to see cases of disobedience and resistance from children. Three "Armenian convert" boys (*Ermeni muhtedilerinden*) from the İzmit CUP Orphanage Talatiye department escaped the orphanage and attempted to go to Adana "with fake documents" (*sahte vesikayla*).

Hasan, a.k.a. (*nam-ı diğer*) Avedis, was from Aleppo; Ali, a.k.a. Krikor, was from Adana; and Osman, a.k.a. Arşag, was from Erzurum. They were caught on a freight train (*marşandiz treni*) in Eskişehir and were held there by the police.[92] When the Aintab Orphanage was closed and a significant number of its boys were transferred to Istanbul, nine Armenian boys escaped from the orphanage where they were held in Istanbul. They went back to Aintab with the hope of repatriating with their family members or at least finding acquaintances.[93]

In circumstances that they could not escape from, they devised other forms of resistance. Cemal Pasha's Antoura Orphanage in Lebanon was not a part of the *darüleytam* network and operated, in a sense, autonomously. It was infamous for the extent of its concentration of Armenian orphans, but not so exceptional in terms of its policy of enforced Turkification. The Armenian orphans, either in other state orphanages or in private households, were subject to the same treatment. The main policy of the Antoura Orphanage administration was to Turkify the orphans, by changing their names to Turkish ones and by forcing them to speak only Turkish. Those children who used their Armenian names or said a word in Armenian were severely punished. Karnig Panian's (1910–89) *Memoirs of Childhood and Orphanhood* (*հուշեր Մանկության եւ որբության*) is a very well-written account of children's experience through different episodes of the genocide, and also a rare account of life at the Antoura Orphanage.[94] Panian said the children knew that they were fighting "an unequal battle," but still they were "determined to resist" by holding on to "their identities, which were all they had left."[95] As part of their firm decision not to give up their identities, they made a remarkable scene of rebellion while welcoming Cemal Pasha in his first visit to the orphanage. The children were told that they should smile and applaud when he arrived, as well as shout "*Yaşasın* (long live) Cemal Paşa." Children obeyed the order, but then one of the older ones spoke and said that they were dying of hunger. Others joined him and cried out, "We're hungry! We're hungry!" Then some of the boldest boys climbed up the trees, jumped on the branches, ate the wild fruits, and made funny noises like monkeys.[96] They were not only disobedient but also creatively rebellious.

Cemal's entourage was going all shades of red, unable to react. Finally, he turned around and gestured to his followers to retreat. A handful of starving children could send the pasha away just by asking for food, not even mentioning anything concerning conversion or Turkification. Later that day, children had the courage to speak Armenian in the classroom and in the courtyard. They assumed they had scored a "victory" in their "battle against the forces of Turkification."[97]

Economies of Survival

One of the main activities that symbolized the continuity of life for the survivors was trade. We know that children familiarized with work rather early in Ottoman society. During the genocidal process, they easily and frequently used their economic minds. Vahram Altounian's genocide journal clearly reveals the importance of possessing something with an exchange value in order to survive in those years.[98] Already in the second line of his narration, he cites his father's advice: "Being idle is not good, let's do something."[99] Then all through their deportation journey, without succumbing to the despair of walking toward their deaths, they managed to find a job to do and acquired commodities with exchange values. Their valuable goods were at times dried meat (*pastırma*), at others attar of roses or their manual labor. Vahram incessantly bought and sold things in order to find food, to have shelter, to get medication, and so forth. In other words, he bought privileges that would help them stay alive.[100] There is no doubt that staying alive was proportional to doing business.

The death of Vahram's father is a striking example of an ongoing "trade." Burying the dead was an exceptional blessing for the deported Armenians. In most cases, the dead were just left behind. But Vahram bribed the responsible officer of their convoy with attar of roses and so delayed their deportation. Then he dug a grave, found an Armenian priest, and gave him five *kuruş* to say the funeral prayer for his father. While reading these lines, the reader is at first surprised that men of religion were accepting money from those unfortunate people, when people were perishing. However, it was also their *trade*. They also needed money to buy lifesaving privileges.

Deported Armenians also realized that having a profession was a chance to stay alive. Some had presented themselves as shoemakers; some as seamstresses, tailors, blacksmiths, or carpenters; and some as doctors. Under the circumstances of the war, there were very few skilled artisans or professionals left. Taking on such identities was believed to be a way to survive. It was common for a boy of sixteen to present himself as a pharmacist or a doctor, if he had worked with a pharmacist or a doctor for six months in his hometown.[101]

Children on the road of deportation would constantly try to make some money from their fellow deportees. They would go to the market, buy baskets of fruits, and bring them to the camp or to the station where the Armenian deportees were and sell them.[102] A survivor boy remembers finding a tin gas can. He cleaned it and then bought a donkey with all the money he had and started selling water to the deported Armenians. As he entered the camp, the thirsty and weak would run to him. He was making ten *kuruş* a day by selling "water to the dying."[103]

Children in the orphanages were also engaged in constant trade.[104] They tried to accumulate capital to exchange their properties when necessary. They sought to barter their valuable items to eat more or different things. They saved raisins to buy bread. They saved bread to buy walnuts. They saved walnuts to buy a spoon (spoons were especially crucial since food was eaten from a common pot). Sometimes several children collected their bread to sell them at the market, and with the money they made they would buy "enough fruit to fill a skirt."[105]

Those children who did not have anything to trade would go into thievery. One survivor admitted that stealing became a habit for him. One day he saw a woman leaving her house without locking the door. He entered the house and drank the unready yogurt (like warm milk). He knew it was bad and sinful, but he was starving. "Staying alive was a relentless struggle for me—so I stole each time I had a chance."[106] One very *carbig* survivor said that he became "a first-class thief" in order to stay alive. One summer night, he noticed a Turkish man and his wife asleep in the courtyard of their house. They had left the door ajar, and the boy sneaked in, grabbed the blanket off them, and ran. He took the blanket to the marketplace the next morning where he exchanged it for some bread.[107]

Children made sense of theft as part of their struggle to survive. Sometimes older friends would inspire and encourage children when they did not have the courage. A ten-year-old child, Mihran, who was ready to make all sorts of sacrifices for his friends and would face any danger, was trying to convince his friends that they had to forget about their fears and go along with him to a nearby vegetable garden: "Whatever happens, we'll keep doing what we do. We're not thieves; we're simply trying to survive. There's no other way."[108] Panian described him as "willful, bold, and enterprising," possessing "not only rare courage, but also the willingness to lead others."[109]

Survival and Adventure

Knowing his grandfather Stepan Miskjian only through his struggle and pain through the genocide, reading his memoirs, published by a small Armenian press in the United States in the 1960s, was a shock for Dawn Anahid Mackeen. She felt like she unfairly has "reduced him to one dimension: he was a survivor." She realized that she never imagined him—or other survivors who endured the genocide—as having a personality, as being funny and enjoying life. The genocide erased all the tiny but meaningful details of survivors' lives. Without his own memoirs that made his daughter and granddaughter giggle, she would have never thought that this sad-looking old man was once "a little prankster."[110]

The available works on the experiences of children during the Armenian genocide also reduce life to survival by solely focusing on suffering and trauma. Without a doubt, there are detailed accounts of the suffering and pain in different types of sources, including narrative sources. However, children were not suffering as a one-dimensional experience; they were also resisting death and remaining alive. Their stories tell us about their survival and how to survive. Within this picture, play, adventure, and children's activities were all very important to provide them with strength and resilience. Either in Muslim households, in orphanages, or at camps and in hiding, children were playing games, making friends, having fun.

Describing his first days on the deportation road, like all other kids who shared his fate, Panian said "farewell to the innocence of his [my] childhood"; he was only five years old.[111] However, he quickly realized that he was still a child. Play was the persistent evidence of their childhood and also their strongest support to cling to life throughout the genocide. Panian says that when they took a break and camped on their deportation journey, children played games every evening "without knowing what fatigue is." They played easy and lively games, such as catch a thief and blind man's bluff, that do not require extra gear. These games pleased, relaxed, and encouraged the adults as well. The parents thought, "They play our games, the ones after them will also play the same games."[112] George Eisen argues that children at play reflected a belief in a future. Play, like all other human activities, served as a tool for survival.[113]

At the orphanage of Hama, as Karnig went out to the courtyard to play, other boys were already separated into different groups and playing "all kinds of games." He thought that their "joyful voices" proved they still had "the ability to enjoy life." Play had a magical capacity to help children adapt to abnormal situations, such that they had "almost forgotten that they were exiles" and that their families were still suffering in the camps; they "were children again."[114] The survival narratives of children are full of tragic events regarding the loss of their families, their own suffering alone, constant hunger, and a longing for home. Still, this general climate of sadness goes hand in hand with play and adventure. There are long depictions of all sorts of adventures in many children's survival narratives that they recount with joy and pride.

> When they [the White Army] evacuated Novorossiysk they left a huge amount of half-destroyed artillery and carloads of ammunition and rifles on the pier which they would not evacuate despite the huge movement of troops. . . . Now—*boys will be mischievous and have fun* and that's what we did. I'm surprised as I think back on it. It was a miracle that none of us was injured or blown up. We took apart the

4. Armenian orphans happily playing together, Maraş (ca. 1919–20). *Source:* "Mrs. Timm's Children, Marash," box 5OV, Cleo A. and Nellie Miller Mann Papers, 1920–2000, HM1-695, Mennonite Church USA Archives, Elkhart, Indiana.

> shells and tried to bury them with dynamite and gunpowder in the ground and then ignite it from a distance to blow it all up—*in addition to lots of other games we devised.*[115]

Despite the dark-toned preface, *Men Deprived of Their Childhood* is an account full of fun and laughter. While describing his best friends, Dzarugyan wrote with pride that "for days, weeks, and months," they learned to ride a bike, played with marbles (*misket*), went to the movies, and skipped school.[116] In Antoura the "tragic life of orphans" could only be "livened up by games and jokes." The children would devise all sorts of funny bets, such as eating their bread without dropping a single crumb. The game was played in the presence of a *referee* and in front of a large *audience.* These sorts of games that Panian regarded as "adventure" were for older boys, while small ones like himself were content to be only watching. But all of them, old or young, would "forget their pain during the game and laugh endlessly."[117]

One boy who was hiding in the premises of American missionaries in Harput tells the story of Enver Pasha's visit to the town in August 1915. Although they were supposed to be hiding in the basement of an American missionary school, as Armenians were deported all over the empire, he was hypnotized by the automobile. He went with his cousin and a friend to the road where Enver Pasha's car was passing. They jumped onto the rear of the car and clung to the spare tire for a ride. After some time, the car stopped, and they were grabbed by the police.[118]

Friendship and solidarity were very important and crucial for children. Panian thought there were great "sincerity and warmth" among his friends and a strong "bond of love." This friendship was born when they were looting the fruit gardens or when they escaped the orphanage and lived in desolate mountains and caves.[119] Children who were fighting to stay alive knew that one could not do this alone. They were aware that they overcame the difficulties in solidarity with their friends.

Finding family members was the most important motivation for children to take risks and embark on an adventure. Reuniting with the family is the one common hope and desire in all survivor accounts. The story of eight-year-old Mgırdiç is quite an adventure, as he traveled very long distances to find his family members.[120] Mgırdiç was from Urfa. In the summer of 1915, the convoys from Diyarbekir, Harput, and Siverek passed through his city. When it was finally their turn, his mother dressed him as a girl. This form of disguise was a very typical survival strategy for Armenian boys and helped Mgırdiç to reach Der Zor. Assuming the role of head of the family there, he bought a horse and a donkey to take his mother and sisters to Mosul. His sisters were mounted on the animals, while he chose to walk beside them with his mother. Hungry and thirsty for days, they passed through the desert. But living conditions in Mosul were not any better. There was a great famine, and the family had nothing to eat but grass. The mother eventually died. Mgırdiç took his sisters and went to Tel Afar. There he heard that his older brothers were alive, working in a garden

5. Armenian orphans on a joyful city tour in the French Quarter, Beirut (1927). *Source*: Maria Jacobsen Collection; courtesy of Houshamadyan.

in Aleppo. He said his "heart jumped" with the news, and he decided to go and find them.

What followed was a remarkable adventure of an eight-year-old doing anything to reunite with the rest of his family. Mingling with a caravan of Arabs, he went to Nusaybin after six or seven days on foot. He found some relatives who cleaned him up, gave him clothes, and helped him recover for a difficult journey ahead. He then went to the train station, where he observed and learned all about traveling without papers, tickets, or money. Despite numerous obstructions on the way, he reached Aleppo and could actually find his brothers. After a couple of peaceful and happy days, he started worrying about his sisters back in Tel Afar. His brother said one of them should go back and bring them. As Mgırdiç thought about it, he knew that his brothers could not find the way back, even though they were considerably older, and that "it had to be him." He volunteered for this difficult mission as the youngest of the brothers, and he successfully accomplished his mission.

6. Armenian orphan girls from the Birds' Nest Orphanage swimming, Jbeil/Byblos (1928). *Source*: Maria Jacobsen Collection; courtesy of Houshamadyan.

All those adventures that one reads with astonishment and exhaustion were part of children's survival. It is as if they actually needed adventure, movement, and accomplishment. Children's play and adventures constituted a part of their quest for survival.[121] As Eisen argues, children's activities had the potential to surround them with "a protective cloak, a spiritual shelter," from which the wounds of the genocide would become invisible, though only for a short time. Through play, they were pursuing a conscious escape. The escape was a promise to transcend their physical limitations and to leave behind their trauma and terror.

It is an especially striking example that Antranig, a ten-year-old boy, who was finally reunited with his mother after four years of separation, runs away from home to return to the orphanage. He finally had a chance to experience the childhood he idealized in a family home and evade the orphanage life, which he called a "never-ending torture." Then why does he refuse to remain with his mother? As he explains in his memoirs, this was *a childish desire* motivated by the train ride and being close to the sea. It was much more attractive for him to make a long journey with his friends and to embark on new adventures in a new city by the sea than to sit idly in his mother's house. The more he thought about how much fun his friends would have on this new adventure, the more unbearable it became to stay at home. "They would all leave, they were all going to get on the train and ride jovially; me, on the other hand, I would be alone in the dirty squares and curved streets of this worn-out city."[122] Before the day of the departure, he spent a very difficult night and finally left the house in the dark and went to the train station.

> We were on a train for the first time and this was a big happiness. The usual things, houses, trees, the whole world had changed for us. As if there was an invisible, a magical hand showing us colorful pictures. Everything was renewed, beautiful, completely different. The wild cries we threw over a bridge, near a small village, or through a cluster of trees, were shaking the freight train. The happiness flowing from the secret fountains opened in our souls could not be contained inside us, it flooded and watered the endless plains of Syria.[123]

Here is a very different picture from the dying and suffering representations of Armenian orphans. A train going at top speed; screaming, cheering, joyful children; the sun, the fields, the trees . . . the depiction of pure happiness!

Enjoying the beautiful scenery around the orphanage in Antoura (bright days, peaks of mountains in the distance to the east, the glittering Mediterranean Sea to the west), Panian also confessed that they "couldn't help but feel a little bit cheerful" that they "had not given up on life yet."[124] Children found the strength they needed to cling to life through play, friendships, adventures, and escapes. A note from Anne Frank's diary perfectly summarizes the needs of children and youth for an escape and their longing for a return to the "normal." "I long to ride a bike, dance, whistle, look at the world, feel young and *know that I'm free*. . . . I sometimes wonder if anyone will ever understand what I mean . . . and merely see me as *a teenager badly in need of some good plain fun*."[125]

A Sedative Called Life

Armenian people, women, men, children, families, the whole population of villages, were wiped out by bullets, disease, starvation, on the roads and in camps and killing fields. Most of them were never to be seen again, either dead or alive. It is a huge story of a loss. There was, and then there was not . . . But the survivors left the dead behind; they continued to live. Most of them were still living under terrible circumstances, but the power of survival helped them not to lose their minds, though many did;[126] not to commit suicide, though it was very common among women;[127] and still laugh despite everything. Survivors carried with them the trauma of the genocide, but it was side by side with their struggle to survive. Life was still going on for them. They suppressed their trauma with a sedative called life.[128] Children repressed their memories, numbed their feelings, and ignored their traumas through play, adventure, friendships, and laughter. These activities also made them take control of their own lives, assume agency for their own survival. They held on to life, but there was always more than holding on. As they lived, they also enjoyed life. They ate their food with appetite, they laughed, and they fell in love.

The stories of these bold and audacious children must have been passed from generation to generation. Although the extent of desolation and deprivation made the listeners weep, they are intended more to making them smile, even laugh, and especially make them proud. Thanks to their assumed agency, adventures, and play, children felt empowered, resilient, and grown up.

Conclusion

Farewell to Childhood?

HISTORIANS OF CHILDREN and youth in the First World War underline the theme of "the end of childhood" prevalent in the discourses of children who witnessed and survived the war.[1] The experience of growing up during wartime had a significant meaning in giving shape to memories of childhood. The narrative sources written by those who were children at the war years almost without exception express the feeling that they ceased to be children. This awareness sometimes came with the recognition of the significance of the world outside their homes. They became conscious of their cities, villages, and the whole world around them. Politicization and socialization of Ottoman children and youth along religious, ethnic, and nationalist lines during the war (chapter 3) can be interpreted as part of this increased awareness of children. In this new settlement of roles, responsibilities, and duties, Ottoman children were both targets and agents of nationalist politics. They were not only functional in *representing* certain nationalist ideals and future dreams, but also *active* in assuming new roles for their nation. Children acquired new identities and exerted agency, either in the form of throwing stones at police forces, getting into fights with other boy gangs, resisting Turkification, traveling to a foreign country for training, or enrolling in boy-scouting organizations. They were more aware of the world outside their homes, such that they became increasingly visible and active in the public sphere.

This sentiment of "ceasing to be a child" is also expressed through the resentment that the war generation never had a childhood, since they had to grow up before their due. The First World War is defined as a "total war" that required the most comprehensive mobilization of all members of the society, regardless of age or gender. Children assumed responsibility for absent adults and became workers in agricultural fields, apprentices in workshops, miners underground, and proletariats in the factories. These war workers were not only laboring children but "little adults." Thousands of orphans in state orphanages (chapter 1) and almost a thousand orphan boys who were sent to Germany as apprentices (chapter 2) need to be regarded from that perspective. By and large, Ottoman authorities treated children in state orphanages as their rightfully owned property over which the state had unrestricted rights of disposal. Their living circumstances remained miserable throughout the war, and they worked *sans cesse* inside the orphanages and also in workshops and factories outside. They were even sent as far as German workshops and mines, even though the opportunities offered to these children or the trades they were trained in were not sufficiently scrutinized. Their work was propagated as sacrifice for the nation, but they also figured as independent agents. They relied on disobedience and escape as their main sources of empowerment. Although the authorities had a hard time comprehending it, these children were not simply lazy, disobedient, or problematic for no reason. They were deeply disillusioned with the limits of care and education with which they were provided. What the authorities saw as "going out of their way" was their search for a way out of their disappointments.

The "loss of childhood" discourse is especially predominant in Armenian survival testimonies (chapter 4). Survivors often commented about their childhood as a sad or a *lost* period in their lives. The "loss" was frequently formulated as growing up precociously and losing one's "childhood innocence" too early. Twelve-year-old Vahan thought that his "childhood ended" when he watched the execution of his two older brothers by gendarmes in Bitlis.[2] Karnig Panian speaks of Armenian children who shared his fate on the deportation road as those children whose "childhood was already dead" and whose "boyhood was in death bed." There was "a barbaric expression on their blackened faces"; they looked both "wretched and wild."[3]

In *Men Deprived of Their Childhood*, Dzarugyan argued that his childhood had been the tragedy of his life. He said his childhood ended even without ever beginning. "We did not have a childhood, because we were Armenians and we were orphans. Was it childhood, our wretched existence, out in the cold and the rain, on the pavements, half naked and barefoot? Was it childhood, our destitution, hunger, tears, the indifference of strangers and the cruelty of those of us [other orphans]?"[4]

The survivors said the best years of their lives were stolen from them. Armenian children's survival narratives are, without doubt, full of such tragic events as the loss of their families, their own suffering alone, constant hunger, and longing for home. However, they are not only tragic stories of *loss*; they are also sagas of courage and resilience. The feeling of "no longer being a child" went hand in hand with what Nazım Hikmet calls living "with great seriousness." Describing himself as a pigeon-livered child, Karnig was extremely proud of the courage and resistance of his friends. Their childhood was "taken away from them"; they were involved with only "matters of life and death." But their hold on life was so splendid that he wanted to "be like them."[5] When it came to survival, acting like a precocious adult was a true talent that Panian praised.

Despite the manifest stress on the "loss," stories of Armenian children also prove that they were more than passive victims. Children were not suffering and surviving as a one-dimensional experience; they were also continuing their lives. They played games, made friends, took part in adventurous journeys. Their "lust for life" was very strong. Both "talented" and resilient, they took control of their own lives, they assumed agency for their own survival.

The public discourse at the time was not only one that pitied children for their "loss of childhood" but also one that was wary of children for their "precocious adulthood." According to Ahmet Emin (Yalman), the orphans of the war, especially the ones who spent long periods of time in state orphanages, saw and felt themselves as being different from the rest of society. Moreover, they were "full of more or less strong feelings of rebellion against the society" (*topluma karşı hafif veya şiddetli isyan duygularıyla dolu*). He even defined this generation of children as "numb" (*hissiz*) and "machinelike" (*makinaya benzer*).[6] The pitiful observant disregarded the fact that children had to numb their feelings, ignore their traumas, in order to take action, in order to survive those terrible years of the war. In his works on the genocide and testimony as a literary form, Marc Nichanian underlines a sense of numbness in the writings of survivors, which made everything look ordinary. It is obvious that they suppressed their feelings, pain, and memories in order to survive. They had to be oblivious; they had to disregard their pain.[7] Dzarugyan underlined that he always felt a big emptiness and a restlessness in his soul, which made him live without thinking of tomorrow.

The war experiences of Ottoman children are especially impressive when seen from a romanticist (prejudiced) perspective, which assumes that children are vulnerable and "special." In this discourse children are "in the making" and thus cannot be considered fully fledged human beings. According to middle-class family values, children would go to school, play in a park, read a children's book. They sound like clichés, but they point to a very general conviction. A child is innocent, ignorant, and defenseless. From this viewpoint, children cannot be subjects, but only victims. The modern bourgeois norm of the nuclear family considers children as precious, but also reduces them to dolls deprived of will and action. The children of the Great War, on the other hand, acted as agents, they felt powerful, and they defined their new selves as "adultlike." In many accounts of childhood during and after the war, it is possible to note the disappearance of parental authority over children, as they were empowered through different new roles they had to assume during the war years.

Despite the firsthand evidence of the strength and resilience of children during the First World War, in numerous successor states in the Middle East the national identity was formed on an infantilized understanding of the nation as a child. There is a lot of discourse and imagery from 1920s Turkey, for instance, that portrays the new state metaphorically as a child needing the support of its founding father.[8] A cartoon published in 1928 features a fatherly figure, Mustafa Kemal, with a young girl, the new nation, seated on his lap. Mustafa Kemal both instructs and protects the nation, with his arms holding the girl. The text above the cartoon reads, "The Republic who has just turned five is learning to read from the Great Ghazi [Warrior]."[9]

Independent and self-sufficient children/nations were not what the interwar states preferred. They would rather have dependents to "teach" and "impose." Nationalist intellectuals and statesmen of the interwar decades probably leaned on their own multinational childhoods as the children of a dismantling Ottoman Empire who were introduced to nationalism for the first time as imperial subjects. Those individuals who founded the nation-states of the post-Ottoman era were precisely the same ones who had grown up and were children during late Ottoman times, particularly World War I. Ironically, in all these nation-states, the elites saw their people as immature, ignorant, innocent children (the masses) to be raised with proper inculcation, despite their own childhood experiences as empowered and active agents.

Glossary
•
Notes
•
Bibliography
•
Index

Glossary

amele: laborer
askeri: military
besleme: foster daughter
Bitarafhane: Neutral House
çırak: apprentice
Darülaceze: the poorhouse of Istanbul
darüleytam: state orphanage
Darüleytam Müdüriyet-i Umumiyesi: General Directorate of Orphanages
Darülmuallimat: Girls Teacher Seminary
Düstur: compilation of regulations
evlad-ı şüheda: children (orphans) of martyrs
evlatlık: foster child
eytam: orphans
eytamhane: orphanage
Eytam ve Eramil Sandığı: Orphans and Widows Aid Fund
fabrika: factory
Genç Dernekleri: Youth League
hamam: public bath
Hamidiye Etfal Hastanesi: children's hospital in Şişli
Himaye-i Etfal Cemiyeti: Children's Protection Society
ırzahane: foundling home, nursing home
ıslah: reform
ıslahhane: vocational state orphanage (literally "reform house")
kabile: midwife
kaymakam: head official of a district
keşşaflık: scouting
kuruş: piaster
lira: Ottoman gold coin
madrassa: Muslim religious school
malul gazi: invalid veterans
Matbaa-i Amire: state printing house
Meclis-i Mebusan: Ottoman parliament
mekteb-i sanayi: vocational school
mekteb-i sultani: high school
millet: officially recognized non-Muslim communities of the Ottoman Empire
millet-i müsellaha: nation in arms
muhacir: refugee, immigrant

muhtar: headman of district

muinsiz aile: soldier families (without male breadwinners)

mutasarrıf: local administrator

müdür: director

mülteci: refugee, immigrant

nafaka: stipend, monthly alimony (for a child)

neseb: lineage, descent

nizamname: regulation

Osmanlı Hilal-i Ahmer Cemiyeti: Ottoman Red Crescent Society

örf: customary law

Rum: Ottoman Greeks

Salname: Ottoman yearbook

sanayi şubesi: industrial section (of an orphanage)

sicil: court case registration

silah: arms

tabakhane: tannery

talebe: student

talim: exercise, drill

Tanzimat: literally reorganizations; an institutionalized process of modernization officially begun in 1839

taşra: provinces, provincial

tebenni: formal adoption

Tersane-i Amire: imperial shipyards

veled: child

veli: guardian

Viladethane: birth/maternity clinic

vilayet: Ottoman province

yetim: orphan

zabtiye: police department, police officer, ministry of police

Notes

Introduction

1. Erik J. Zürcher, "Between Death and Desertion: The Experience of the Ottoman Soldier in World War I," 235.

2. Erik J. Zürcher, "The Ottoman Conscription System in Theory and Practice, 1844–1918," "Little Mehmet in the Desert: The Ottoman Soldier's Experience," "Ottoman Labor Battalions in World War I," and "Refusing to Serve by Other Means: Desertion in the Late Ottoman Empire."

3. Yücel Yanıkdağ, "Ill-Fated Sons of the Nation: Ottoman Prisoners of War in Russia and Egypt, 1914–1922" and *Healing the Nation: Prisoners of War, Medicine and Nationalism in Turkey, 1914–1939*.

4. Except for already mentioned works by Zürcher and Yanıkdağ, the available literature is mostly transcribed memoirs of the POWs, such as Mehmet Arif Ölçen, *Vetluga Memoir: A Turkish Prisoner of War in Russia, 1916–1918*. More general analyses include Cemalettın Taşkıran, *Ana Ben Ölmedim: Birinci Dünya Savaşı'nda Türk Esirleri*; Cemil Kutlu, "I. Dünya Savaşı'nda Rusya'daki Türk Savaş Esirleri ve Bunların Yurda Döndürülmeleri Faaliyetleri"; and Serkan Tuna and Eminalp Malkoç, "The Problem of Turkish Captives in Russia from Moscow Treaty to the First Years of the Turkish Renovation." There is also new literature on the Ottoman POW camps. See Kate Ariotti, *Captive Anzacs: Australian POWs of the Ottomans during the First World War*.

5. The genre turned into a major field in publishing in Turkey, and innumerable diaries appeared in the past decades. Publishing houses, such as İş Kültür Yayıncılık, Timaş, and Arba Yayınevi, published a series of World War I diaries, but the interest on the issue is not limited to them.

6. However, as Salim Tamari underlines, "the power of wartime diaries lies in their exposure of the texture of daily life." Those individuals who could write a few lines on a regular basis were mostly the ones who could stay in towns close to where the actual fighting took place. They had a chance to observe the daily life of the civilians as well.

See Salim Tamari, *Year of the Locust: A Soldier's Diary and the Erasure of Palestine's Ottoman Past*, 4–5; and *The Great War and the Remaking of Palestine*.

7. Mehmet Beşikçi, "When a Military Problem Became a Social Issue: Ottoman Desertions and Deserters in World War I."

8. Mehmet Beşikçi notes that the public sphere was characterized by these "semiofficial" civil society associations, such as the Donanma Cemiyeti (Fleet Society), the Müdafaa-i Milliye Cemiyeti (National Defense League), and the Osmanlı Hilal-i Ahmer Cemiyeti (Ottoman Red Crescent Society). Nadir Özbek also points out that philanthropic associations were used as instruments to expand control over society and consolidate legitimacy. Nadir Özbek, "Defining the Public Sphere during the Late Ottoman Empire: War, Mass Mobilization and the Young Turk Regime (1908–18)."

9. Erol Köroğlu, *Ottoman Propaganda and Turkish Identity: Literature in Turkey during World War I*; Gizem Tongo, "The Ottoman Society of Painters during the First World War," paper presented at the international conference "Not All Quiet on the Ottoman Fronts: Neglected Perspectives on a Global War (1914–1918)," Istanbul, Apr. 2014; Özde Çeliktemel-Thomen, "Osmanlı İmparatorluğu'nda Sinema ve Propaganda, 1908–1922."

10. Ömer Faruk Şerifoğlu, *Ressam Mehmet Ruhi Bey'in "Seferberlik Kartpostalları"*; Gizem Tongo, "Ottoman Painting and Painters during the First World War."

11. Stéphane Audoin-Rouzeau and Annette Becker, *14–18, Understanding the Great War*, 226–36.

12. Elizabeth Thompson, *Colonial Citizens: Republican Rights, Paternal Privileges, and Gender in French Syria and Lebanon*, 18–38; Melanie Tanielian, "The War of Famine: Everyday Life in Wartime Beirut and Mount Lebanon." Tanielian has published extensively on the issue. See her "Feeding the City: The Beirut Municipality and the Politics of Food during World War I," "Politics of Wartime Relief in Ottoman Beirut (1914–1918)," and *The Charity of War: Famine, Humanitarian Aid, and World War I in the Middle East*.

13. M. Talha Çiçek, *War and State Formation in Syria: Cemal Pasha's Governorate during World War I, 1914–1917*; Martin Strohmeier, "Fakhri (Fahrettin) Paşa and the End of Ottoman Rule in Medina (1916–1919)"; Yuval Ben-Bassat and Dotan Halevy, "A Tale of Two Cities and One Telegram: The Ottoman Military Regime and the Population of Greater Syria during WWI."

14. Yiğit Akın, "War, Women, and the State: The Politics of Sacrifice in the Ottoman Empire during the First World War," 13.

15. See by Nicole A. N. M. van Os, "Nurturing Soldiers and Girls: Osmanlı Kadınları Cemiyet-i Hayriyesi," "Aiding the Poor Soldiers' Families: The Asker Âilelerine Yardımcı Hanımlar Cemiyeti," "Gendering Jihad: Ottoman Muslim Women and War during the Early Twentieth Century," and "Taking Care of Soldiers' Families: The Ottoman State and the '*Muinsiz Aile Maaşı*.'"

16. Yiğit Akın, *When the War Came Home: The Ottomans' Great War and the Devastation of an Empire*; Elif Mahir Metinsoy, *Ottoman Women during World War I: Everyday Experiences, Politics, and Conflict*; Zeynep Kutluata, "Ottoman Women and the State during World War I," 92–127.

17. Nazan Maksudyan, *Orphans and Destitute Children in the Late Ottoman Empire*, 3.

18. Michael Geyer, "Militarization of Europe, 1914–1945," 74; Belinda Davis, "Experience, Identity, and Memory: The Legacy of World War I," 115.

19. See Y. Doğan Çetinkaya, "Illustrated Atrocity: The Stigmatisation of Non-Muslims through Images in the Ottoman Empire during the Balkan Wars" and "Atrocity Propaganda and the Nationalization of the Masses in the Ottoman Empire during the Balkan Wars (1912–13)."

20. Stefan Ihrig underlines in his recent book that the Armenian genocide "was and is of towering importance for German history." Stefan Ihrig, *Justifying Genocide: Germany and the Armenians from Bismarck to Hitler*.

21. Beşikçi, *Ottoman Mobilization*; Akın, *When the War Came Home*.

22. BOA, Meclis-i Vükela Mazbataları (MV.), 245/84, 25/Z/1334 (23.10.1916). Akın's *When the War Came Home* provides a detailed account of the parliamentary discussions regarding this temporary law (103–4).

23. Mahir Metinsoy, *Ottoman Women during World War I*, 175–76.

24. Donald Quataert, *Miners and the State in the Ottoman Empire: The Zonguldak Coalfield, 1822–1920*, 145.

25. Yavuz Selim Karakışla, *Women, War and Work in the Ottoman Empire: Society for the Employment of Ottoman Muslim Women, 1916–1923*.

26. BOA, Dahiliye, Şifre Kalemi (DH.ŞFR.), 55/230, 03/Za/1333 (14.09.1915). The document refers to them as "children" (çocuklar) with a gender-neutral term. Although the girls were more numerous in yarn factories, boys were also employed.

27. Mahir Metinsoy, *Ottoman Women during World War I*, 103.

28. Turkish girls gave the emperor flowers at the station. "Emperor Visits Istanbul," *New York Times*, 17 Oct. 1917.

29. "Ben çocuklara çocuk gibi davranmam. Bir çocukla ilişkim, dostluğum, arkadaşlığım varsa, o benim arkadaşımdır, çocuk değildir. Çocuk gibi bakmam. Ayrı bir insan türü gibi bakmam. Niye bu böyle? İnanmadım hiçbir zaman çocukların, insanların çocuklara davrandığı gibi çocuk olduklarına. Basbayağı insandır onlar." Yaşar Kemal's interview with Kemal Özer, 13 Sept. 1975, in *Çocuklar İnsandır*, 17 (emphasis mine; translation mine).

30. Olivier Faron, *Les enfants du deuil: Orphelins et pupilles de la nation de la Première Guerre Mondiale*; Maureen Healy, *Vienna and the Fall of the Habsburg Empire: Total War and Everyday Life in World War I*; Manon Pignot, *La guerre des crayons: Quand les petits Parisiens dessinaient la grande guerre*; Andrew Donson, *Youth in the Fatherless Land: War

Pedagogy, Nationalism, and Authority in Germany, 1914–1918; Susan Fisher, *Boys and Girls in No Man's Land: English-Canadian Children and the First World War*; Rosie Kennedy, *The Children's War: Britain, 1914–1918.*

1. The Great War and State Orphanages (*Darüleytams*)

1. Yakup Kadri, "Darüleytamlara Dair," *Tasvir-i Efkar*, 13 Eylül 1332 (26.09.1916), 1.

2. "Darüleytamlar Müdüriyet-i Umumiyesi Teşkili ve Müteferruatı Hakkında Kanun, 10 Cemaziyelahir 1335 (2 Apr. 1917)," *Düstur*, Tertib 2 (Istanbul: Evkaf Matbaası, 1928), 9:575–76; "Maarif Nezareti'ne Merbut Darüleytamlar Müdüriyet-i Umumiyesi Teşkili Hakkında Layiha-yı Kanuniye," in *Meclis-i Mebusan Encümen Mazbataları ve Levayih-i Kanuniye, vol. 9 (1332–1333)* (Devre: 3, İctima: 3, no. 240), 1–7, https://acikerisim.tbmm.gov.tr/xmlui/handle/11543/2400.

3. The priority of children whose fathers died or were wounded during combat was underlined in several documents. BOA, Dahiliye Nezareti, Umur-ı Mahalliye-i Vilayet Müdüriyeti (DH.UMVM.), 70/40, 03/Ra/1334 (08.02.1916).

> Millet ve Devlet-i Osmaniye'nin saadet ve selameti namına ifna-yı hayat eden gerd-bad şuun ve hadisat arasında aile ve yurtları tar-ı mar olan fedakar İslam ve Türk şehitlerinin hamisiz kalmış olan evlad-ı yetimesine mahsus şefkat ve terbiye müessesesidir. Çocuklar için hariçte mevcut olmayan aileyi darüleytam kendi muhitinde tesis etmiş ve çocukların evvela muhafaza-yı hayatını saniyen terbiye-yi ahlakiyesini salisen tedris ve talimini temin için mümkün kadar aile esaslarına müstenid bir teşkilat vücuda getirilmiştir. *Taht-ı Himaye-i Mufahhama-i Hazret Hilafet-penahi-i Azamide Darüleytam Çağlayan Kız Şubesi* (n.p., n.d.), 1.

There are also numerous examples in the Ottoman Archives of children who were admitted to the *darüleytam* as an "orphan of a martyr." BOA, DH.UMVM., 70/18, 9/Ra/1336 (22.01.1918): registration of a girl from Salonika, whose father was a martyr.

4. For further information, see Roderic H. Davison, *Reform in the Ottoman Empire, 1856–1876.*

5. For a detailed analysis of nineteenth-century provisions for needy children in the Ottoman Empire, see Maksudyan, *Orphans and Destitute Children.*

6. "Memalik-i şahanenin bazı mahallerinde bulunan etfal-i yetimenin devletce yapılacak mekteblerde terbiyelerine ecanibin bir şey demeğe bir güna hak ve salahiyetleri olamayacağına . . . ," BOA, Yıldız Sadaret Resmi Maruzat Evrakı (Y.A.RES.), 101/39, 19/S/1317 (29.06.1899).

7. BOA, Sadaret Mühimme Kalemi Evrakı (A.MKT.MHM.), 702/30, 25/Z/1316 (06.05.1899). In many of these documents on the discussion, the Ottoman term for orphanage took a number of forms: *eytamhane*, *yetimhane*, *darütterbiye*, and *darüttalim.*

8. BOA, Y.A.RES., 101/39, 19/S/1317 (29.06.1899).

9. BOA, Yıldız Mütenevvi Maruzat Evrakı (Y.MTV.), 193/44, 7/R/1317 (15.08.1899).

10. The building plan was prepared by the famous Italian architect Raimondo D'Aronco (1857–1932). He was the chief palace architect of Abdülhamid II for sixteen years. BOA, Yıldız Perakende Evrakı Başkitabet Dairesi (Y.PRK.BŞK.), 62/70, 28/R/1318 (26.07.1900).

11. BOA, Y.MTV., 193/44, 7/R/1317 (15.08.1899).

12. *Salname-i Nezaret-i Maarif-i Umumiye 1319* (Istanbul: Matbaa-i Amire, 1319 [1901]), 14.

13. BOA, İrade, Hususi (İ.HUS.), 109/37, 8/Ca/1321 (01.09.1903); Nadir Özbek, "II. Abdülhamid ve Kimsesiz Çocuklar: Darülhayr-ı Âlî"; Nadir Özbek, *Osmanlı İmparatorluğu'nda Sosyal Devlet: Siyaset, İktidar ve Meşrutiyet, 1876–1914*, 247.

14. BOA, Zabtiye Nezareti (ZB.), 320/123, 18/Şu/1322 (03.03.1907).

15. *Düstur*, Tertib 2, vol. 1, no. 133, 648–49; *Takvim-i Vekayi*, vol. 2, no. 349, 21 Ramazan 1327 (06.10.1909), 7.

16. Mahir Metinsoy, *Ottoman Women during World War I*, 101; Akın, *When the War Came Home*, 82–83, 142.

17. *Minutes of the Grand National Assembly*, 2nd Parliament, 1st Legislative Year (11.08.1923–28.02.1924), 15th Session (08.09.1339) [1923]) (hereafter *TBMM ZC*), 448–79, http://www.tbmm.gov.tr/tutanaklar/TUTANAK/TBMM/d02/c001/tbmmo2001015.pdf, 469.

18. "Darüleytam," *İkdam* 6846 (5 Mar. 1916), 1. İsmail Mahir Efendi was sometimes referred to as the founder of the orphanages, even as the "father of orphans," for his efforts in opening several branches in Istanbul. Upon his death, a circular was sent to all orphanages, noting that the institutions were now "orphaned" with the death of İsmail Mahir (the father) and that the last wish of "this great man" was the "immortality" (*payidar*) of his "beloved establishment." BOA, Maarif Nezareti Darüleytam Dosyaları (MF.EYT.), 5/60, no. 15, 1 Haziran 1332 (14.06.1916).

19. Osman Nuri Ergin, *Türkiye Maarif Tarihi*, 1548.

20. Necdet Sakaoğlu, "Darüleytamlar."

21. BOA, MF.EYT., 6/110, 6/Za/1335 (23.09.1917). The second article further explained that the educational purpose of the institution was to enhance the Islamic and national feelings of the children and to provide them an industrial education (both theoretical and practical) in view of their abilities and also the needs of the country.

22. For instance, Ahmet Niyazi noted that the most sacred duty of the state was to take care of the children of martyrs, those who reached "the highest rank as Muslims." Ahmed Niyazi, "Şehit Kardeşime," *İslam Mecmuası* 39, 6 Teşrinisani 1331 (19.11.1915), 823–25.

23. Capitulations of the Ottoman Empire were contracts between the Ottoman Empire and European powers, particularly France. They were generally bilateral acts whereby definite arrangements were entered into by each contracting party toward the other. According to these capitulations, traders entering the Ottoman Empire were exempt from local prosecution, local taxation, local conscription, and search of their domicile.

24. On allocation of buildings belonging to "foreigners," see BOA, MF.MKT., 1203/30, 14/M/1333 (02.12.1914); and Ergin, *Türkiye Maarif Tarihi*, 1548.

25. The Dominican School in Yedikule was appropriated and turned into an orphanage for boys. BOA, MF.MKT., 1207/70, 30/C/1333 (15.04.1915). Later, it became one of the largest orphanages in Istanbul, with seven hundred boys trained in trades.

26. BOA, MF.MKT.,1209/93, 5/N/1333 (16.06.1915).

27. As part of the same process, some factories were also confiscated during the war in order to make use of the free orphan labor. One of these factories was the basket factory in Divanyolu, which was taken over from the National Defense Society. "Sepet Fabrikasının Darüleytama Devri," *İleri*, 1 Eylül 1336 (01.09.1920), 2. A more interesting example was a silk factory in Kartal (Istanbul), which was supposedly donated to the *darüleytam* by Hacı Yunus Efendi. During the Allied occupation of the city, two Armenian women claimed that they were the rightful owners of the factory and demanded its release. BOA, Dahiliye, İdare-i Umumiye (DH.İ.UM.), 7-7/1-24, 20/L/1339 (27.06.1921).

28. BOA, MF.MKT., 1207/70, 30/C/1333 (15.04.1915).

29. New research on the Armenian genocide underlines "nonlethal forms of violence." As Polatel, Üngör, Onaran, and Kurt have discussed, genocide also involved taking over wealth and property together with demographic resources. Mehmet Polatel and Uğur Ümit Üngör, *Confiscation and Destruction: The Young Seizure of Armenian Property*; Nevzat Onaran, *Emval-i Metruke Olayı: Osmanlı'da ve Cumhuriyette Ermeni ve Rum Mallarının Türkleştirilmesi*; Ümit Kurt, "The Plunder of Wealth through Abandoned Properties Laws in the Armenian Genocide."

30. Raymond Kévorkian, *The Armenian Genocide: A Complete History*, 755.

31. Theodore P. Ion and Carroll N. Brown, *Persecutions of the Greeks in Turkey since the Beginning of the European War*, 6.

32. BOA, Babıali Evrak Odası (BEO), 4396/329676, 26/Re/1334 (01.02.1916).

33. Elli Kohen describes how the estrangement from France (and rapprochement to Germany) came as an utter shock to Frenchified Jews. After the unimaginable rupture with France, the French had to go and with them left brothers and sisters of French schools. Joseph's high-class French school, Lycée Saint Michel, was discontinued. Elli Kohen, *The Kohens del de Campavias: A Family's Sweet and Sour Story in Ottoman and Republican Turkey*, 35.

34. "Fener'de Darüleytam," *Tasvir-i Efkar*, 11, 19, 25 Teşrinisani 1330 (24.11.1914, 02.12.1914, 08.12.1914).

35. BOA, Maarif Nezareti İstanbul Maarif Müdüriyeti (MF.İMF.), 49/84, 19/S/1335 (15.12.1916).

36. "Fener'de Darüleytam," *Tasvir-i Efkar*, 11, 19, 25 Teşrinisani 1330 (24.11.1914, 02.12.1914, 08.12.1914); İsmet Binark, "Maarif Tarihimize Ait Bir Rapor," *Yeni Türkiye* 2/7 (1996): 490.

37. BOA, MF.EYT., 1/17, 16 Mart 1331 (29.03.1915). The first director of the orphanages, İsmail Mahir Efendi, was using first the Kadıköy Orphanage as his "headquarters," and then he moved his office to the Galata Industrial Orphanage.

38. "1334 Senesi Darüleytam Müdüriyet-i Umumiyesi Bütçesi Muvazene-i Maliye Encümeni Mazbatası," in *Meclis-i Mebusan Encümen Mazbataları ve Levayih-i Kanuniye, vol. 10 (1333–1334)* (Devre: 3, İctima: 4, no. 409), 3 (abbreviated as "1334 Senesi Darüleytam Müdüriyet-i Umumiyesi Bütçesi," the document has thirty pages in total).

39. BOA, Dosya Usulü İradeler Tasnifi (İ.DUİT.), 87/44, 04/Re/1336 (18.12.1917).

40. "1333 Senesi Darüleytamlar Müdüriyet-i Umumiyesi Masraf Bütçesinin Birinci Faslının İkinci ve Dördüncü Maddeleri ile Maliye Nezareti'nin Sene-i Mezkure Bütçesinin Ondokuzuncu Darüleytamlar Faslı Tahsisatına 42.060.402 Kuruş İlavesi Hakkında Layiha-yı Kanuniye," in *Meclis-i Mebusan Encümen Mazbataları ve Levayih-i Kanuniye, vol. 10 (1333–1334)* (Devre: 3, İctima: 4, no. 459), 1–6, https://acikerisim.tbmm.gov.tr/xmlui/handle/11543/2400.

41. BOA, Sadaret Evrakı (A.VRK.), 806/71, doc. 1, 8 Teşrinievvel 1332 (21.10.1916). Later this institution was simply called Bebek Girls Industrial Orphanage (Kız Sanayi).

42. BOA, MF.EYT, 4/6, 17 Eylül 1332 (30.09.1916).

43. "1334 Senesi Darüleytam Müdüriyet-i Umumiyesi Bütçesi," 3.

44. Ibid.

45. BOA, MF.EYT., 6/110, 23/Ca/1333 (08.05.1915).

46. BOA, MF.MKT., 1227/20, 19/S/1335 (15.12.1916).

47. BOA, DH.UMVM., 70/2, 28/N/1333 (11.07.1915); "1334 Senesi Darüleytam Müdüriyet-i Umumiyesi Bütçesi," 4–5; Yakup Kadri, "Darüleytamlar İdaresi I," *Tasvir-i Efkar*, 20 Kanunusani 1335 (20.01.1919), 1; Yakup Kadri, "Darüleytamlar İdaresi II," *Tasvir-i Efkar*, 29 Kanunusani 1335 (29.01.1919), 1; "Darüleytamlar İdaresi III," *Tasvir-i Efkar*, 31 Kanunusani 1335 (31.01.1919), 1.

48. BOA, DH.UMVM., 70/1, 6/B/1333 (20.05.1915); DH.UMVM, 70/2, 28/N/1333 (11.07.1915).

49. The province of Kastamonu mentioned donations collected from the people. BOA, DH.UMVM., 23/3, 28/Re/1332 (24.02.1914).

50. A lottery was organized in Söğüt, and the revenue was used for the establishment of the orphanage. BOA, DH.UMVM., 20/19, 26/Ca/1334 (30.04.1916).

51. "1334 Senesi Darüleytam Müdüriyet-i Umumiyesi Bütçesi," 4.

52. Okur, "Darüleytamlar"; Hakan Aytekin, "1914–1924 Yılları Arasında Korunmaya Muhtaç Çocuklar ve Eğitimleri."

53. *MMZC*, vol. 1, session 14, 6 Kanunuevvel 1333 (06.12.1917), 197.

54. The table prepared by the directorate in mid-1917 gives the exact numbers in orphanages. But this document has a missing page; see table 3. BOA, MF.EYT., 7/51, 5/L/1335 (25.07.1917).

55. The financial burden of doubling the budget to meet the needs of those children outside orphanages was beyond the financial capacity of the Ottoman state. *Meclis-i Mebusan Encümen Mazbataları ve Levayih-i Kanuniye, vol. 10 (1333–1334)* (Devre: 3, İctima: 4, no. 409), 1–30, https://acikerisim.tbmm.gov.tr/xmlui/handle/11543/2400.

56. "1334 Senesi Darüleytam Müdüriyet-i Umumiyesi Bütçesi," 11.

57. Mahir Metinsoy, *Ottoman Women during World War I*, 101–6.

58. Ahmed Emin Yalman, *Turkey in the World War*, 259.

59. Ibid., 258.

60. Karnig Panian, *Goodbye, Antoura: A Memoir of the Armenian Genocide*, 98–119.

61. In a novel by Hüseyin Rahmi Gürpınar, *Hakka Sığındık* (1919) (*We Seek Refuge in God*), orphaned siblings try to survive in the streets by selling things, begging, and stealing. Then the eleven-year-old sister is forced into prostitution to save her sick brother.

62. In 1917 Kadıköy Girls Orphanage had eight hundred girls, while Bebek Girls Industrial orphanage had two hundred. BOA, MF.EYT., 7/51, 5/L/1335 (25.07.1917).

63. BOA, MF.EYT., 7/51, 5/L/1335 (25.07.1917). See table 3.

64. See chap. 3 for detail.

65. BOA, MF.MKT., 1213/71, 13/Re/1334 (19.01.1916).

66. Ibid., doc. 2, 6 Kanunusani 1331 (19.01.1916).

67. Ibid., doc. 3, 12 Kanunusani 1331 (25.01.1916).

68. BOA, MF.MKT., 1217/34, 18/N/1334 (19.07.1916).

69. "Darüleytamlar Müdüriyet-i Umumiyesinin Teşkili ve Müteferruatı Hakkında Kanun, 10 Cemaziyelahir 1335 (2 April 1917)" *Düstur*, Tertib 2 (Istanbul: Evkaf Matbaası, 1928), 9:575–76.

70. Reşat Özalp, *Milli Eğitimle İlgili Mevzuat (1857–1923)*, 118–19.

71. Hüseyin Ragıp, "Meclis-i Mebusanda Şehit Çocukları I," *Muallim*, vol. 1, no. 9, 11 Nisan 1333 (11.04.1917), 283.

72. BOA, MF.MKT., 1225/64, 1/B/1335 (23.04.1917); BOA, MF.MKT., 1225/51, 28/Ca/1335 (21.04.1917).

73. BOA, MF.MKT., 1225/40, 26/Ca/1335 (19.04.1917).

74. BOA, MF.MKT., 1229/24, 21/Za/1335 (08.09.1917).

75. BOA, MF.MKT., 1227/22, 20/N/1335 (11.06.1917); BOA, MF.MKT., 1233/15, 10/B/1336 (21.04.1918).

76. *Tanin*, 5 Kanunusani 1331 (18.01.1916), 3.

77. The Ministry of Interior, on the other hand, was constantly sending new children to orphanages. For instance, the ministry asked each and every province to find a vacant place for an orphan boy named Abbasoğlu Hasan. BOA, DH.UMVM., 70/14, 5/M/1336 (21.10.1917).

78. BOA, DH.KMS., 38/3, 29/C/1334 (03.04.1916).

79. For example, BOA, MF.MKT., 1215/63, 04/B/1334 (07.05.1916); BOA, Dahiliye, Kalem-i Mahsus Müdüriyeti (DH.KMS.), 38/3, 29/C/1334 (03.04.1916); and BOA, MF.MKT., 1229/46, 24/Za/1335 (12.09.1917).

80. BOA, MF.EYT., 9/61, 7 Teşrinisani 1333 (07.11.1917).

81. For instance, İzmit Reşadiye had 262 boys, though its quota was 200; Efkere Boys Orphanage had 335 children, while its quota was 300. BOA, MF.EYT., 7/51, 5/L/1335 (25.07.1917).

82. *TBMM ZC*, 461; BOA, MF.EYT., 6/131 (report) cited in Safiye Kıranlar, Aynur Soydan Erdemir, "Köyün Modernleştirilmesine Dair Bir Uygulama ve Proje: Kimsesiz Köy Çocuklarının Köyde Eğitimi."

83. Hasan İzzettin Dinamo, *Öksüz Musa*, 14–16.

84. BOA, MF.EYT., 7/57, 1 Ağustos 1333 (01.08.1917).

85. İrfan Orga notes in his memoirs that his little brother became ill owing to constant hunger in the orphanage in Kadıköy. Their mother put them there in 1916, assuming that they would be properly fed. However, the circumstances greatly deteriorated within two years, and their mother took them out in 1918. İrfan Orga, *Portrait of a Turkish Family*, 176–90; Nissim M. Benezra, *Une enfance Juive à Istanbul, 1911–1929*.

86. BOA, İrade, Meclis-i Mahsus (İ.MMS.), 198/1333-N-10, 06/N/1333 (19.07.1915); BOA, İrade, Meclis-i Umumi (İ.MLU.), 10/1334-S-34, 24/S/1334 (01.01.1916); BOA, MF.MKT., 1227/20, 19/Ş/1335 (09.06.1917).

87. BOA, MF.EYT., 10/20, doc. 15, 18 Mayıs 1334 (18.05.1918).

88. Ibid. This time he was heard, and the ministry sent 43,782 *kuruş*.

89. In the report prepared for the budget of 1334, it was noted that the costs were assumed to be lower in the provinces as opposed to the center (Istanbul). While calculating the income, orphanages in the provinces were given 100 *kuruş* per child per month, while the ones in Istanbul received 150. "1334 Senesi Darüleytam Müdüriyet-i Umumiyesi Bütçesi," 5; Ersin Müezzinoğlu, "I. Dünya Savaşı Esnasında Yetim ve Öksüz Çocukların Himayesi ve Eğitimi: Darüleytamlar," *History Studies* 4, no. 1 (2012): 403–4.

90. BOA, MF.MKT., 1227/20, 19/S/1335 (15.12.1916).

91. BOA, MF.EYT., 16/145, 8 Ağustos 1336 (08.08.1920); BOA, MF.EYT., 16/143, 2 Ağustos 1336 (02.08.1920); BOA, MF.EYT., 17/62, 15 Ağustos 1336 (15.08.1920).

92. BOA, MF.EYT., 7/65, 6 Teşrinievvel 1333 (06.10.1917).

93. Panian, *Goodbye, Antoura*, 98–119.

94. BOA, MF.EYT., 7/23, doc. 1, 5 Mayıs 1333 (05.05.1917).

95. BOA, MF.MKT., 1227/12, 16/N/1335 (07.06.1917).

96. For an example of a health check prior to the admittance, see BOA, MF.EYT., 2/84, doc. 7, 28 Nisan 1332 (11.05.1916). For an example of a vaccination certificate, see BOA, MF.EYT., 9/46, doc. 2, 15 Apr. 1334 (1918).

97. *TBMM ZC*, 448–79.

98. BOA, MF.EYT., 6/131 (report) cited in Kıranlar and Erdemir, "Köyün Modernleştirilmesine Dair Bir Uygulama," 98–99.

99. Dinamo, Öksüz Musa, 18–20.

100. BOA, MF.EYT., 5/60, doc. 46, 16 Teşrinievvel 1332 (29.10.1916).

101. BOA, MF.EYT., 10/20, doc. 10, 21 Mart 1334 (21.03.1918).

102. BOA, MF.MKT., 1225/98, 10/B/1335 (02.05.1917).

103. BOA, Dahiliye Nezareti İdare-i Umumiye Ekleri (DH.İ.UM.EK.), 25/92, 28/S/1335 (24.12.1916).

104. Ibid. doc. 5, 2 Teşrinievvel 1332 (15.12.1916).

105. BOA, MF.MKT., 1225/97, 10/B/1335 (02/05/1917).

106. *TBMM ZC*, 461.

107. *TBMM ZC*, 453.

108. BOA, MF.EYT., 10/15, doc. 1, 21 Eylül 1334 (21.09.1918).

109. "1334 Senesi Darüleytam Müdüriyet-i Umumiyesi Bütçesi," 11: "1333 senesi ibtidasından bugüne kadar alınan malumata nazaran 32'si merkezde ve 48'i mülhakat darüleytamlarında olmak üzere maalesef 80 çocuk vefat etmiştir. . . . [V]efatın nisbeti % 1 farz olunabilir."

110. *Takvim-i Vekayi* 3200, 4 Nisan 1334 (04.04.1918), 2.

111. The first group of forty-five orphans who were transported from Anatolia by train arrived there in September 1918. BOA, MF.EYT., 10/119, doc. 29, 11 Eylül 1334 (01.09.1918).

112. His suggestions were based on common sense such as to provide enough food for children, to separate the sick from the healthy, and to bring sick children immediately to the hospital. BOA, MF.EYT., 16/126, 3 Haziran 1336 (03.06.1920).

113. BOA, MF.EYT., 6/131 (report) cited in Kıranlar and Erdemir, "Köyün Modernleştirilmesine Dair Bir Uygulama," 98–99.

114. Some parliamentarians were criticizing the Ministry of Education that the orphanages did not have clear rules about education and training, since the institution did not have a clear regulation on these issues. The minister, Ahmet Şükrü Bey, objected and explained that children should be educated along the lines of already existing regulations. Little children would be subject to the Regulation of Kindergartens (Ana Mektepleri Nizamnamesi), primary school children would be subject to the Primary Schools Regulation (Tedrisat-ı İbtidaiye Kanun-ı Muvakkati), and children older than twelve would receive industrial training based on the regulations of vocational

schools (*sanayi mektepleri için yapılmış talimatnameler*). *MMZC*, vol. 1, session 33, 14 Jan. 1918, 595.

115. BOA, MF.EYT., 10/15, doc. 1, 21 Eylül 1334 (21.09.1918).

116. BOA, MF.EYT., 6/110, 6/Za/1335 (23.09.1917).

117. Taylan Esin, "Savaş, Tehcir, Ütopya: Darüleytamların Yükselişi ve Çözülüşü"; "1334 Senesi Darüleytam Müdüriyet-i Umumiyesi Bütçesi," 3, 10, 14.

118. Hüseyin Ragıp, "Meclis-i Mebusanda Şehit Çocukları II," *Muallim*, vol. 1, no. 11, 1 Haziran 1333 (01.06.1917), 344–45.

119. The exhibit in June 1920 had been discussed extensively in the press. "Divan Yolunda Darüleytam Sergisi," *İleri*, 1 June 1336 (1920), 3.

120. "Darüleytamlarımız ve Yavrularımız Hakkında," *İkdam*, 7 July 1337 (1921), 3.

121. BOA, MF.MKT., 1230/7, 09/Z/1335 (26.09.1917). The orphanage also requested exemption from tithing (öşür), a canonical levy for Muslim villagers. The same demand was also made by the Adana orphanage and refused. BOA, MF.MKT., 1230/111, 5/M/1336 (21.10.1917).

122. While these orphanages initially planned to provide mixed education, they did not exist long enough to admit girls.

123. BOA, MF.MKT., 1230/55, 20/Z/1335 (07.10.1917).

124. BOA, İ.MMS., 198/9, 6/R/1333 (18.07.1915).

125. BOA, MF.EYT., 19/62, 6 Teşrinievvel 1337 (06.10.1921).

126. BOA, MF.EYT., 15/131, 17 Teşrinisani 1337 (17.11.1921).

127. MF.EYT., 17/78; Safiye Kıranlar, "Savaş Yıllarında Türkiye'de Sosyal Yardım Faaliyetleri (1914–1923)," 85. The dissertation is also published as a book: Safiye Kıranlar and Savaş Yıllarında, *Türkiye'de Sosyal Yardım Faaliyetleri (1914–1923)* (Ankara: Türk Tarih Kurumu, 2013).

128. Hüseyin Ragıp, "Meclis-i Mebusanda Şehit Çocukları II," 344–45.

129. BOA, MF.MKT., 1229/44 24/Za/1335 (11.09.1917); BOA, MF.MKT., 1230/36, 16/Z/1335 (03.10.1917).

130. "Çocuğun Harekat-ı Hariciyesi Hakkında Kontrole Memur Mürebbi ve Mürşidin Mütalaat ve Meşhudatı." Such registers were found in two different files relating to two different orphans: BOA, MF.EYT., 17/78; and BOA, MF.EYT., 17/96, 25 Mayıs 1337 (25.05.1921).

131. BOA, MF.EYT., 17/96, 25 Mayıs 1337 (25.05.1921).

132. Yavuz S. Karakışla, "Kadınları Çalıştırma Cemiyeti Himayesi'nde Savaş Yetimleri ve Kimsesiz Çocuklar: 'Ermeni' mi, 'Türk' mü?."

133. "1334 Senesi Darüleytam Müdüriyet-i Umumiyesi Bütçesi," 9.

134. BOA, MF.MKT., 1229/52, 24/Za/1335 (11.09.1917).

135. BOA, MF.EYT., 7/51, 5/L/1335 (25.07.1917).

136. The reasons behind the opening of orphanages are consistently said to be the care and education of orphans of martyrs, Muslim orphans, Turkish orphans, and

so on. Okur, "Darüleytamlar"; Kıranlar, "Savaş Yıllarında Türkiye'de Sosyal Yardım"; Neslihan Can, "Atatürk ve İnönü Dönemi Sosyal Yardım Politikalarının Karşılaştırmalı Bir Analizi, 1923–1950."

137. Uğur Ümit Üngör, "Orphans, Converts, and Prostitutes: Social Consequences of War and Persecution in the Ottoman Empire, 1914–1923," 175.

138. Ara Sarafian, "The Absorption of Armenian Women and Children into Muslim Households as a Structural Component of the Armenian Genocide," 210–11.

139. There are innumerable orders sent to the provinces for the admittance (or in the postwar period "release") of Armenian orphans to state orphanages. For instance, BOA, DH.ŞFR., 59/150, 21/S/1334 (29.12.1915); BOA, DH.ŞFR., 68/95, 25/Za/1334 (23.09.1916); and BOA, DH.ŞFR., 96/77, 04/Ca/1337 (07.03.1919).

140. Even denialist historians underline that Armenian orphans were taken care of in Ottoman state orphanages, in other state institutions such as the Ottoman Red Crescent or the Islamic Society for the Employment of Women, and were distributed to private households. They underline that Armenian orphans were handed over to the care of Muslims as a central state policy. Önder Duman, "Mütareke İstanbul'unda Ermeni Faaliyetleri," 159–60.

141. Taner Akçam, *Ermenilerin Zorla Müslümanlaştırılması: Sessizlik, İnkâr ve Asimilasyon.*

142. Üngör, "Orphans, Converts, and Prostitutes," 175–76.

143. Ümit Kurt, "Cultural Erasure: The Absorption and Forced Conversion of Armenian Women and Children, 1915–1916."

144. BOA, DH.ŞFR., 54/150, 13/N/1333 (26.06.1915).

145. BOA, DH.ŞFR., 54/411, 29/N/1333 (12.07.1915): "Children who became parentless during the transportation of Armenians" ("Ermenilerin nakil ve sevkleri esnasında velisiz kalmış çocuklar") were to be placed in state orphanages.

146. The Ministry of Interior openly promised an additional allocation to the orphanages that accepted Armenian children. BOA, DH.KMS., 39/4, 8/N/1334 (10.06.1916).

147. BOA, MF.EYT., 6/110, 6/Za/1335 (24.08.1917); Kıranlar, "Savaş Yıllarında," 60.

148. İbrahim E. Atnur, *Türkiye'de Ermeni Kadınları ve Çocukları Meselesi, 1915–1923*, 51, 54–55.

149. BCA, Toprak İskan Genel Müdürlüğü Kataloğu (272-0-0-12/MUHACIRIN), 37/20/1, doc. 2, 1 Mayıs 1332 (14.05.1916).

150. Kıranlar, "Savaş Yıllarında," 60.

151. Kévorkian, *Armenian Genocide*, 674.

152. BOA, DH.ŞFR., 64/67, 15/B/1334 (18.05.1916). The orphanage was finally opened by the municipality. Because of financial difficulties, children were then sent to

Istanbul in 1919. There, 339 children were greeted in the Haydarpaşa train station by the Armenian and Allied authorities, who claimed that they were all Armenians. After a long period of controversy, 200 children were given back to the authority of *darül-eytam*. *MMZC*, vol. 1, İctima-ı Fevkalade, session 17, 1 Mart 1336 (01.03.1920), 303.

153. BOA, DH.ŞFR., 95/261, 23/Ra/1337 (26.01.1919). In a controversy in the postwar period, it was underlined that Armenian children in Muslim households in Kayseri were in a miserable state.

154. BOA, DH.ŞFR., 61/20, 10/Ra/1334 (15.02.1916).

155. Watenpaugh, "League of Nations Rescue of Armenians," 1329.

156. Murat Bardakçı, *Talât Paşa'nın Evrak-ı Metrukesi: Sadrazam Talât Paşa'nın Özel Arşivinde Bulunan Ermeni Tehciri Konusundaki Belgeler ve Hususî Yazışmalar*, 88–89; Fuat Dündar, *Modern Türkiye'nin Şifresi: İttihat ve Terakki'nin Etnisite Mühendisliği, 1913–1918*, 307.

157. The report was most probably prepared for Talat Pasha's private use and not for publication. The report survived because Talat took it into exile when he fled the Ottoman Empire in 1918. It was obtained from his widow by a Turkish historian shortly before her death in 1982. Ara Sarafian, *Talaat Pasha's Report on the Armenian Genocide*. For a detailed discussion of Talat Pasha and the Armenian genocide, see the new biography by Hans-Lukas Kieser that defines him as the "architect of the Armenian Genocide," *Talaat Pasha: Father of Modern Turkey, Architect of Genocide*.

158. BOA, DH.ŞFR., 74/165, 25/C/1335 (19.03.1917).

159. BOA, MF.EYT., 10/22, doc. 2, 19 Teşrinievvel 1334 (19.10.1918); MF.EYT., 10/23, doc. 3, 19 Teşrinievvel 1334 (19.10.1918).

160. Dinamo, *Öksüz Musa*, 78.

161. Kévorkian, *Armenian Genocide*, 759.

162. "Eytamhane Küşadı," *Sabah*, 15 Kanunusani 1334 (15 Jan. 1918), 2.

163. BOA, DH.İ.UM., 7/1, 5/S/1338 (30.11.1919).

164. Aram Haigaz wrote, "Any Armenian who survived seemed to have gone to Sivas. Once there, I found relatives and countrymen that I did not know were alive." Aram Haigaz, *Four Years in the Mountains of Kurdistan: An Armenian Boy's Memoir of Survival*, 322–23.

165. BOA, Maarif Nezareti, Tedrisat-ı Hususiye Kalemi (MF.HUS.), 21/50, doc. 1, 21 Temmuz 1334 (21.07.1918).

166. "Şüheda Vesaire Evladlarının Leyli Mekatib-i İdadiye-i Askeriyeye Kayıt ve Kabulü Hakkında Nizamname," *Düstur*, Tertib 2, vol. 7 (Dersaadet: Matbaa-i Amire, 1336 [1920]), 743–45.

167. Anna Welles Brown, "Orphanages in Constantinople," 233.

168. BOA, DH.İ.UM., 19-20/1-2, doc. 2, 23/Ca/1340 (21.02.1922).

169. This attitude is discussed in more detail in chapter 2.

170. Üngör, "Orphans, Converts, and Prostitutes," 178–79.

171. See Emre Erol, "Organized Chaos as Diplomatic Ruse and Demographic Weapon: The Expulsion of the Ottoman Greeks (Rum) from Foça 1914," for more information on forced migration of the Ottoman Greeks from the Aegean.

172. BOA, DH.UMVM., 136/61, 29/R/1334 (04.02.1916).

173. BOA, MF.EYT., 6/131; "1334 Senesi Darüleytam Müdüriyet-i Umumiyesi Bütçesi," 3.

174. Kıranlar and Erdemir, "Köyün Modernleştirilmesine"; Kıranlar, "Savaş Yıllarında Türkiye'de Sosyal Yardım Faaliyetleri," 60–62.

175. "Darüleytamlara Dair," *Tasvir-i Efkar*, 22 Eylül 1333 (22.09.1917), 2.

176. Hüseyin Ragıp, "Meclis-i Mebusanda Şehit Çocukları II," 344–45.

177. BOA, DH.İ.UM., 22/25, 11/N/1336 (22.05.1918).

178. Ibid; BOA, MF.EYT., 9/65, docs. 1–2, 26 Mayıs 1334 (26.05.1918). The list consisted of the following orphanages: Edirne Orphanages (Asım Bey, Edirne Girls, CUP orphanage), Kırklareli (Ömer Naci Bey Darüleytamı), Tekirdağ (Tekfurdağı Gazi Fazıl Darüleytamı), Adana (Enver Pasha), Adana Girls, Kozan, Mersin, Dörtyol, Tarsus, Ekbaz, Kars, Ankara, Yozgat, Aydın (Aydın center, Alaçatı), Manisa, Kilis, Bursa, Tirilye, Söğüt, Diyarbekir, Mardin, Sivas, Amasya, Merzifon, Kastamonu, Konya, Niğde, Canik, Kala-yı Sultaniye, Bolu, Antalya, Maraş, Aintab, Balıkesir, Urfa, Karahisar-ı Sahip, and Kayseri (Kayseri center, Efkere).

179. For Edirne, see BOA, DH.İ.UM., 5/1, 19/L/1336 (28.07.1918); for Bursa, see BOA, MF.MKT., 1235/13, 22/L/1336 (31.07.1918); for Adana, see MF.MKT., 1235/16, 23/L/1336 (01.08.1918).

180. Orphanage directors, with the assistance of architects and under the supervision of the representatives of the Allied forces, prepared reports on the damage and the cost for reparations and reconstruction. BOA, MF.EYT., 10/119, doc. 40, 4 Kanunuevvel 1334 (4 Dec. 1918).

181. Abdurrahman Şeref recounts that French brothers themselves chucked the orphans out of Kadıköy Orphanage, their Collège de Saint Joseph. *TBMM ZC*, 465.

182. "Taşra Darüleytamlarının Dersaadete Suret-i Nakilini Mübeyyin Talimatname": BOA, MF.EYT., 1/116 (n.d.), BOA, MF.EYT., 10/19 (n.d.). The directorate determined three geographical and inspectional areas. The Black Sea region comprised the orphanages of Kastamonu (girls and boys), Sivas boys, Bolu boys, Samsun boys, Merzifon (girls and boys), Amasya boys, Kayseri boys, and Efkere boys. Central Anatolia comprised the orphanages of Ankara and Karahisar. The Mediterranean area included the *vilayet* of Adana: Adana (girls and boys), Ekbaz, Kars, Dörtyol, Tarsus, Kozan, Mersin, Konya Boys Orphanage, and Niğde Orphanages (girls and boys).

183. "Harb Yetimleri-Darüleytamdan Evlerine Gönderiliyor," *İleri*, 16 Eylül 1336 (16.09.1920), 1.

184. The directorate approved the fostering of children before 1920 as well. For instance, a certain Şükriye was given away with a certain Ayşe Hanım as a foster daughter (*evlatlık*) in July 1919. BOA, MF.EYT., 13/5, 3 Temmuz 1335 (03.07.1919).

185. Kıranlar, "Savaş Yıllarında Türkiye'de Sosyal Yardım," 82.

186. Nazan Maksudyan, "Foster-Daughter or Servant, Charity or Abuse: *Beslemes* in the Late Ottoman Empire."

187. BOA, MV., 220/85, 28/Z/1338 (12.09.1920).

188. Although probably only 10 percent of the orphans from orphanages in Anatolia ended up in Istanbul, the "danger" of moving rural children to the biggest urban center of the empire had been fiercely criticized in the 1920s. This move had not only endangered order and security in Istanbul, but also decreased the population of Anatolia. "Yetimlerin Hakkı," *İleri*, 26 Teşrinievvel 1336 (26.10.1920), 2.

189. BOA, MF.EYT., 10/23, doc. 1, 19 Teşrinievvel 1334 (19.10.1918), doc. 2, 23 Teşrinievvel 1334 (23.10.1918).

190. BOA, DH.ŞFR., 96/276, 22/Ca/1337 (25.03.1919).

191. Ten children from Samsun Orphanage were admitted to Bebek Orphanage after this standard procedure. BOA, MF.EYT., 11/23, doc. 1, 25 Şubat 1335 (25.02.1919).

192. "Darüleytamlar," *Vakit*, 18 Teşrinievvel 1336 (18.10.1920), 1.

193. *TBMM ZC*, 452–53.

194. Dinamo, Öksüz Musa, 29.

195. Ibid., 13–30.

196. Ibid., 36.

2. Ottoman Orphan Apprentices in Germany

1. Börte Sagaster, *Achmed Talib: Stationen des Lebens eines türkischen Schuhmachermeisters in Deutschland von 1917–1983*.

2. The sending of children from Ottoman orphanages to work as apprentices in German handicrafts, mines, and farms during the First World War is reminiscent of the "Orphan Train" movement of the mid-nineteenth-century United States. The Children's Aid Society and the New York Foundling Hospital were the two main institutions responsible for this mass emigration of children. The scheme roughly meant taking orphans from the street, sending them to the West on trains, and "placing them out" to families at the various stops along the way who were willing to adopt them. The visionary behind the plan, Charles Loring Brace (1826–90), argued these orphans had a better chance at life with placement in a new home "out west" than they did remaining on the streets of New York. The Orphan Trains are estimated to have relocated between 150,000 and 200,000 orphan and destitute children of New York to new homes in the West over the span of seventy-five years, from 1854 to the 1930s. Marilyn Holt, *The Orphan Trains: Placing Out in America*.

3. Mustafa Gencer, *Nationale Bildungspolitik, Modernisierung und kulturelle Interaktion: Deutsch-türkische Beziehungen (1908–1918)*, 268–69.

4. Dr. Hans Hermann Russack, "Die türkischen Lehrlinge," 60.

5. "Die Ausbildung der Handwerks- und Bergwerkslehrlinge erfolgt für die Türkei ganz kostenlos durch das deutsche Handwerk und den deutschen Bergbau." "Tätigkeitsbericht der DTV (für das Jahr 1917)," Political Archive (PA) of the Auswärtiges Amt (AA) (hereafter PA AA), R63454.

6. The Political Archive of the Auswärtiges Amt (PA AA) (Kurstraße 36, 10117 Berlin) comprises rich documentation on the German Foreign Service. It has almost complete files on the meetings of the DTV.

7. Ernst Friedrich Wilhelm Jäckh (born 22 February 1875 in Urach and died 17 August 1959 in New York City) was a journalist, managing director of the German Work Federation, and professor at the German Hochschule für Politik in Berlin, the New Commonwealth Institute in London, and Columbia University in New York. Jäckh, also known as "Turk Jäckh," was the main proponent of German-Ottoman alliance in the German media. He also wrote an influential book on the Ottoman Empire, *The Rising Crescent* (1911). Ihrig, *Justifying Genocide*, 84.

8. Malte Fuhrmann, "Germany's Adventures in the Orient: A History of Ambivalent Semicolonial Entanglements."

9. When Ottoman-German relations strengthened after the Balkan Wars, the Ottoman Empire wanted to modernize its educational system based on the German model. For this purpose, the German Foreign Office was asked for a specialist. As a result, Professor Dr. Franz Schmidt, director of educational services abroad and an expert of education, was commissioned to the service of the Ottoman Empire. He came to Istanbul in December 1914, appointed as an adviser of the Ottoman Ministry of Education. Dr. Schmidt's mission was "to organize the school system based on the German model." Mustafa Çolak, *Alman İmparatorluğu'nun Doğu Siyaseti Çerçevesinde Kafkasya Politikası (1914–1918)*, 59.

10. Malte Fuhrmann, "Germany's Adventures in the Orient," 135.

11. Ingeborg Böer, Ruth Haerkötter, and Petra Kappert, eds., *Türken in Berlin, 1871–1945: Eine Metropole in den Erinnerungen osmanischer und türkischer Zeitzeugen*, 107–17.

12. To give a few examples from the many: Hâki, "Almanya Darü'l-Fünunları" (German Universities), *Mektep*, vol. 4, no. 31, 18 Nisan 1312 (30.04.1896), 483–86; "Almanya'da Çocuk Yuvaları" (Kindergartens in Germany), *Servet-i Fünun*, vol. 51, no. 1319, 10 Eylül 1332 (23.09.1916), 225; "Almanya'da Tamim-i Maarif" (Public Education in Germany), *Servet-i Fünun*, vol. 35, no. 893, 22 Mayıs 1324 (04.06.1908), 132–34; Abdullah Zühdü, "Almanya'da Yeni Sanayi Mektepleri" (New Vocational Schools in Germany), *Servet-i Fünun*, vol. 30, no. 777, 2 Mart 1322 (15.03.1906), 350–51; Yusuf

Osman, "Almanya'nın Terakkiyyat-i Ahiresi: Sanayi-i Hadidiyye" (Latest Progresses in Germany: Iron Industry), *Donanma*, vol. 7, no. 62, 1 Teşrinievvel 1331 (14.10.1915), 984–86; Yusuf Osman, "Almanya'nın Terakkiyyat-i Ahiresi: Şehirler" (Latest Progresses in Germany: Cities), *Donanma*, vol. 7, no. 60, 17 Eylül 1331 (30.09.1915), 954–55; Yusuf Osman, "Almanya'nın Terakkiyyat-i Ahiresi: Vesait-i Nakliye, Şimendiferler, Nehirler" (Latest Progresses in Germany: Vehicles of Transportation, Trains, Rivers), *Donanma*, vol. 7, no. 61, 24 Eylül 1331 (07.10.1915), 970–72; Yusuf Osman, "Almanya'nın Terakkiyyat-i Hazırası: Servet ve Para" (Current Progress in Germany: Wealth and Money), *Donanma*, vol. 7, no. 58, 20 Ağustos 1331 (02.09.1915), 923–25.

13. Gencer, *Nationale Bildungspolitik*, 265.

14. Adnan Şişman, *Tanzimat Döneminde Fransa'ya Gönderilen Osmanlı Öğrencileri (1839–1876)*.

15. Other accounts put the number of Ottoman students in Europe at three thousand. Safiye Kırbaç [Kıranlar], "Almanya'ya Gönderilen Darüleytam Öğrencileri." The Ministry of Foreign Affairs also reported that there were about 3,000 students (üç bine yakın talebe) in December 1918. BOA, Hariciye, Siyasi (HR.SYS.), 2653/3 (19.12.1918).

16. Muslihiddin Adil gave an interview on his inspection visit, "Avrupa'daki Talebemiz," *Zaman* 116, 31.07.1918, 3.

17. For students in Switzerland, see Hans-Lukas Kieser, *Türklüğe İhtida*, 99, 130.

18. BOA, HR.SYS., 2653/3, (05.12.1918).

19. Gencer, *Nationale Bildungspolitik*, 268–69.

20. Charles Albert Paul Rohrbach (born in 1869 in Irgen at Goldingen, died in 1956 in Langenburg in Württemberg) was a Protestant theologian, political writer, colonial administrator, and travel writer. From 1914 to 1918, Rohrbach was employed first in the Imperial Naval Office and then in the Foreign Office, where he distinguished himself as a spokesman for an anti-Russian policy. He took part of the DTV Board as a representative of the Foreign Office. As Ihrig noted, he was also among the prominent "Protestant pro-Armenian activists." He joined Jäckh, along with Schacht, in a trip to Adana shortly after the massacres in the city in 1909. After he found out about the Armenian massacres in 1915, he even wrote to Jäckh that he wanted to quit the DTV. Ihrig, *Justifying Genocide*, 84, 145–46.

21. Dr. Hjalmar Horace Greeley Schacht (22 January 1877–3 June 1970) was a German economist, banker, liberal politician, and cofounder of the German Democratic Party. In 1903 he joined the Dresdner Bank, where he became deputy director from 1908 to 1915. He was then a member of the committee of direction of the Deutsche Bank for the next seven years, until 1922. He was part of the DTV Board as the director of the Deutsche Bank. He became the minister of economy in the Third Reich. Ihrig, *Justifying Genocide*, 84.

22. Hans Hermann Russack (born 18 December 1887 in Weissenborn [Droyßig], died in the twentieth century) was a German art historian. Together with Jäckh and Ryll, he was one of the decision-making figures of the DTV.

23. Gerhard Ryll (1884–?) was the inspector of Turkish students in Germany from 1916 onward. He inspected the students and consulted with school principals and host families. He also became the director of the Schülerheim for Ottoman students, which was opened in 1917 in Grunewald. Together with Jäckh and Russack, he was one of the decision-making figures of the DTV.

24. Dr. Nazım (1870–26 August 1926), physician and politician, was a CUP central committee member and had an important role in the Ottoman "Special Organization" (Teşkilat-ı Mahsusa). He had a say in the decision making until the end of World War I. He became the minister of education in Talat Pasha's cabinet in 1918.

25. "Abschrift Nr. III d 1854, 5.März.1917, Report über die DTV von Schmidt," PA AA, R63063. The TDV Committee was composed of parliament's vice president Hüseyin Cahid (Yalçın), the famous novelist Halid Ziya (Uşaklıgil), CUP central committee member Dr. Nazım, and director general of the Ministry of Education Muslihiddin Adil (Taylan). As the German members, Professor Bergsträsser, school principal Tominski, and teacher Gabel of the German high school in Istanbul were on the committee.

26. Mustafa Çolak, "Alman-Türk Dostluk Cemiyeti'nin İstanbul'da Bir 'Dostluk Yurdu' Kurma Çabaları (1915–1918)."

27. "Türkische Jugend in Berlin," *Berliner Tageblatt* 216, 06.05.1917.

28. BOA, MF.EYT, 2/117, 29/Ş/1334 (01.07.1916); Aytekin, "1914–1924 Yılları arasında Korunmaya Muhtaç Çocuklar ve Eğitimleri," 108–10; Nurdan Şafak, "Darüleytam'da Çocuk Olmak: On Çocuk On Portre."

29. After Austria declared war on Serbia, the Orient Express came to a standstill, and Germany and its allies started running their own luxury train between Berlin and Istanbul from January 1916 onward.

30. Russack, "Die türkischen Lehrlinge," 50.

31. "Türkische Jugend in Berlin."

32. "From die DTV to Dr. Söhring, Auswärtiges Amt, 13.Juni.1917, Berlin," PA AA, R63063.

33. Ibid.

34. Russack, "Die türkischen Lehrlinge," 54.

35. BOA, MF.MKT., 1229/46, 24/Za/1335 (12.09.1917).

36. BOA, MF.MKT., 1230/82, 28/Z/1335 (16.10.1917). Still in late October, the Ministry of Education was sending orders for the completion of necessary documentation. BOA, MF.MKT., 1231/7, 09/M/1336 (26.10.1917).

37. BOA, MF.EYT., 7/57, 1 Ağustos 1333 (01.08.1917).

38. "Sitzung des Ausschusses für türkische Schüler und Lehrlinge der DTV, 17.Sept.1917, Berlin," PA AA, R63063.

39. "30. Vorstandsitzung der DTV, am 29.Oktober.1917, Berlin," PA AA, R63064. Dr. Nazım was a very significant person in the sending of Ottoman orphans to Germany. He was a member of the selection committee of the TDV from the beginning. In July 1918, he was appointed to the Ministry of Education. Just before his assignment to his post, the DTV was rendered ineffective in the student-selection procedure; now the Ministry of Education was the sole organ deciding who could leave for Germany or other Allied countries (BOA, MF.MKT., 1235/10, 21/L/1336, (30.07.1918).

40. A smaller group of 36 orphans was sent by the province of Konya, and a bigger group was supported by the Ottoman Ministry of War (104 trainees). "37. Vorstandsitzung der DTV am 3.August.1918, in der Deutschenbank, Berlin," PA AA, R63454.

41. In the future, those boys willing could even take other classes (for example, math) or even attend a vocational school. Russack, "Die türkischen Lehrlinge," 62.

42. BOA, MF.MKT., 1238/91, 05/N/1337 (04.06.1919).

43. Already in mid-1916, the DTV arranged for more than eighteen hundred families to accommodate scholarship-holding Turkish pupils. "20. Vorstandsitzung der Deutsch-Türkischen Vereinigung am 15.Juli.1916 in der Nationalbank für Deutschland, Berlin," PA AA, R63435. Such a great number raises doubt about the motivations and "quality" of these families. As I will touch upon later, some critics claimed that these were usually poor soldier families, who volunteered to receive Turkish boys in order to have access to some financial means.

44. Gencer, *Nationale Bildungspolitik*, 278.

45. "An die Königlichen Provinzialschulkollegien, Der Minister der geistlichen und Unterrichts, Berlin, den 14. Oktober 1916," PA AA, R63062; "Maarif Şuunu," *Muallim*, 15 Kanunuevvel 1332 (28.12.1916), 190–92.

46. "[Report] Deutscher Handwerks- und Gewerbekammertag (E.V.): Unterbringung von jugendlichen Türken in deutschen Handwerksbetrieben, Hannover, 25.Juni.1917," PA AA, R63063.

47. BOA, MF.MKT., 1225/38, 26/C/1335 (18.04.1917).

48. "[Letter] Reichsbekleidungsstelle an das Auswärtiges Amt, 27.Sept.1917," PA AA, R 63063.

49. "28. Vorstandsitzung der Deutsch-Türkischen Vereinigung am 26.Juni.1917 in der Deutschenbank, Berlin," PA AA, R63063.

50. "Sitzung des Ausschusses für türkische Schüler und Lehrlinge der DTV, 17.Sept.1917, Berlin," PA AA, R63063.

51. The Städtische Irrenverpflegungsanstalt Dalldorf had been established in 1862 and was expanding steadily during the following decades to a capacity of much more than a thousand inmates.

52. "Sitzung des Ausschusses für türkische Schüler und Lehrlinge der DTV, 2. August 1917, Berlin," PA AA, R63063.

53. Russack, "Die türkischen Lehrlinge," 49.

54. "Sitzung des Ausschusses für türkische Schüler und Lehrlinge der DTV, 2. August 1917, Berlin," PA AA, R63063.

55. "[Report] Deutscher Handwerks- und Gewerbekammertag (E.V.): Unterbringung von jugendlichen Türken in deutschen Handwerksbetrieben, Hannover, 25.Juni.1917," PA AA, R63063.

56. "Sitzung des Ausschusses für türkische Schüler und Lehrlinge der DTV, 20.Juli.1917, Berlin," PA AA, R63063.

57. Muslihiddin Adil [Taylan], *Alman Hayat-ı İrfanı*, 229–31. Muslihiddin Adil Bey was actually very critical regarding the success of sending students and apprentices to Germany. After visiting German educational institutions in Berlin, Leipzig, Heidelberg, Munich, Dresden, and Chemnitz, he wrote that the education of Ottoman youth in Germany, or in other Western countries, was a serious national problem. He criticized the fact that most of the boys were of secondary school age. This age was the ideal time to teach the history and traditions of a country, together with the fundamentals of the native language. Those boys who did not have enough knowledge about their own national history and language could not "represent Turkishness and country's national ideals in the future." He argued that student exchange programs should not involve teenage boys. Sending high school graduates for the purposes of improving and expanding their professional knowledge would be of more importance. Muslihiddin Adil Bey also underlined the significance and necessity of constant supervision of these young boys, owing to the endless possibilities (and vices) of nightlife in European cities. He wrote that the danger of these inexperienced boys falling into crime and debauchery was his biggest fear and concern.

58. "Ein kleines Wörterbuch, das wir auf Wunsch des deutschen Handwerks- und Gewerbekammertags für die Handwerkslehrlinge herausgegeben haben. 24.Juli.1917," PA AA, R 63063.

59. Russack, "Die türkischen Lehrlinge," 59–60.

60. Although Muammer Tuksavul was among the relatively rich student group and had enough funds to stay in pensions, he was unable to eat the soup served by his host. Muammer Tuksavul, *Eine bittere Freundschaft: Erinnerung eines türkischen Jahrhundertzeugen*, 162–63.

61. "Sitzung des Ausschusses für türkische Schüler und Lehrlinge der DTV, 20. Juli 1917, Berlin," PA AA, R63063.

62. "Sitzung des Ausschusses für türkische Schüler und Lehrlinge der DTV, 2. August 1917, Berlin," PA AA, R63063.

63. There is actually evidence for transfer of food from the Ottoman Empire to Germany for students. The DTV arranged with İsmail Hakkı Pasha, the head of the

Army Provisioning Office, for the procurement of 120 kg rice, 100 kg beans, 200 kg raisins, and 32 kg oil (and paid for them) in October 1917, though their arrival was delayed until February 1918, owing to lengthy negotiations. The DTV also attempted to arrange with the Ottoman Ministry of Education the sending of foodstuffs at regular intervals. "Lebensmitteln für die türkischen Schüler in Deutschland, From Kaiserlich Deutsche Botschaft, Pera, 19.Juli.1918," PA AA, R63065.

64. "Was ein aus Deutschland kommender Reisender erzählt, *Akşam*, 5.12.1918 [Übersetzung, Gabel]," PA AA, R63066. This article represented a very critical view on the Ottoman students' experiences in Germany. The author argued that many coffeehouses were filled with Ottoman students who hung around as vagrants in a depraved state. Sadly, many of them did not even learn the German language. Because of prolonged residence in "places of terrible debauchery," such as Berlin, many got accustomed to the vulgarities of this life, many contracted sexually transmitted diseases, and some became completely Germanized. He also assured his readers that the issue of students and apprentices was "the biggest villainy that Germany inflicted upon [the Ottoman Empire] during this war."

65. "From Königliches Provinzialschulkollegium der Provinz Hannover, 25.mai.1917," PA AA, R63063. However, some masters reported that most of them did not abstain from eating pork. Gencer, *Nationale Bildungspolitik*, 278.

66. "Jahresbericht des Schülerheims, 1.Nov.1918," PA AA, R 63065.

67. Captain Hüsni tells of a report by the Turkish supervisor Hasan in Mülheim that four mine apprentices from the company of Altenberg in Unter-Eschbach asked for pocket money and, when refused, escaped. "Sitzung des Ausschusses für türkische Schüler und Lehrlinge der DTV, 2. August 1917, Berlin," PA AA, R63063.

68. "Sehr zahlreich sind leider aber die Klagen, dass die jungen Leute Ansprüche stellen hinsichtlich der Entlohnung, hinsichtlich der freien Zeit u.s.w., die mit den Pflichten eines Lehrlings schlechthin nicht zu vereinbaren sind." "[Report] Deutscher Handwerks- und Gewerbekammertag (E.V.): Unterbringung von jugendlichen Türken in deutschen Handwerksbetrieben, Hannover, 25.Juni.1917," PA AA, R63063.

69. "Hauptsächlich ist allgemein die Klage, dass man anscheinend den Lehrlingen in ihrer Heimat die Meinung beigebracht hat, als sollten sie in Deutschland in Fabrikbetrieben ausgebildet werden und dabei von vornherein möglichst hohe Löhne verdienen" (ibid.).

70. Russack, "Die türkischen Lehrlinge," 59.

71. "Sitzung des Ausschusses für türkische Schüler und Lehrlinge der DTV, 2. August 1917, Berlin," PA AA, R63063.

72. Russack, "Die türkischen Lehrlinge," 60.

73. "Sitzung des Ausschusses für türkische Schüler und Lehrlinge der DTV, 17.Sept.1917, Berlin," PA AA, R63063.

74. "Sitzung des Ausschusses für türkische Schüler und Lehrlinge der DTV, 20.Juli 1917, Berlin," PA AA, R63063.

75. Ibid.

76. A key to many postcolonial texts, colonial or imperial gaze is the dominating look of the "imperialist," who assigns an inferior quality (as "barbarians," "savages," or as "untamed") to the colonized. Pramod K. Nayar, *Colonial Voices: The Discourses of Empire*; Ann Laura Stoler, *Carnal Knowledge and Imperial Power: Race and the Intimate in Colonial Rule*.

77. Russack, "Die türkischen Lehrlinge," 61.

78. "Dank türkischer Untertanen an Deutschland," *Hamburger Fremdenblattes* 113, 9 Aug. 1919 (my translation).

79. There is need to note that while poor orphans were hastily called back, sons of affluent and pro-CUP families were rushing into Germany. As the war was approaching its end, there was a marked increase in the number of Ottoman students and subjects in Germany. According to the famous novelist Halid Ziya, who was accompanying his son (also a student) at the time in Berlin, one of Enver Pasha's "frenzies" (çılgınlık) was "to pile" (*yığmak*) hundreds of Turkish children into Germany. Halid Ziya Uşaklıgil, *Bir Acı Hikâye*, 63. There was also a substantiated rumor that Talat Pasha was "shipping men" from Istanbul to Europe after the armistice. Arif Cemil Denker, *İttihatçı Şeflerin Gurbet Maceraları*, 45.

80. "Die gesamten kosten für türkische Schüler, 24.April.1919," PA AA, R14044.

81. "Dank türkischer Untertanen an Deutschland," *Hamburger Fremdenblattes* 113, 9 Aug. 1919.

82. "Aus politischen Gründen ist aber weiter Wert darauf zu legen, dass sie ihre Ausbildung ungestört fortsetzen können und erst nach deren Abschluss oder wenn ihre Eltern sie rufen, noch früh zurückkehren." "Die gesamten *kosten* für türkische Schüler, 24 April 1919," PA AA, R14044.

83. "Kehren dagegen die jungen Leute nach beendeter Ausbildung mit nützlichen Kenntnissen ausgerüstet und zufrieden nach der Heimat zurück, so wird das zur Erfüllung und Wahrung unseres Ansehens im Orient beitragen und uns voraussichtlich auch auf wirtschaftlichem Gebiete nützen bringen" (ibid.).

84. Muammer Tuksavul was among the relatively rich student group. In order to pass his *Abitur* exam and also to study chemistry in the technical high school in Darmstadt, he remained in Germany. Tuksavul, *Eine bittere Freundschaft*, 162–63.

85. Sagaster, *Achmed Talib*, 36–37. Some other children, who returned, also had better memories of their days in Germany, although they did not dare to stay in a foreign country any longer. In a short interview with the grandson of an orphan apprentice in Germany, he said that his grandfather always kept the hammer he made in Germany as a souvenir of his days there and that he also encouraged the future generations of the

family to go and work or study in Germany. "Interview with Arif Bodur," Feb. 2015. Bodur took the recommendations and advice of his grandfather regarding Germany seriously. He went to the German school in Istanbul and then lived and worked in Germany.

86. "Jahresbericht der DTV für 1918 [–1919], 11.Dezember.1919," PA AA, R63443.

87. BOA, DH.İ.UM., 19-16/1-28, doc. 4, 25/Re/1339 (07.12.1920).

88. Ibid., doc. 2, 18/Ca/1339 (27.02.1921).

89. BOA, DH.UMVM., 119/15, 16/N/1337 (15.06.1919).

90. Dinamo, Öksüz Musa, 37–38.

91. BOA, DH.UMVM., 119/26, 12/B/1340 (11.03.1922).

92. Gencer, *Nationale Bildungspolitik*, 265.

93. All major industrial powers during the war, except for the United States, had a severe shortage of skilled workers. Industry redesigned work so that it could be done by unskilled men and women (termed the "dilution of labor") so that war-related industries grew rapidly.

94. Colin Nicholson, *The Longman Companion to the First World War*, 248.

95. On 28 January 1918, there was a massive strike in Berlin, where one hundred thousand workers took to the streets, demanding an end to the war on all fronts. Within a few days, the number was up to four hundred thousand. Gerald D. Feldman, *Army, Industry and Labour in Germany, 1914–1918*, 326–36.

96. For further information on the concept "semicolonial mentality," see Fuhrmann, "Germany's Adventures in the Orient," 123–45.

97. Ibid., 133.

98. Ulrich Trumpener, *Germany and the Ottoman Empire, 1914–1918*, 319.

99. BOA, MF.MKT., 1230/54, 20/Z/1335 (08.10.1917).

100. "Türkische Schüler in deutschen Familien," *Tägliche Rundschau*, 3.Juli.1916.

101. "An die Königlichen Provinzialschulkollegien, Der Minister der geistlichen und Unterrichts, Berlin, den 14. Oktober 1916," PA AA, R63062.

102. "Immer mehr wächst bei Freunden und Kennern unserer Arbeit—und zwar ebenso auf türkischer wie auf deutscher Seite—die Erkenntnisse, dass ihr Erfolg nicht davon abhängt, ob die Zahl der in Deutschland studierenden jungen Leute sich alljährlich um einige Hundert vermehrt, dass es viel mehr darauf ankommt, die 'besten Köpfe der türkischen Schulen' (wie es in unseren Leitsätzen heisst) auszusondern und sie, die allein die Träger einer besseren türkischen Zukunft sein können, in unserem Lande zu bilden und zu erziehen. Dabei mag man zunächst ruhig an die 'besten Familien' d.h. an die soziale Oberschicht der türkischen Gesellschaft denken, die bisher die politisch führende Rolle gespielt hat und vorläufig auch wohl weiter spielen wird." Dr. Ryll, "Quantität oder Qualität?: Kritische Bemerkungen zur dritten Schülerentsendung, 31.Juli 1918," PA AA, R63065 (my translation).

3. Children as Agents and Targets of Nationalist Politics

1. See Stéphane Audoin-Rouzeau, "Children and the Primary Schools of France, 1914–1918"; Faron, *Les enfants du deuil*; Manon Pignot, *La Guerre des Crayons*; Fisher, *Boys and Girls in No Man's Land*; Kennedy, *The Children's War*; and Donson, *Youth in the Fatherless Land.*

2. See Bedross Der Matossian, *Shattered Dreams of Revolution: From Liberty to Violence in the Late Ottoman Empire.*

3. See Cynthia Enloe, *Maneuvers: The International Politics of Militarizing Women's Lives*, 145–49, 189–91.

4. Ibid., 219.

5. Ayşe Gül Altınay and Yeşim Arat, *Violence against Women in Turkey: A Nationwide Survey*, 1–5.

6. Roger Chickering and Stig Förster, eds., *Great War, Total War: Combat and Mobilization on the Western Front, 1914–1918*, 1–15.

7. He also touches on the class dimension of conscription. Their rich neighbors' son was exempted after paying a very high exemption fee (*devlete oğlumun ağırlığınca altın ödedik*). The author also hints that being close to the CUP also brought about different forms of privileges. Hasan İzzettin Dinamo, *Savaş ve Açlar*, 196–200. A well-known folk song tells the story of boys conscripted from Tokat at the age of fifteen to fight in the Gallipoli in 1915. Mahir Metinsoy, *Ottoman Women during World War I*, 176.

8. Colmar von der Goltz had advocated systematic premilitary training of primary school students since 1876. He was the founder of the Young German League (*Jungdeutschlandbund*) of 1911. His book *Das Volk in Waffen* (1883) was translated immediately into Ottoman, *Millet-i Müsellaha: Asrımızın Usul ve Ahvali Askeriyesi.*

9. The semiofficial character of the National Defense League was obvious, and its organic ties with the government were quite visible. The league propagated the idea that the home front was essential in supporting the war effort. It underlined the significance of supporting the civilian population and the families left behind. See Mehmet Beşikçi, *The Ottoman Mobilization of Manpower in the First World War: Between Voluntarism and Resistance*, 75.

10. For further information, see Zeynep Kutluata, "Geç Osmanlı ve Erken Cumhuriyet Dönemi'nde Toplumsal Cinsiyet ve Savaş: Kara Fatma(lar)."

11. For further information, see Erdoğan Altınkaynak, "Sarıkamış Harekatı ve Çevresinde Oluşan Destanlar, Hatıralar."

12. See Çetinkaya, "Atrocity Propaganda."

13. In his PhD dissertation on the role of sports, Murat C. Yıldız discusses the increasing importance of physical activities for all communities from the late nineteenth century onward. Murat C. Yıldız, "Strengthening Male Bodies and Building Robust

Communities: Physical Culture in the Late Ottoman Empire"; Palmira Johnson Brummett, *Image and Imperialism in the Ottoman Revolutionary Press, 1908–1911*, 199.

14. Toprak, "II. Meşrutiyet Döneminde Paramiliter Gençlik Örgütleri," 531–36; Beşikçi, *Ottoman Mobilization*, 226–32.

15. On the development of the boy scouting among Turkish Muslim youth in the early Republican period, see Yiğit Akın, *Gürbüz ve Yavuz Evlatlar*; and Rıfat N. Bali, *Sports and Physical Education in Turkey in the 1930s*.

16. Yıldız, "Strengthening Male Bodies," 72.

17. Ibid., 162.

18. Ibid., 113.

19. Ibid., 283.

20. For a detailed account of paramilitary youth organizations, see Beşikçi, *Ottoman Mobilization*, 203–45.

21. Toprak, "II. Meşrutiyet Döneminde Paramiliter Gençlik Örgütleri."

22. Tahsin Kuzucuoğlu, "Güççülük," *Türk Yurdu* 66 (28 May 1914) translit. ed., vol. 3, 308–9.

23. *Güç Dernekleri'nin Programı* (Istanbul: Matbaa-i Askeriye, 1330 [1914]); BOA, Dahiliye, İdari Kısım (DH. İD.), 224/3, 19/S/1333 (06.01.1915).

24. *Harb Mecmuası* 24, Kanunuevvel 1333 (Dec. 1917), 381. The Ottoman Strength Association promised a license for those participants who attended the training activities and who proved themselves capable of carrying out various military exercises. The license holders also had certain privileges, such as being sent to more agreeable fronts, earlier promotion to the rank of corporal, and a yearly leave of a month and a half.

25. BOA, Dahiliye, Emniyet-i Umumiye Müdüriyeti, Muhasebe Kalemi (DH. EUM.MH.), 87/137, 24/Ş/1332 (18.07.1914); Sadık Sarısaman, "Osmanlı Güç Dernekleri."

26. "Osmanlı Milletine Harbiye Nezareti'nin Beyannamesi," BOA, Dahiliye, Mebani-i Emiriye, Hapishaneler Müdüriyeti Müteferrik Evrakı (DH.MB.HPS.M.), 15/30, 6/N/1332 (29.07.1914).

27. BOA, MF.MKT., 1215/23, 28/Ca/1334 (02.05.1916).

28. BOA, DH.UMVM., 121/34, 8/N1334 (9.7.1916).

29. BOA, MF.MKT., 1230/38, 16/Z/1335 (3.10.1917); BOA, MF.MKT., 1228/61, 27/L /1335 (16.8.1917).

30. Beşikçi, *Ottoman Mobilization*, 226.

31. Nazan Maksudyan, "'Öldürmeden utan, ölmeden usan!': Geç Osmanlı İmparatorluğu'nda Savaş Karşıtı Hissiyatın Açık ve Örtük Dışavurumları."

32. "Turkish Women Revolt," *New York Times*, 14 Dec. 1914.

33. "Riots Reported in Turkey," *New York Times*, 6 Mar. 1916.

34. Mahir Metinsoy, *Ottoman Women during World War I*, 178–81.

35. Ibid., 181–84.

36. Sadık Sarısaman, "Birinci Dünya Savaşında İhtiyat Kuvveti Olarak Kurulan Osmanlı Genç Dernekleri," 461–63.

37. On women's self-empowerment during the war, see Akın, "War, Women, and the State"; Ehir Mahir Metinsoy, "Writing the History of Ordinary Ottoman Women during World War I"; and Kutluata, "Ottoman Women and the State during World War I."

38. BOA, DH.UMVM., 146/109, 30/C/1335 (24.03.1917).

39. Ibid.

40. Heinrich von Hoff, "Jugendpflege und Turnen in der Türkei," *Zeitschrift für Schulgesundheitpflege* 31 (1918): 204–5.

41. For a similar development in France, see Audoin-Rouzeau, "Children and the Primary Schools of France, 1914–1918," 39–52.

42. BOA, MF.MKT., 1212/63, 02/Z/1333 (11.10.1915).

43. Ibid.

44. BOA, MF.MKT., 1215/23, 28/Ca/1334 (02.05.1916).

45. "Terbiye-i Bedeniye Mektebi," *Tedrisat-ı İbtidaiye Mecmuası* 4/23 (14.04.1913), 42.

46. BOA, MF.MKT., 1214/83, 11/Ca/1334 (15.04.1916).

47. BOA, MF.MKT., 1235/107, 19/Z/1336 (25.09.1918).

48. Kazım Karabekir, *Çocuk Davamız*.

49. One of the earliest Armenian initiatives was organized by the Armenian community in Plovdiv (Bulgaria). The consular authorities noted that following the examples of Bulgarians, Greeks, and Jews, Armenians also established a gymnastics association in the city, providing military training to the idle youth. BOA, HR.SFR.04., 17 July 1906. The establishment of an Armenian sport club in Ruse (Bulgaria), Troshag (Flag), which provided physical education and military drills for the youth, also got the attention of the Ottoman authorities. BOA, HR.SFR.04., 827/59, 14 July 1908.

50. Yıldız, "Strengthening Male Bodies," 69.

51. Chrissian was among the Armenian intellectuals who were arrested on 24 April 1914. He was sent to Ayaş prison and killed there.

52. Yıldız, "Strengthening Male Bodies," 56.

53. For further information, see Hayk Demoyan, *Haygagan Sportı yev Marmnagırtutyunı Osmanyan Gasyrutyunum* (*Armenian Sport and Physical Gymnastics in the Ottoman Empire*).

54. Yıldız, "Strengthening Male Bodies," 162–63.

55. BOA, DH.ŞFR., 414/105, 25/Re/1325 (08.05.1907), BOA, DH.MKT., 2836/58, 19/Ce/1327 (08.06.1909).

56. BOA, DH.MKT., 2840/90, 23/Ce/1327 (12.06.1909).

57. BOA, DH.ŞFR., 407/38, 12/R/1324 (30.10.1906).

58. BOA, Teftişat-ı Rumeli Evrakı Manastır Evrakı (TFR.I.MN.), 87/8663, 16/M/1324 (12.03.1906).

59. BOA, DH.EUM.THR., 105/9, 27/Ca/1328 (06.07.1909); BOA, DH.EUM. THR., 40/40, 28/Ca/1328 (07.07.1909).

60. BOA, Dahiliye Hukuk Müşavirliği (DH.HMŞ.), 30/89, 5/N/1332 (29 June 1914).

61. BOA, Dahiliye Hapishaneler Müdüriyeti Müteferrik (DH.MB.HPS.M.), 14/25, 5/N/1332 (29.06.1914).

62. BOA, Dahiliye Emniyet-i Umumiye Memurin Kalemi (DH.EUM.MEM.), 49/74, 8/N/1332 (2 July 1914); BOA, Dahiliye Emniyet-i Umumiye Muhasebe Kalemi (DH.EUM.MH.), 87/44, 8/N/1332 (2 July 1914).

63. "Instruction for the establishment of scouting organizations that will prepare the youth for the army." BOA, DH.EUM.MH., 86/58, 23/B/1332 (17 June 1914).

64. BOA, DH.EUM.6.Şb., 7/47, 09/B/1334 (12.05.1916).

65. BOA, DH.KMS., 49/34, 06/L/1337 (05.07.1919).

66. BOA, DH.KMS., 49/35, 07/L/1337 (06.07.1919).

67. BOA, Dahiliye, Emniyet-i Umumiye Müdüriyeti, Asayiş Kalemi (DH.EUM. AYŞ.), 16/84, 27/L/1337 (26.07.1919).

68. BOA, DH.EUM.AYŞ., 10/27, 26/Ş/1337 (25.05.1919).

69. Biz Çatalcalılar istavrozu gark-ı belaya çıkarıb Türklerin camilerini yıkacağız / Haydin yıkalım haydin yıkalım / Bombalarla köpek İslamları mahvedelim / Biz Çatalcalılar Yunan evlatları bulunduğumuzdan / Yunan askeri ahvali üzere talim etmek ve öğrenmek icab eder / Zira Çatalca sancağı ve civarı artık Yunan oldu ve Yunanistan'ındır.

70. Doumanis notes that the ideal of coexistence started to shatter already from 1908 onward and turned into multiple "catastrophes" during the war. Nicholas Doumanis, *Before the Nation: Muslim-Christian Coexistence and Its Destruction in Late-Ottoman Anatolia*, 131–69.

71. Dimitris Kamouzis, "Elites and the Formation of National Identity: The Case of the Greek Orthodox Millet Mid-19th Century to 1922," 34.

72. http://asbarez.com/53076/the-history-of-homenetmen/.

73. Based on the biography written by his son, Aram Arax was one of those boy scouts who even worked on an anthem for Armenian boy scouts. When he was leaving for the United States in May 1920, the boy-scout band played for the departing boat. Mark Arax, *In My Father's Name*, 106.

74. "The World Brotherhood of Boys," *Boys' Life* 10/3 (1920): 37.

75. "The World Brotherhood of Boys," *Boys' Life* 12/2 (1922): 29.

76. Thomas G. Aved, *Toomas, the Little Armenian Boy: Childhood Reminiscence of Turkish-Armenia*, 160–77.

77. Ibid., 160.

78. BOA, Dahiliye, Emniyet-i Umumiye Müdüriyeti, Seyrüsefer Kalemi (DH. EUM.SSM.), 39/57, 22/Ra/1338 (15 Dec. 1919).

79. Aved, *Toomas*, 164.

80. BOA, Hariciye, Siyasi (HR.SYS.), 2605/4, 7 June 1919; BOA, HR.SYS., 2605/5, 5 Jan. 1921. Apart from these huge files compiling information on a number of voluntary organizations of non-Muslims, there were also smaller investigations. For an example of an investigation of the Jewish Gymnastics Society Maccabi, see BOA, DH.EUM.VRK., 29/61, 10/L/1338 (27.06.1920).

81. The Armenian authorities noted that they would like to believe in the good intentions of Grand Vizier Tevfik's government, but they could not help but notice that the state itself was still entirely controlled by the Unionists. Kévorkian, *Armenian Genocide*, 750.

82. The daily experience of children in the Ottoman Empire resembled the ones in the Habsburg Empire. See Healy, *Vienna and the Fall of the Habsburg Empire*, 211–14.

83. Mehmet Ö. Alkan, *Tanzimat'tan Cumhuriyet'e Modernleşme Sürecinde Eğitim İstatistikleri, 1839–1924*, 165–66.

84. BOA, MF.MKT., 1207/38, 19/Ca/1333 (4.5.1915); BOA, MF.MKT., 1227/48, 23/Ş/1335 (14.6.1917).

85. Mehmet Akdokur (born in 1910 in Kilis) writes that he spent his childhood mostly with threshing and later as an apprentice to a carpenter. Neither he nor his elder brother ever attended school. Mine Tan et al., *Cumhuriyet'te Çocuktular*, 306–9.

86. A document relating to the dismissal in November 1914 of a British teacher, employed as a specialist of boy scouting, underlines that it was no longer possible to hire a British national. BOA, MF.MKT., 1202/29, 6/Z/1332 (26 Oct. 1914). He was paid a "compensation and per diem" (*tazminat and harcırah*) and was dismissed in November 1914. BOA, MV, 194/34, 22/Z/1332 (11 Nov. 1914).

87. Alliance schools had to make a number of applications so that they could continue their activities in the empire. The school in Edirne was first allowed to continue its activities. DH.EUM.5.Şb., 25/49, 26/N/1334 (28 June 1916). But when it was discovered that the school was registered as belonging to a French citizen named Gaston Mayer, it was ordered to be closed, as all other "institutions belonging to the subjects of warring states" (*muhasım devlet tebasına ait müesseseler*). BOA, DH.EUM.5.Şb., 29/46, 28/Z/1334 (26 Oct. 1916). Other Alliance schools in Jaffa, Bursa, and Jerusalem also had similar problems. BOA, DH.EUM.5.Şb., 5/24, 16/M/1333 (4 Dec. 1914); BOA, DH.ŞFR., 47/348, 18/M/1333 (6 Dec. 1914).

88. As part of this change of authority, the American College for Girls in Üsküdar, for instance, began to give a Turkish diploma to the graduates in addition to the Latin diploma. "College in Turkey Grows Despite War," *New York Times*, 14 Nov. 1916.

89. BOA, DH.ŞFR., 54/261, 18/N/1333 (01.07.1915).

90. Taner Akçam, Ümit Kurt, *Kanunların Ruhu*. The ruination comprised educational prohibitions, targeting of children, and prohibitions on the use of the Armenian language. Üngör, "Orphans, Converts, and Prostitutes," 177.

91. The second half of the nineteenth century was a period in which children were declared to be unwanted in public spaces. By opening vocational state orphanages in all provincial capitals and collecting vagrant children from the streets, the state relatively succeeded in its objective of making unattended children invisible in the cities. See Nazan Maksudyan, "Orphans, Cities, and the State: Vocational Orphanages (Islahhanes) and 'Reform' in the Late Ottoman Urban Space" and "Children as a Transgressors in Urban Space: Delinquency, Public Order and Philanthropy in the Ottoman Reform Era."

92. See Fortna, "Kindergarten in the Ottoman Empire," 264.

93. BOA, MF.MKT., 1205/14, 3/Ra/1333 (19.01.1915).

94. "Dilenci Çocuklar Toplanıyor," *İkdam*, 28 July 1336 (1920), 2.

95. BOA, MF.EYT., 13/163, 11/Za/1337 (8 Aug. 1919).

96. BOA, DH.İ.UM., 19-19/1-20, doc. 2, 4 Kanunusani 1338 (04.01.1922).

97. Şevket Süreyya Aydemir, *Suyu Arayan Adam*, 7–15 (emphasis added; translation mine).

> Mahallemizin sokaklarında . . . oyunlarımız, daha ziyade kavgalardan, baskınlardan, savaşlardan oluşurdu. . . . Oyunlarımızın en başında gene, çetecilik, komitacılık oyunları gelirdi. Bunun için önce kaptanlar, voyvodalar seçilirdi. Bu sözcükler, Rum, Bulgar çetecilerinin reislerine verilen isimlerdir. Kaptanlar, voyvodalar, çocukların en kuvvetlilerinden, en gözü pek olanlarından seçilirdi. Bunlar bizi birkaç kola ayırırlardı. . . . Sonra silahlanma başlardı. Bellerimize bıçak, tabanca vazifesini görecek çubuklar, tahta parçaları takardık. Ceplerimize, kuşaklarımıza bomba yerine taşlar doldururduk. Bazen altımıza bir değnek çekip onu at gibi sıçrattığımız da olurdu. . . .
>
> Sonra kaptan işareti verince, birden, gürültüler, bağrışlarla düşman çetesi üzerine çullanarak, göğüs göğse bir çarpışmadan sonra zaferi kazanmak lazımdı. . . .
>
> Bazen mahallenin bir ucunda başlayan savaşın öbür mahalleye yayıldığı görülürdü. O zaman oyuna iki taraftan yeni kuvvetler karışırdı. Güya ölenler, yaralananlar, esir edilenler olurdu. Bazen de bu esirler, bir baskınla kurtarılırdı. . . .
>
> Bu çetecilik oyunlarının en heyecanlısı, bizim mahallenin çocuklarıyla, bitişik Hıristiyan mahalle çocukları arasında yapılanlarıydı. Bunlar gerçek bir çete çatışması gibi geçerdi. . . . Bu artık bir oyun değildi. Sınır

mahalleler arasında bir kavgaydı. Bütün bunlar, aynı devletin uyruğu, fakat yüzyıllardan beri birbirine kaynaşmayan ırkların çocukları arasında, ilerde olacak kanlı hesaplaşmaların küçük hazırlığıydı.

Bu gibi kavgalar, ya Rum veya Bulgar mahallesinden geçen bir Müslüman çocuğunun taşa tutulması, yahut da Müslüman mahallesine giren bir Hıristiyan çocuğuna dayak atılmasıyla başlardı. İki tarafın da tanınmış elebaşıları, gözü pek savaşçıları vardı. Bunlar kendi mahallelerinin, âdeta talim görmüş çocuklarını takım takım etraflarına toplarlardı. Şehrin kenarına seğirtirler savaşa sürerlerdi. Şehir kenarındaki sırtlarda geniş Müslüman ve Hıristiyan mezarlıkları vardı. . . .

Taşlar yığarak, sipercikler, barikatlar hazırlayarak toplanırdık. Nöbetçiler, öncüler yerlerini alırlardı. Keşif kolları çıkarılırdı. Yer yer taş kavgaları başlardı . . . uzun, yuvarlak mezar taşlarını, siperler, istihkâmlar üzerine yatırarak düşmana doğru taklit toplar yerleştirenler ve Bom! Bom! diye patlatanlar olurdu.

Kendi aramızdaki çete baskını oyunlarında, her nedense hepimiz güya Rumca, Bulgarca konuşuyormuşuz gibi ağzımızda birtakım anlaşılmaz sözlerle bağrışıp dururken, bu mahallelerarası milli kavgalarda biz, yalnız Türkçe konuşurduk. Hep "Allah! Allah! Hücum!" diye bağırırdık. . . .

Bir defasında, kavgayı ayırmaya gelenler de birbirlerine girmişlerdi. Bıçaklar sıyrılmış, kafalar yarılmıştı. . . . Sanki iki taraf da, nasıl olsa ergeç girişecekleri son, kesin hesaplaşmaya, beklenmedik bir kıvılcımla, şimdiden başlamışlardı.

98. Mobilization of children for the war effort was already strong from 1908 onward. See Cüneyd Okay, "War and Child in the Second Constitutional Period."

99. As recently discussed by Fortna, Ottoman children were introduced to contradicting and mixed messages from their reading materials. On the one hand, they were exposed to a fanciful world of sweets and dolls. On the other, there was the stark world of warfare, sacrifice, and service to the homeland. See Benjamin C. Fortna, "Bonbons and Bayonets: Mixed Messages of Childhood in the Late Ottoman Empire and the Early Turkish Republic."

100. Celia M. Kingsbury, *For Home and Country: World War I Propaganda on the Home Front*, 169–217.

101. Boy gangs were active in urban settings in the late Ottoman period. Reşat Ekrem Koçu wrote about "gangs of child thieves" and gave detailed accounts of especially the Pıtır Ali gang of 1883–84 and Shiny Joze gang of 1908–9. Children in these gangs were all destitute and idle on the streets, between the ages of thirteen and fifteen. Reşat Ekrem Koçu, "Çocuk Hırsız Çeteleri," 4076–78.

102. Mark Mazower, *Salonica: The City of Ghosts*, 157.

103. Kohen, *Kohens del de Campavias*, 36.

104. Antranig Dzarugyan, *Çocukluğu Olmayan Adamlar*, 117–18, 123–27.

105. Tan et al., *Cumhuriyet'te Çocuktular*, 271.

106. BOA, MV, 215/129, 27/Ş/1337 (26.05.1919).

107. Ibid.

108. See Çetinkaya, "Illustrated Atrocity."

109. Emre Erol, "Organized Chaos."

110. BOA, DH.ŞFR., 49/2, 27/S/1333 (14.01.1915).

111. The story was based on the experiences of the author, who was born in Ayvalık in 1904. During World War I, he lived on the neighboring island of Lesbos/Midilli, where his family sought refuge. Vangelis Calotychos, *The Balkan Prospect: Identity, Culture, and Politics in Greece after 1989*, 132.

112. Ibid., 133.

113. "La misère à Constantinople," *La Tribune de Genève* 223, 17 September 1917.

114. "Le gouvernement turc, sous prétexte de sauver une partie de ces orphelins, les enfermait dans des lieux des quartiers de Harbiye Nişantaşı ou on les forçait à embrasser la religion musulmane" (ibid.).

115. Ion and Brown, *Persecutions of the Greeks*, 72.

116. "Bikes Etfal Hakkında Saadettin Bey'in Beyanatı," *İkdam*, 30 Teşrinisani 1337 (30 Nov. 1921), 3.

117. "Harbiye Mektebi'ndeki Çocuklar," *Sabah*, 14 Mayıs 1333 (14 July 1917), 3.

118. Ion and Brown, *Persecutions of the Greeks*, 20.

119. Ibid., 19; "Turkish Cruelty Bared by the Greeks," *New York Times*, 16 June 1918.

120. BOA, DH.UMVM., 160/ 27, 13 Mayıs 1335 (13.05.1919).

121. Konstantina Adrianopoulou, "Social Policy and 'National Mission': 'Little Ethnomartyrs' in the Christian Orthodox Community of Istanbul during the First World War," paper presented at the Boğaziçi University History Department, 24 Oct. 2007.

122. BOA, DH.ŞFR., 94/137, 11/Ra/1337 (14.01.1919); BOA, DH.ŞFR., 97/284, 23/C/1337 (24.02.1919).

123. "Sent to Harems," *Liverpool Echo*, 4 Aug. 1917, 3; "For Turkish Harems: 8000 Serbian Girls Deported," *Yorkshire Evening Post*, 4 Aug. 1917, 6; "Sent to Slavery. 8,000 Serbian Girls for Turkish Harems," *Sheffield Independent*, 4 Aug. 1917, 1; "Serbia's Horrors: Girls Carried Off to Turkish Harems," *Daily Record* (Lanarkshire, Scotland), 4 Aug. 1917, 3.

124. The booklet claimed that the Germans "collected eight thousand of them, the prettiest, and patting them paternally on the cheek, with a big laugh, they sold them to the Turk to be put in a cage and to serve for the relaxation of the Pashas of the Committee of 'Union and Progress,' who will hand them on no doubt later on to

some Kurdish soldier of the Guards. That is the gift of Wilhelm II to his friends at Constantinople." *Appeal of the Serbian Women to All Societies of Women.*

125. BOA, HR.SYS., 2438/83, 16 Aug. 1917.

126. Nationalist competition over the possession of unattended children went back to the late nineteenth century (Nazan Maksudyan, "The Fight over Nobody's Children: Religion, Nationality and Citizenship of Foundlings in the Late Ottoman Empire," 151–80) as much as forward to World War II (Tara Zahra, *Kidnapped Souls: National Indifference and the Battle for Children in the Bohemian Lands, 1900–1948*).

127. For instance, it was probably impossible that "almost a hundred thousand" Greek refugees arrived in Istanbul during the war years. Population flow to the capital was among the scariest nightmares of the CUP government, and they did all in their power to prevent it.

4. Survival of Children during the Armenian Genocide

1. Avedis Albert Abrahamian, *Avedis' Story: An Armenian Boy's Journey*, 70.

2. Writing the biography of her mother, Iskouhi Parounagian of Sivas, Alice A. Tashjian stresses that the main theme in this story was the will to survive. *Silences: My Mother's Will to Survive.*

3. David Oswell, *The Agency of Children: From Family to Global Human Rights.*

4. Testimonial production of the educated writers in the Armenian language was numerous. Some of them were published soon after the events, such as Aram Andonian's *Medz Vochirı* (*The Great Crime*) and Garabed Kapiguian's Եղեռնապատում (*Tales of the Yeghern*). Quite a few of them have been translated into English and other European languages: Grigoris Balakian, *Armenian Golgotha: A Memoir of the Armenian Genocide*; Yervant Odyan, *Accursed Years: My Exile and Return from Der Zor, 1914–1919*; Aram Andonian, *En ces sombres jours*; Aram Andonian, *Sur la route de l'exil*; M. Salbi (Aram Sahakian), *Our Cross*; Paylazu Kaptanyan, *1915 Ermeni Soykırımı: Bir Tanığın Anıları*; Mikael Shamdanjian, *The Fatal Night: An Eyewitness Account of the Extermination of Armenian Intellectuals in 1915*.

5. Marc Nichanian, *The Historiographic Perversion*, 104.

6. This is the case regarding the diary of Vahram Altounian, titled "Everything I endured from 1915 to 1919." The notebook, written in Turkish with the Armenian alphabet, was discovered in 1978 and was translated into French in 1980. Vahram Altounian, Janine Altounian, and Krikor Beledian, *Mémoires du génocide arménien: héritage traumatique et travail analytique*. The memoir was translated into Turkish based on the original manuscript. Vahram Altounian and Janine Altounian, *Geri Dönüşü Yok: Bir Babanın Güncesinde ve Kızının Belleğinde Ermeni Soykırımı*.

7. For further information, see Nazan Maksudyan, "Self, Family, and Society: Individual and Communal Reflections on the Armenian Genocide"; and Vahé Tachjian, *Daily Life in the Abyss: Genocide Diaries, 1915–1918*.

8. Aram Andonian, *Medz Vochirı*, 9. Between 1919 and 1922, Andonian was prolifically active as a historian-journalist, concerned with the telling of the event in all its aspects. After 1922 he devoted his life to a possible history of the extermination on the basis of testimonies that he never stopped collecting throughout his life. The entirety of the Andonian dossier remains, to this day, unpublished.

9. See mainly Matthias Bjørnlund, "'A Fate Worse than Dying': Sexual Violence during the Armenian Genocide"; Rubina Peroomian, *And Those Who Continued Living in Turkey after 1915: The Metamorphosis of the Post-Genocide Armenian Identity as Reflected in Artistic Literature*; Vahé Tachjian, "Gender, Nationalism, Exclusion: The Reintegration Process of Female Survivors of the Armenian Genocide"; Vahram L. Shemmassian, "The Reclamation of Captive Armenian Genocide Survivors in Syria and Lebanon at the End of World War I"; Katharine Derderian, "Common Fate, Different Experience: Gender-Specific Aspects of the Armenian Genocide, 1915–1917"; Vahram L. Shemmassian, "The League of Nations and the Reclamation of Armenian Genocide Survivors"; and Sarafian, "Absorption of Armenian Women and Children."

10. Asya Darbinyan and Rubina Peroomian, "Children: The Most Vulnerable Victims of the Armenian Genocide."

11. Donald E. Miller and Lorna Touryan Miller, *Survivors: An Oral History of the Armenian Genocide.*

12. Vahakn N. Dadrian, "Children as Victims of Genocide: The Armenian Case"; Dawn Anahid Mackeen, *The Hundred-Year Walk: An Armenian Odyssey*, 178–79.

13. Dadrian, "Children as Victims of Genocide," 421.

14. Other narrative sources also make reference to this method. Mackeen, *Hundred-Year Walk*, 178–79.

15. Dadrian, "Children as Victims of Genocide."

16. Haigaz, *Four Years in the Mountains of Kurdistan*, 228, 318; Mackeen, *Hundred-Year Walk*, 178–79.

17. Keith D. Watenpaugh, "'Are There Any Children for Sale?': Genocide and the Transfer of Armenian Children (1915–1922)."

18. BOA, DH.ŞFR., 54/411, 29/N/1333 (12 July 1915). The practice was the continuation of the long-lived *besleme* tradition, through which better-off families adopted the daughters of poorer families, yet only in name. They actually used them as maidservants or concubines. See Maksudyan, "Foster-Daughter or Servant."

19. BOA, DH.ŞFR., 63/142, 26/Ca/1334 (30 Apr. 1916).

20. BOA, DH.ŞFR., 56/209, 19/Za/1333 (28 Sept. 1915); BOA, Dahiliye, Emniyet-i Umumiye Müdüriyeti, 2. Şube (DH.EUM.2.Şb), 25/25, 05/L/1334 (05.08.1916); BOA, DH.EUM.2.Şb, 30/7, 05/M/1335 (01.11.1916); BOA, Dahiliye, Emniyet-i Umumiye Müdüriyeti, Seyr ü Sefer Kalemi (DH.EUM.SSM.), 10/Ş/1335 (01.06.1917).

21. BOA, DH.ŞFR., 61/23, 11/R/1334 (17.01.1916).

22. After Fethiye Çetin's memorable book, *Anneannem*, more and more personal accounts have appeared on grandparents with an Armenian origin. Ayşe Gül Altınay and Fethiye Çetin, eds., *Torunlar*; Erhan Başyurt, *Ermeni Evlatlıklar: Saklı Kalmış Hayatlar*; Baskın Oran (ed.), *M. K. Adlı Çocuğun Tehcir Anıları: 1915 ve Sonrası*; İbrahim Ethem Atnur, *Türkiye'de Ermeni Kadınları ve Çocukları Meselesi (1915–1923)*; İrfan Palalı, *Tehcir Çocukları: Nenem bir Ermeni'ymiş*; Kemal Yalçın, *Sarı Gelin—Sari Gyalin.*

23. The society was established in 1916 by Minister of War Enver Pasha. See Yavuz S. Karakışla, "Kadınları Çalıştırma Cemiyeti."

24. BOA, DH.ŞFR., 59/150, 21/S/1334 (29.12.1915). There is a significant body of scholarly research on the subject of Islamicized Armenians in present-day Turkey. See mainly Ayşe Gül Altınay, "In Search of Silenced Grandparents: Ottoman Armenian Survivors and Their (Muslim) Grandchildren"; and Ayşe Gül Altınay and Yektan Türkyılmaz, "Unraveling Layers of Gendered Silencing: Converted Armenian Survivors of the 1915 Catastrophe." An international conference was organized on "Islamized Armenians" in November 2013 in Istanbul by the Hrant Dink Foundation and Boğaziçi University's History Department.

25. Watenpaugh, "The League of Nations' Rescue," 1329. According to the personal registers of Talat, of the 10,314 Armenian orphans who had been reported by different provinces, 6,858 had been distributed to Muslim families, while 3,456 were in state orphanages. Bardakçı, *Talât Paşa'nın Evrak-ı Metrukesi*, 88–89; Dündar, *Modern Türkiye'nin Şifresi*, 307.

26. Sarafian, "Absorption of Armenian Women and Children," 209–21.

27. Tara Zahra, *The Lost Children: Reconstructing Europe's Families after World War II*, 36.

28. Works by Ekmekçioğlu, Watenpaugh, and Tachjian largely focus on the post-genocide period in their discussion of the experiences of genocide survivors. See Lerna Ekmekçioğlu, "A Climate for Abduction, a Climate for Redemption: The Politics of Inclusion During and After the Armenian Genocide" and *Recovering Armenia: The Limits of Belonging in Post-Genocide Turkey*; Keith D. Watenpaugh, *Bread from Stones: The Middle East and the Making of Modern Humanitarianism*; Watenpaugh, "The League of Nations' Rescue"; and Vahé Tachjian, "Gender, Nationalism, Exclusion: The Reintegration Process of Female Survivors of the Armenian Genocide."

29. Mabel Evelyn Elliott, *Beginning Again at Ararat*, 35.

30. BOA, DH.ŞFR., 93/300, 23/S/1337 (28.11.1918); BOA, DH.ŞFR., 95/212, 19/R/1337 (23.12.1918); BOA, DH.ŞFR., 94/56, 01/Ra/1337 (04.01.1919).

31. "Hıristiyan ailelerine mensup kızların ve çocukların Müslüman aileler nezdinde cebren alıkonulduğu haber alındığından, tahkikat yapılarak derhal aile veya akrabalarına teslimlerine dair." BOA, DH.ŞFR., 92/196, 15/M/1337 (21.10.1918); BOA, DH.ŞFR., 95/212, 19/R/1337 (23.12.1918); Ekmekçioğlu, "A Climate for Abduction," 533.

32. BOA, DH.ŞFR., 94/56, 01/Re/1337 (05.12.1918): Telegram from the Ministry of Interior to Adana Province (*vilayet*); BOA, DH.ŞFR., 95/163, 15/Ra/1337 (18.01.1919): Telegram from the Ministry of Interior to the provinces.

33. BOA, DH.ŞFR., 96/76, 04/Ce/1337 (05.02.1919): Telegram from the Ministry of Interior to Kayseri Province (*mutasarrıflık*).

34. BOA, DH.ŞFR., 96/87, 05/Ce/1337 (06.02.1919): Telegram from the Ministry of Interior to the provinces; BOA, DH.ŞFR., 96/96, 07/Ce/1337 (08.02.1919): Telegram from the Ministry of Interior to Canik Province (*mutasarrıflık*).

35. BOA, DH.ŞFR., 93/300, 23/S/1337 (28.11.1918); BOA, DH.ŞFR., 94/56, 1/Ra/1337 (04.01.1919).

36. The news also appeared in a Turkish newspaper, *Söz*, 17 Teşrinisani 1334 (17.11.1918).

37. *Sabah*, 9 Kanunusani 1335 (09.01.1919).

38. *Yeni İstanbul*, 9 Kanunusani 1335 (09.01.1919).

39. Similar activities already started in Sinai, Palestine, Syria, and Iraq in late 1917, after the arrival of the British. Ekmekçioğlu cites a memoir of a *vorpahavak* officer in Mesopotamia, Iskhan Jinbashian and Levon Parian, eds., *Crows of the Desert: The Memoirs of Levon Yotnakhparian*, 109–13. Despite the open reference to orphans (որբ), the campaign to retrieve and reintegrate the Armenian survivors in Muslim households comprised also Armenian women, who were as numerous as children. Vahé Tachjian, “Mixed Marriage, Prostitution, Survival.”

40. Dinamo, *Öksüz Musa*, 11–12.

41. Ibid., 26.

42. Ibid., 24–25.

43. Archives of the League of Nations, United Nations Organization, Geneva (ALON-UNOG), A.35.1921.IV, C.281.M.218.1921. IV, Memorandum by the Secretary-General on the Work of the Commission of Enquiry with Regard to the Deportation of Women and Children, Report by Dr. Kennedy, Letter from Miss E. D. Cushman to the Secretary-General.

44. Zaven Der Yeghiayan, *My Patriarchal Memoirs*, 181.

45. BOA, DH.KMS., 52-2/79, 28 Nisan 1335 (28.04.1919).

46. (ALON-UNOG), A.35.1921.IV, C.281.M.218.1921. IV, Memorandum by the Secretary-General on the Work of the Commission of Enquiry with Regard to the Deportation of Women and Children, Report by Dr. Kennedy, Letter from Miss E. D. Cushman to the Secretary-General.

47. Der Yeghiayan, *My Patriarchal Memoirs*, 186.

48. The patriarchate provided the following numbers: six thousand women and children in the regions of Istanbul, İzmit, Bursa, and Eskişehir; two thousand in Karahisar; fifteen hundred in the district of Bolu; three thousand in Konya; five thousand in Kastamonu; two thousand in Trabzon; thirty-five hundred in Sivas; thirty-five

hundred in Kayseri; three thousand in Erzurum; twenty-five thousand in Diyarbekir-Mardin; three thousand in Harput; and five thousand in the vilayets of Bitlis and Van. Kévorkian, *Armenian Genocide*, 759.

49. Der Yeghiayan, *My Patriarchal Memoirs*, 181.

50. All four were to receive monthly salaries, in addition to their expenses. The British embassy gave each of them a letter of introduction addressed to the Allied authorities, requesting their assistance in need. Ibid., 182.

51. BOA, DH.KMS., 52-2/79, 22 Mayıs 1335 (22.05.1919). The society filed a complaint that the registers were taken by Çakıryan and never returned.

52. Der Yeghiayan, *My Patriarchal Memoirs*, 181–82.

53. Levon Marashlian, "Finishing the Genocide: Cleansing Turkey of Armenian Survivors, 1920–1923," 122; Der Yeghiayan, *My Patriarchal Memoirs*, 183, 185.

54. (ALON-UNOG), A.35.1921.IV, C.281.M.218.1921. IV, Memorandum by the Secretary-General on the "Work of the Commission of Enquiry with Regard to the Deportation of Women and Children in Turkey and Adjacent Countries," Report by Dr. Kennedy, Letter from Miss E. D. Cushman to the Secretary-General.

55. Marashlian, "Finishing the Genocide," 120; Kévorkian, *Armenian Genocide*, 760–61.

56. On 12 January 1919, an Armenian search committee with the support of French soldiers went to the house of the retired medical officer Kaymakam (district governor) İsmail Tevfik in Bakırköy to find an Armenian girl. BOA, Dahiliye, Emniyet-i Umumiye, 6. Şube (DH.EUM.6.Şb.), 47/61, 09/Ra/1337 (12.01.1919). In a similar instance, an Armenian search committee went into the house of Captain Kemal Bey and demanded the release of a young girl, named Şerife. BOA, DH.EUM.6.Şb., 48/11, 15/Ra/1337 (18.01.1919). In mid-1919 there was a series of complaints by Major Süleyman Bey in Arnavutköy, Dr. Kamil Bey in Üsküdar, the head of the Committee of Purchasing (Mubayaa Komisyonu) Şekib in Ortaköy, and Lieutenant Mehmet Nuri Efendi in Bakırköy that their foster daughters were forcefully taken away by Armenian patriarchal officers. BOA, DH.İ.UM., 19-7/1-5, 08/R/1337 (07.06.1919).

57. Zaruhi Bahri, a prominent writer, feminist, and a founding member of the Armenian Red Cross, acted for a long time as the Armenian representative at the Neutral House. Her memoirs provide contemporary Armenian discussions of the Neutral House's operations. Watenpaugh, *Bread from Stones*, 142; Ekmekçioğlu, *Recovering Armenia*, 85.

58. Several sources suggest that the institution was superintended by Americans and that there was a supervisory board of two attendants—an Armenian and a Turkish lady. The Rum presence in the institution might have been just on paper. Der Yeghiayan, *My Patriarchal Memoirs*, 182.

59. Watenpaugh, *Bread from Stones*, 142.

60. Der Yeghiayan, *My Patriarchal Memoirs*, 182; Watenpaugh, *Bread from Stones*, 143, 224n40. "Index of Children Brought to the Neutral House," 7 Aug. 1919, ALON-UNOG, 12/15100/4631(1).

61. "From the Armenian Patriarch to Major Arnold, Managing Director to the American Relief Committee in the Near East, 7 Aug. 1919," ALON-UNOG, 12/15100/4631(2).

62. Ibid.

63. ALON-UNOG, A.35.1921.IV, C.281.M.218.1921. IV, Memorandum by the Secretary-General on the Work of the Commission of Enquiry with Regard to the Deportation of Women and Children, Report by Dr. Kennedy, Letter from Miss E. D. Cushman to the Secretary-General:

> The child, a boy of twelve years, was placed for treatment in an international eye hospital, an American institution. He was sent in with other boys from a Turkish orphanage. He came with a Turkish name and a history of Turkish parentage. For two months, he had been in this institution, had mixed with children of various nationalities and no one suspected that he was not a Turkish child. Suddenly, he began to sing Armenian hymns, and to speak in Armenian, not fluently of course, but a few words. When asked where he learned the hymns and also to speak Armenian, he said, "I spoke that language when I was little, then I sang these hymns." He was asked what his name was at that time, and he readily gave an Armenian name. I may add that this condition was not brought about by suggestion or persuasion, as no one had doubted that the child was of Turkish origin; a change of environment had brought about a mental change, and the child had discovered himself.

64. The League of Nations' Fifth Committee's investigations also focused on the work of the Neutral House. Therefore, there is significant discussion of the House in League of Nations reports. *The Humanitarian Activities of the League; Book 6 of a Series of Text Books Specially Prepared for Study Circles*, 22 (emphasis added).

65. ALON-UNOG, A.35.1921.IV, C.281.M.218.1921. IV, Memorandum by the Secretary-General on the Work of the Commission of Enquiry with Regard to the Deportation of Women and Children, Report by Dr. Kennedy, Letter from Miss E. D. Cushman to the Secretary-General.

66. The same theme was also relevant for "hidden Jewish children" during the Holocaust who tried to survive by pretending to be Christians. Nechama Tec, introduction to *Children during the Holocaust*.

67. "Index of Children Brought to the Neutral House," 28 April 1920, ALON-UNOG, 12/15100/4631(1).

68. Ibid., 3.

69. Ibid., 12.

70. Ibid., 5–6.

71. Ibid., 14–15.

72. Ibid., 16.

73. Ibid., 3.

74. Der Yeghiayan, *My Patriarchal Memoirs*, 182.

75. "From the Armenian Patriarch to Major Arnold, Managing Director to the American Relief Committee in the Near East, 7 Aug. 1919," ALON-UNOG, 12/15100/4631(2).

76. Stanley E. Kerr, *Lions of Marash: Personal Experiences with American Near East Relief, 1919–1922*, 49.

77. Miller and Touryan Miller, *Survivors*, 113.

78. The book has been translated into French as *Des hommes sans enfance*, into English as *Men without Childhood*, and into Turkish as *Çocukluğu Olmayan Adamlar*.

79. My references are based on the Turkish translation. Dzarugyan, *Çocukluğu Olmayan Adamlar*, 11, 16, 31, 33, 49, 74.

80. Papken Injarabian, *Azo the Slave Boy and His Road to Freedom*, 93.

81. Haigaz, *Four Years in the Mountains of Kurdistan*, 30.

82. Dirouhi Kouymjian Highgas describes in *Refugee Girl* how hard her parents tried to hide her so that the gendarmes would not take her away.

83. Miller and Touryan Miller, *Survivors*, 109.

84. Ibid., 113.

85. Haigaz, *Four Years in the Mountains of Kurdistan*, 303.

86. Miller and Touryan Miller, *Survivors*, 112.

87. Injarabian, *Azo the Slave Boy*, 1–14. Kerop Bedoukian was also nine when the deportations in Sivas started. *The Urchin: An Armenian's Escape*.

88. Injarabian, *Azo the Slave Boy*, 83.

89. Food scarcity and hunger were common problems in all orphanages, in Turkish, Armenian, or American alike.

90. Ramela Martin, who was a very little girl during the genocide, had been in different Near East Relief orphanages in Aleppo, Beirut, Istanbul, and Corinth. Her accounts of each were equally sad, filled with accounts of children dying from hunger and several illnesses. Ramela Martin, *Out of Darkness*.

91. Haigaz, *Four Years in the Mountains of Kurdistan*, 303.

92. BOA, DH.EUM.2.Şb, 48/56, 28/Ra/1336 (10.02.1918).

93. BOA, MF.MKT., 1238/71, 13/N/1337 (14.05.1919).

94. The abridged memoirs were published a few years ago in English (with a different title). Karnig Panian, *Goodbye, Antoura: A Memoir of the Armenian Genocide*. The

recent Turkish edition is the unabridged version: Karnig Panyan, *Elveda Antura: Bir Ermeni Yetimin Anıları.*

95. Panian, *Goodbye, Antoura*, 83.

96. Ibid., 85–89.

97. Ibid., 97.

98. Altounian and Altounian, *Geri Dönüşü Yok*, 14–24.

99. Born in 1908 in Aintab, Euphoria Halebian Meymerian stresses the "business skills" of her father in her family's survival. Thanks to her father's service to the Ottoman army, he knew the right people to assist the family's escape to Lebanon. Euphoria Halebian Meymerian, *Housher: My Life in the Aftermath of the Armenian Genocide.*

100. "Boş durmak eyi deyil bir iş yapalım." Altounian and Altounian, *Geri Dönüşü Yok*, 14.

101. Haigaz, *Four Years in the Mountains of Kurdistan*, 123.

102. Abrahamian, *Avedis' Story*, 72.

103. Mackeen, *Hundred-Year Walk*, 118.

104. Dzarugyan, *Çocukluğu Olmayan Adamlar*, 21–26; Injarabian, *Azo the Slave Boy*, 99; Panian, *Goodbye, Antoura*, 117.

105. Miller and Touryan Miller, *Survivors*, 119.

106. Injarabian, *Azo the Slave Boy*, 34.

107. Miller and Touryan Miller, *Survivors*, 114.

108. Panian, *Goodbye, Antoura*, 101.

109. Ibid.

110. Mackeen, *Hundred-Year Walk*, 14.

111. Panian, *Goodbye, Antoura*, 33.

112. Karnig Panyan, *Elveda Antura: Bir Ermeni Yetimin Anıları*, 101–2.

113. George Eisen, *Children and Play in the Holocaust: Games among the Shadows*, 10.

114. Panian, *Goodbye, Antoura*, 67.

115. Abrahamian, *Avedis' Story*, 70 (emphasis added).

116. Dzarugyan, *Çocukluğu Olmayan Adamlar*, 200.

117. Panyan, *Elveda Antura*, 184–85.

118. Abrahamian, *Avedis' Story*, 39.

119. Panyan, *Elveda Antura*, 302.

120. Miller and Touryan Miller, *Survivors*, 115–17.

121. Eisen, *Children and Play in the Holocaust*, 42.

122. Dzarugyan, *Çocukluğu Olmayan Adamlar*, 167.

123. Ibid., 176.

124. Panian, *Goodbye, Antoura*, 108.

125. From Friday, 24 December 1943. Anne Frank, *The Diary of a Young Girl: The Definitive Edition*, 310.

126. Those who lost their minds, like Gomidas Vartabed, were also elevated to a degree of spiritual martyrdom. It was as if ordinary people were aware that going mad was the most dignified thing to do, but they only knew how to survive and were not as "special" as those who went mad. Rita Soulahian Kuyumjian, *Archeology of Madness: Komitas, Portrait of an Armenian Icon*.

127. Suicide appears once and again in survivor testimonies, especially in the case of raped girls, pregnant women, and young (unmarried) mothers. The gendered character of suicide during the genocide points to its "moral" character. To give only a few examples, Bertha Nakshian Ketchian recounts women hurling themselves from cliffs in *In the Shadow of the Fortress: The Genocide Remembered*, 17; Abrahamian, *Avedis' Story*, 31; Haigaz, *Four Years in the Mountains of Kurdistan*, 234.

128. Krikor Beledian and Janine Altounian stress the numbness and the absence of graphic descriptions of pain in Vahram Altounian's diary. Régine Waintrater also underlines the overall respect for the "craft of survival" in the narrative. Altounian and Altounian, *Geri Dönüşü Yok*, 103, 122, 124, 160.

Conclusion

1. Kennedy, *Children's War*, 1–2; Manon Pignot, "Entrer en guerre, sortir de l'enfance? Les 'ado-combattants' de la Grande Guerre."

2. Adam Baghdasarian, *Forgotten Fire*.

3. Panyan, *Elveda Antura*, 92.

4. Dzarugyan, *Çocukluğu Olmayan Adamlar*, 10.

5. Panyan, *Elveda Antura*, 194.

6. Ahmed Emin (Yalman), "Yetimler Meselesi, Bugünlerde Mebuslarımız Yetimleri Konuşacaklar," *Vakit*, 29 Kanunusani 1334 (29.01.1918), 1.

7. Marc Nichanian, *Entre l'art et le témoignage: Le roman de la catastrophe*.

8. Duygu Köksal, "İsmayıl Hakkı Baltacıoğlu, İnkilap ve Terbiye: Ulusun 'Çocukluğu.'"

9. Yasemin Gencer, "We Are Family: The Child and Modern Nationhood in Early Turkish Republican Cartoons (1923–28)," 304.

Bibliography

Published Official Documents

"1333 Senesi Darüleytamlar Müdüriyet-i Umumiyesi Masraf Bütçesinin Birinci Faslının İkinci ve Dördüncü Maddeleri ile Maliye Nezareti'nin Sene-i Mezkure Bütçesinin Ondokuzuncu Darüleytamlar Faslı Tahsisatına 42.060.402 Kuruş İlavesi Hakkında Layiha-yı Kanuniye." In *Meclis-i Mebusan Encümen Mazbataları ve Levayih-i Kanuniye (1333–1334)* (Devre: 3, İctima: 4, no. 459), 10:1–6. Retrievable from https://acikerisim.tbmm.gov.tr/xmlui/handle/11543/2400.

"1334 Senesi Darüleytam Müdüriyet-i Umumiyesi Bütçesi Muvazene-i Maliye Encümeni Mazbatası." In *Meclis-i Mebusan Encümen Mazbataları ve Levayih-i Kanuniye (1333–1334)* (Devre: 3, İctima: 4, no. 409), 10:1–30. Retrievable from https://acikerisim.tbmm.gov.tr/xmlui/handle/11543/2400.

"Darüleytamlar Müdüriyet-i Umumiyesinin Teşkilatı Hakkındaki 2 Nisan 1333 tarihli kanuna müzal Layiha-yı Kanuniye." In *Meclis-i Mebusan Encümen Mazbataları ve Levayih-i Kanuniye (1333–1334)* (Devre: 3, İctima: 4, no. 401), 10:1–3. Retrievable from https://acikerisim.tbmm.gov.tr/xmlui/handle/11543/2400.

"Darüleytamlar Müdüriyet-i Umumiyesinin Teşkili ve Müteferruatı Hakkında Kanun." *Düstur*, Tertib 2, vol. 9, 575–76. Istanbul: Evkaf Matbaası, 1928.

"Darüleytam Müdüriyeti Teşkilatı Hakkındaki 2 Nisan 1333 tarihli Kanunun birinci maddesini muadil Layiha-yı Kanuniye." In *Meclis-i Mebusan Encümen Mazbataları ve Levayih-i Kanuniye (1333–1334)* (Devre: 3, İctima: 4, no. 431), 10:1–4. Retrievable from https://acikerisim.tbmm.gov.tr/xmlui/handle/11543/2400.

The Humanitarian Activities of the League, Book 6 of a Series of Text Books Specially Prepared for Study Circles. London: League of Nations Union, 1922.

"Maarif Nezareti'ne Merbut Darüleytamlar Müdüriyet-i Umumiyyesi Teşkili Hakkında Layiha-yı Kanuniye." In *Meclis-i Mebusan Encümen Mazbataları ve Levayih-i Kanuniye (1332–1333)* (Devre: 3, İctima: 3, no. 240), 9:1–7. Retrievable from https://acikerisim.tbmm.gov.tr/xmlui/handle/11543/2400.

Minutes of the Grand National Assembly, 2nd Parliament, 1st Legislative Year (11.08.1923–28.02.1924), 15th sess. (08.09.1339) [1923]), 448–79. Retrievable from http://www.tbmm.gov.tr/tutanaklar/TUTANAK/TBM/d02/c001/tbmm02001015.pdf.

Russack, Dr. Hans Hermann. "Die türkischen Lehrlinge." In *Türkische Jugend in Deutschland: Jahresbericht der Schülerabteilung der Deutsch-Türkischen Vereinigung*, 47–65. Berlin: Deutsch-Türkische Vereinigung e.V., 1918.

Salname-i Nezaret-i Maarif-i Umumiye 1319. Istanbul: Matbaa-i Amire, 1319 [1901].

"Şüheda Vesaire Evladlarının Leyli Mekatib-i İdadiye-i Askeriyeye Kayıt ve Kabulü Hakkında Nizamname." *Düstur*, Tertib 2, vol. 7, 743–45. Dersaadet: Matbaa-i Amire, 1336 [1920].

Other Sources

Abrahamian, Avedis Albert. *Avedis' Story: An Armenian Boy's Journey*. Edited by Carolann S. Najarian. London: Gomidas Institute, 2014.

Akçam, Taner. *Ermenilerin Zorla Müslümanlaştırılması: Sessizlik, İnkâr ve Asimilasyon*. Istanbul: İletişim Yayınları, 2014.

Akçam, Taner, and Ümit Kurt. *Kanunların Ruhu*. Istanbul: İletişim Yayınları, 2012.

Akın, Yiğit. *Gürbüz ve Yavuz Evlatlar*. Istanbul: İletişim, 2004.

———. "War, Women, and the State: The Politics of Sacrifice in the Ottoman Empire during the First World War." *Journal of Women's History* 26/3 (2014): 12–35.

———. *When the War Came Home: The Ottomans' Great War and the Devastation of an Empire*. Stanford, CA: Stanford Univ. Press, 2018.

Alkan, Mehmet Ö. *Tanzimat'tan Cumhuriyet'e Modernleşme Sürecinde Eğitim İstatistikleri, 1839–1924*. Ankara: Başbakanlık Devlet İstatistik Enstitüsü, 2000.

Altınay, Ayşe Gül. "In Search of Silenced Grandparents: Ottoman Armenian Survivors and Their (Muslim) Grandchildren." In *Der Völkermord an den Armeniern, die Türkei und Europa: The Armenian Genocide, Turkey and Europe*, edited by Hans-Lukas Kieser and Elmar Plozza, 117–32. Zurich: Chronos, 2006.

Altınay, Ayşe Gül, and Yeşim Arat. *Violence against Women in Turkey: A Nationwide Survey*. Istanbul: Punto, 2009.

Altınay, Ayşe Gül, and Fethiye Çetin, eds. *Torunlar*. Istanbul: Metis, 2009.

Altınay, Ayşe Gül, and Yektan Türkyılmaz. "Unraveling Layers of Gendered Silencing: Converted Armenian Survivors of the 1915 Catastrophe." In *Untold Histories of the Middle East: Recovering Voices from the 19th and 20th Centuries*, edited by Amy Singer, Christoph K. Neumann, and Selçuk Akşin Somel, 25–53. London: Routledge, 2011.

Altınkaynak, Erdoğan. "Sarıkamış Harekatı ve Çevresinde Oluşan Destanlar, Hatıralar." In *Savaş Çocukları: Öksüzler ve Yetimler*, edited by Emine Gürsoy-Naskali and Aylin Koç. Istanbul: n.p., 2003.

Altounian, Vahram, and Janine Altounian. *Geri Dönüşü Yok: Bir Babanın Güncesinde ve Kızının Belleğinde Ermeni Soykırımı*. Istanbul: Aras Yayıncılık, 2015.

Altounian, Vahram, Janine Altounian, and Krikor Beledian. *Mémoires du génocide arménien: Héritage traumatique et travail analytique*. Paris: Presses Universitaires de France—PUF, 2009.

Andonian, Aram. *En ces sombres jours*. Translated by Hervé Georgelin. Geneva: MétisPresses, 2007.

———. *Medz Vochirı (The Great Crime)*. Boston: Hayrenik, 1921.

———. *Sur la route de l'exil*. Geneva: MétisPresses, 2007.

Appeal of the Serbian Women to All Societies of Women. Geneva: Ligue Nationale des Femmes Serbes, 1917.

Arax, Mark. *In My Father's Name*. New York: Pocket Books, 1997.

Ariotti, Kate. *Captive Anzacs: Australian POWs of the Ottomans during the First World War*. Cambridge: Cambridge Univ. Press, 2018.

Ateş, Sanem Yamak. *Asker Evlatlar Yetiştirmek: II. Meşrutiyet Dönemi'nde Beden Terbiyesi, Askeri Talim ve Paramiliter Gençlik Örgütleri*. Istanbul: İletişim Yayınları, 2012.

Atnur, İbrahim Ethem. *Türkiye'de Ermeni Kadınları ve Çocukları Meselesi (1915–1923)*. Ankara: Babil Yayıncılık, 2005.

Audoin-Rouzeau, Stéphane. "Children and the Primary Schools of France, 1914–1918." In *State, Society and Mobilization in Europe during the First World War*, edited by John Horne, 39–52. Cambridge: Cambridge Univ. Press, 1997.

Audoin-Rouzeau, Stéphane, and Annette Becker. *14–18, Understanding the Great War*. New York: Hill and Wang, 2002.

Aved, Thomas G. *Toomas, the Little Armenian Boy: Childhood Reminiscence of Turkish-Armenia*. Fresno: Pioneer, 1979.

Aydemir, Şevket Süreyya. *Suyu Arayan Adam*. Istanbul: Remzi Kitabevi, 2010.

Aytekin, Hakan. "1914–1924 Yılları Arasında Korunmaya Muhtaç Çocuklar ve Eğitimleri." Master's thesis, Marmara Univ., 2006.

Baghdasarian, Adam. *Forgotten Fire*. New York: DK, 2000.

Balakian, Grigoris. *Armenian Golgotha: A Memoir of the Armenian Genocide*. Translated by Peter Balakian and Aris Sevag. New York: Vintage, 2010.

Bali, Rıfat N. *Sports and Physical Education in Turkey in the 1930s*. Istanbul: ISIS Press, 2009.

Bardakçı, Murat. *Talât Paşa'nın Evrak-ı Metrukesi: Sadrazam Talât Paşa'nın Özel Arşivinde Bulunan Ermeni Tehciri Konusundaki Belgeler ve Hususî Yazışmalar*. Istanbul: Everest Yayınları, 2008.

Başyurt, Erhan. *Ermeni Evlatlıklar: Saklı Kalmış Hayatlar*. Istanbul: Karakutu, 2006.

Bedoukian, Kerop. *The Urchin: An Armenian's Escape*. London: Butler and Tanner, 1978.

Ben-Bassat, Yuval, and Dotan Halevy. "A Tale of Two Cities and One Telegram: The Ottoman Military Regime and the Population of Greater Syria during WWI." *British Journal of Middle East Studies* 45/2 (2018): 212–30.

Benezra, Nissim M. *Une enfance Juive à Istanbul, 1911–1929*. Istanbul: Isis, 1996.

Beşikçi, Mehmet. *Ottoman Mobilization of Manpower in the First World War: Between Voluntarism and Resistance*. Leiden: Brill, 2012.

———. "When a Military Problem Became a Social Issue: Ottoman Desertions and Deserters in World War I." In *War and Collapse: World War I and the Ottoman State*, edited by M. Hakan Yavuz and Feroz Ahmad, 480–91. Salt Lake City: Univ. of Utah Press, 2016.

Bihl, Wolfdieter. *Die Kaukasus-Politik der Mittelmächte.* 2 vols. Vienna: Böhlau, 1975–92.

Binark, İsmet. "Maarif Tarihimize Ait Bir Rapor." *Yeni Türkiye* 2/7 (1996): 477–93.

Bjørnlund, Matthias. "'A Fate Worse than Dying': Sexual Violence during the Armenian Genocide." In *Brutality and Desire: War and Sexuality in Europe's Twentieth Century*, edited by Dagmar Herzog, 16–58. Basingstoke: Springer, 2009.

Böer, Ingeborg, Ruth Haerkötter, and Petra Kappert, eds. *Türken in Berlin, 1871–1945: Eine Metropole in den Erinnerungen osmanischer und türkischer Zeitzeugen.* Berlin: de Gruyter, 2002.

Brown, Anna Welles. "Orphanages in Constantinople." In *Constantinople Today; or, The Pathfinder Survey of Constantinople: A Study in Oriental Social Life*, edited by Clarence Richard Johnson, 227–57. New York: Macmillan, 1922.

Brummett, Palmira Johnson. *Image and Imperialism in the Ottoman Revolutionary Press, 1908–1911.* Albany: SUNY Press, 2000.

Calotychos, Vangelis. *The Balkan Prospect: Identity, Culture, and Politics in Greece after 1989.* New York: Palgrave Macmillan, 2013.

Can, Neslihan. "Atatürk ve İnönü Dönemi Sosyal Yardım Politikalarının Karşılaştırmalı Bir Analizi, 1923–1950." PhD diss., Marmara Univ., Istanbul, 2014.

Çeliktemel-Thomen, Özde. "Osmanlı İmparatorluğu'nda Sinema ve Propaganda, 1908–1922." *Kurgu Online International Journal of Communication Studies* 2 (2010): 1–17.

Çetinkaya, Doğan Y. "Atrocity Propaganda and the Nationalization of the Masses in the Ottoman Empire during the Balkan Wars (1912–13)." *International Journal of Middle East Studies* 46 (2014): 759–78.

———. "Illustrated Atrocity: The Stigmatisation of Non-Muslims through Images in the Ottoman Empire during the Balkan Wars." *Journal of Modern European History* 12 (2014): 460–78.

Chickering, Roger, and Stig Förster, eds. *Great War, Total War: Combat and Mobilization on the Western Front, 1914–1918.* Washington, DC: German Historical Institute, 2000.

Çiçek, M. Talha. *War and State Formation in Syria: Cemal Pasha's Governorate during World War I, 1914–1917.* New York: Routledge, 2014.

Çolak, Mustafa. *Alman İmparatorluğu'nun Doğu Siyaseti Çerçevesinde Kafkasya Politikası (1914–1918).* Ankara: Türk Tarih Kurumu, 2006.

———. "Alman-Türk Dostluk Cemiyeti'nin İstanbul'da Bir 'Dostluk Yurdu' Kurma Çabaları (1915–1918)." In *I. Uluslararası Tarihi ve Kültürel Yönleriyle Türk-Alman İlişkileri Sempozyumu (8–10 Ekim 2009)*, edited by Ramazan Çalık, 182–87. Konya: Konya Valiliği, İl Kültür ve Turizm Müdürlüğü, 2010.

Darbinyan, Asya, and Rubina Peroomian. "Children: The Most Vulnerable Victims of the Armenian Genocide." In *Plight and Fate of Children during and following Genocide*, edited by Samuel Totten, 57–84. New York: Routledge, 2018.

Dadrian, Vahakn N. "Children as Victims of Genocide: The Armenian Case." *Journal of Genocide Research* 5/3 (2003): 421–37.

Davis, Belinda. "Experience, Identity, and Memory: The Legacy of World War I." *Journal of Modern History* 75 (2003): 111–31.

Davison, Roderic H. *Reform in the Ottoman Empire, 1856–1876.* Princeton, NJ: Princeton Univ. Press, 1963.

Demoyan, Hayk. *Haygagan Sportı yev Marmnagırtutyunı Osmanyan Gasyrutyunum* (*Armenian Sport and Physical Gymnastics in the Ottoman Empire*). Yerevan: Armenian Genocide Museum-Institute, 2009.

Denker, Arif Cemil. *İttihatçı Şeflerin Gurbet Maceraları.* Edited by Y. Demirel. Istanbul: Arma, 1992.

Derderian, Katharine. "Common Fate, Different Experience: Gender-Specific Aspects of the Armenian Genocide, 1915–1917." *Holocaust and Genocide Studies* 19/1 (2005): 1–25.

Der Matossian, Bedross. *Shattered Dreams of Revolution: From Liberty to Violence in the Late Ottoman Empire.* Stanford, CA: Stanford Univ. Press, 2014.

Der Yeghiayan, Zaven. *My Patriarchal Memoirs.* Translated by Ared Misirliyan. Barrington, RI: Mayreni, 2002.

Dinamo, Hasan İzzettin. *Öksüz Musa.* Istanbul: Heyamola Yayınları, 2005.

———. *Savaş ve Açlar.* Istanbul: May Yayınları, 1980.

Donson, Andrew. *Youth in the Fatherless Land: War Pedagogy, Nationalism, and Authority in Germany, 1914–1918.* Cambridge, MA: Harvard Univ. Press, 2010.

Doumanis, Nicholas. *Before the Nation: Muslim-Christian Coexistence and Its Destruction in Late-Ottoman Anatolia.* Oxford: Oxford Univ. Press, 2013.

Duman, Önder. "Mütareke İstanbul'unda Ermeni Faaliyetleri." *Ermeni Araştırmaları* 16–17 (2004–5): 151–73.

Dündar, Fuat. *Modern Türkiye'nin Şifresi: İttihat ve Terakki'nin Etnisite Mühendisliği, 1913–1918*. Istanbul: İletişim, 2008.

Dzarugyan, Antranig. *Çocukluğu Olmayan Adamlar.* Istanbul: Aras Yayıncılık, 2016.

———. *Des hommes sans enfance*. Paris: Les Éditeurs Français Réunis, 1977.

———. *Men without Childhood*. New York: Ashod Press, 1985.

Eisen, George. *Children and Play in the Holocaust: Games among the Shadows.* Amherst: Univ. of Massachusetts Press, 1988.

Ekmekçioğlu, Lerna. "A Climate for Abduction, a Climate for Redemption: The Politics of Inclusion during and after the Armenian Genocide." *Comparative Studies in Society and History* 55/3 (2013): 522–53.

———. *Recovering Armenia: The Limits of Belonging in Post-Genocide Turkey.* Stanford, CA: Stanford Univ. Press, 2016.

Elliott, Mabel Evelyn. *Beginning Again at Ararat.* New York: Fleming H. Revell, 1924.

Enloe, Cynthia. *Maneuvers: The International Politics of Militarizing Women's Lives.* Berkeley: Univ. of California Press, 2000.

Ergin, Osman Nuri. *Türkiye Maarif Tarihi.* Vols. 3–4. Istanbul: Eser Matbaası, 1977.

Erol, Emre. "Organized Chaos as Diplomatic Ruse and Demographic Weapon: The Expulsion of the Ottoman Greeks (Rum) from Foça, 1914." *Tijdschrift Voor Sociale en Economische Geschiedenis* 10/4 (2013): 66–96.

Esin, Taylan. "Savaş, Tehcir, Ütopya: Darüleytamların Yükselişi ve Çözülüşü." *Toplumsal Tarih* 258 (June 2015): 50–61.

Faron, Olivier. *Les enfants du deuil: Orphelins et pupilles de la nation de la Première Guerre Mondiale.* Paris: La Découverte, 2001.

Feldman, Gerald D. *Army, Industry and Labour in Germany, 1914–1918.* Princeton, NJ: Princeton Univ. Press, 1966.

Fisher, Susan. *Boys and Girls in No Man's Land: English-Canadian Children and the First World War.* Toronto: Univ. of Toronto Press, 2011.

Fortna, Benjamin C. "Bonbons and Bayonets: Mixed Messages of Childhood in the Late Ottoman Empire and the Early Turkish Republic." In *Childhood in the Late Ottoman Empire and After*, edited by Benjamin C. Fortna, 173–88. Leiden: Brill, 2015.

———. "The Kindergarten in the Ottoman Empire and the Turkish Republic." In *Kindergartens and Cultures: The Global Diffusion of an Idea*, edited by Roberta Lyn Wollons, 251–73. New Haven, CT: Yale Univ. Press, 2000.

Frank, Anne. *The Diary of a Young Girl: The Definitive Edition.* Translated by Susan Massotty. Edited by Otto H. Frank and Mirjam Pressler. New York: Doubleday, 1995.

Fuhrmann, Malte. "Germany's Adventures in the Orient: A History of Ambivalent Semicolonial Entanglements." In *German Colonialism: Race, the Holocaust, and Postwar Germany*, edited by Volker Max Langbehn and Mohammad Salama, 123–45. New York: Columbia Univ. Press, 2011.

Gencer, Mustafa. *Nationale Bildungspolitik, Modernisierung und kulturelle Interaktion: Deutsch-türkische Beziehungen (1908–1918).* Münster: LiT, 2002.

Gencer, Yasemin. "We Are Family: The Child and Modern Nationhood in Early Turkish Republican Cartoons (1923–28)." *Comparative Studies of South Asia, Africa and the Middle East* 32/2 (2012): 294–309.

Geyer, Michael. "Militarization of Europe, 1914–1945." In *The Militarization of the Western World*, edited by John Gillis, 65–102. New Brunswick, NJ: Rutgers Univ. Press, 1989.

Gruesshaber, Gerhard. *The German Spirit in the Ottoman and Turkish Army, 1908–1938: A History of Military Knowledge Transfer.* Berlin: Walter de Gruyter, 2018.

Gürpınar, Hüseyin Rahmi. *Hakka Sığındık* (*We Seek Refuge in God* [1919]). Istanbul: Ayrıntı, 2018.

Haigaz, Aram. *Four Years in the Mountains of Kurdistan: An Armenian Boy's Memoir of Survival.* Translated by Iris Haigaz Chekenian. Bronxville, NY: Maiden Lane Press, 2015.

Healy, Maureen. *Vienna and the Fall of the Habsburg Empire: Total War and Everyday Life in World War I.* Cambridge: Cambridge Univ. Press, 2004.

Highgas, Dirouhi Kouymjian. *Refugee Girl.* Watertown, MA: Baykar, 1985.

Holt, Marilyn. *The Orphan Trains: Placing Out in America.* Lincoln: Univ. of Nebraska Press, 1992.

Ihrig, Stefan. *Justifying Genocide: Germany and the Armenians from Bismarck to Hitler.*. Cambridge, MA: Harvard Univ. Press, 2016.

Injarabian, Papken. *Azo the Slave Boy and His Road to Freedom.* London: Gomidas Institute, 2015.

Ion, Theodore P., and Carroll N. Brown. *Persecutions of the Greeks in Turkey since the Beginning of the European War.* New York: Oxford Univ. Press, 1918.

Jinbashian, Iskhan, and Levon Parian, eds. *Crows of the Desert: The Memoirs of Levon Yotnakhparian.* Tujunga, CA: Parian Photographic Design, 2012.

Jones, Heather. "Imperial Captivities: Colonial Prisoners of War in Germany and the Ottoman Empire, 1914–1918." In *Race, Empire and First World War Writing*, edited by Santanu Das, 175–93. Cambridge: Cambridge Univ. Press, 2011.

Kamouzis, Dimitris. "Elites and the Formation of National Identity: The Case of the Greek Orthodox Millet, Mid-19th Century to 1922." In *State-Nationalisms in the Ottoman Empire, Greece and Turkey: Orthodox and Muslims, 1830–1945*, edited by Benjamin C. Fortna, Stefanos Katsikas, Dimitris Kamouzis, and Paraskevas Konortas, 13–46. New York: Routledge, 2013.

Kapiguian, Garabed. Եղեռնապատում (*Tales of the Yeghern*). Boston: Hayrenik, 1924.

Kaptanyan, Paylazu. *1915 Ermeni Soykırımı: Bir Tanığın Anıları.* Translated by Fatma Özgen. Istanbul: Pencere Yayınları, 2012.

Karabekir, Kazım. *Çocuk Davamız.* Edited by Faruk Özerengin. Istanbul: Emre Yayınları, 1995.

Karakışla, Yavuz S. "Kadınları Çalıştırma Cemiyeti Himayesi'nde Savaş Yetimleri ve Kimsesiz Çocuklar: 'Ermeni' mi, 'Türk' mü?" *Toplumsal Tarih* 6 (1999): 46–55.

———. *Women, War and Work in the Ottoman Empire: Society for the Employment of Ottoman Muslim Women, 1916–1923.* Istanbul: Osmanlı Bankası Arşiv ve Araştırma Merkezi, 2005.

Kemal, Yaşar. *Çocuklar İnsandır.* Istanbul: Yapı Kredi Yayınları, 2013.

Kennedy, Rosie. *The Children's War: Britain, 1914–1918.* Houndmills: Palgrave Macmillan, 2014.

Kerr, Stanley E. *Lions of Marash: Personal Experiences with American Near East Relief, 1919–1922.* Albany: State Univ. of New York Press, 1975.

Ketchian, Bertha Nakshian. *In the Shadow of the Fortress: The Genocide Remembered.* Cambridge, MA: Zoryan Institute, 1988.

Kévorkian, Raymond. *The Armenian Genocide: A Complete History.* New York: I. B. Tauris, 2011.

———. *Le génocide des Arméniens.* Paris: Odile Jacob, 2006.

Kieser, Hans-Lukas. *Talaat Pasha: Father of Modern Turkey, Architect of Genocide*. Princeton, NJ: Princeton Univ. Press, 2018.

———. *Türklüğe İhtida*. Istanbul: İletişim, 2008.

Kingsbury, Celia M. *For Home and Country: World War I Propaganda on the Home Front*. Lincoln: Univ. of Nebraska Press, 2010.

Kırbaç, Safiye. "Almanya'ya Gönderilen Darüleytam Öğrencileri." In *Savaş Çocukları, Öksüzler ve Yetimler*, edited by Emine Gürsoy-Naskali and Aylin Koç, 87–101. Istanbul: n.p., 2003.

———. "Savaş Yıllarında Türkiye'de Sosyal Yardım Faaliyetleri (1914–1923)." PhD diss., Istanbul Univ., 2005.

Kıranlar, Safiye, and Aynur Soydan Erdemir. "Köyün Modernleştirilmesine Dair Bir Uygulama ve Proje: Kimsesiz Köy Çocuklarının Köyde Eğitimi." *Yakın Dönem Türkiye Araştırmaları* 8 (2005): 94–113.

Koçu, Reşat Ekrem. "Çocuk Hırsız Çeteleri." In *İstanbul Ansiklopedisi*, 8:4076–78. Istanbul: Koçu Yayınları, 1966.

Kohen, Elli. *The Kohens del de Campavias: A Family's Sweet and Sour Story in Ottoman and Republican Turkey*. Istanbul: ISIS, 2004.

Köksal, Duygu. "İsmayıl Hakkı Baltacıoğlu, İnkilap ve Terbiye: Ulusun 'Çocukluğu.'" *Toplumsal Tarih* 40 (1997): 7–12.

Köroğlu, Erol. *Ottoman Propaganda and Turkish Identity: Literature in Turkey during World War I*. London: I. B. Tauris, 2007.

Kurt, Ümit. "Cultural Erasure: The Absorption and Forced Conversion of Armenian Women and Children, 1915–1916." *Études Arméniennes Contemporaines*. http://journals.openedition.org/eac/997. doi:10.4000/eac.997.

———. "The Plunder of Wealth through Abandoned Properties Laws in the Armenian Genocide." *Genocide Studies International* 10 (2016): 37–51.

Kutlu, Cemil. "I. Dünya Savaşı'nda Rusya'daki Türk Savaş Esirleri ve Bunların Yurda Döndürülmeleri Faaliyetleri." PhD diss., Erzurum, Atatürk Univ., 1997.

Kutluata, Zeynep. "Geç Osmanlı ve Erken Cumhuriyet Dönemi'nde Toplumsal Cinsiyet ve Savaş: Kara Fatma(lar)." *Kültür ve Siyasette Feminist Yaklaşımlar* 2 (2007). http://www.feministyaklasimlar.org/ozet/?postid=476.

———. "Ottoman Women and the State during World War I." PhD diss., Sabancı Univ., 2014.

Kuyumjian, Rita Soulahian. *Archeology of Madness: Komitas, Portrait of an Armenian Icon*. London: Gomidas Institute, 2001.

Larcher, Maurice. *La Guerre Turque dans la Guerre Mondiale*. Paris: Étienne Chiron, 1926.

Mackeen, Dawn Anahid. *The Hundred-Year Walk: An Armenian Odyssey*. New York: Houghton Mifflin Harcourt, 2016.

Mahir Metinsoy, Elif. *Ottoman Women during World War I: Everyday Experiences, Politics, and Conflict*. Cambridge: Cambridge Univ. Press, 2017.

———. "Writing the History of Ordinary Ottoman Women during World War I." *Aspasia* 10 (2016): 18–39.

Maksudyan, Nazan. "Agents or Pawns? Nationalism and Ottoman Children during the Great War." *Journal of the Ottoman and Turkish Studies Association* 3 (2016): 147–72.

———. "Children as Transgressors in Urban Space: Delinquency, Public Order and Philanthropy in the Ottoman Reform Era." In *Expertise and Juvenile Violence, 19th–21st Century*, edited by Aurore François, Veerle Massin, and David Niget, 21–39. Louvain: Presses Universitaires de Louvain, 2011.

———. "The Fight over Nobody's Children: Religion, Nationality and Citizenship of Foundlings in the Late Ottoman Empire." *New Perspectives on Turkey* 41/2 (2009): 151–80.

———. "Foster-Daughter or Servant, Charity or Abuse: *Beslemes* in the Late Ottoman Empire." *Journal of Historical Sociology* 21 (2008): 488–512.

———. "La jeunesse ottomane, enjeu des luttes nationales (1914–1919)." *Le Mouvement Social* 261 (2017): 9–29.

———. "Orphans, Cities, and the State: Vocational Orphanages (*Islahhanes*) and 'Reform' in the Late Ottoman Urban Space." *International Journal of Middle East Studies* 43/3 (2011): 493–511.

———. *Orphans and Destitute Children in the Late Ottoman Empire*. Syracuse: Syracuse Univ. Press, 2014.

———. "'Öldürmeden utan, ölmeden usan!': Geç Osmanlı İmparatorluğu'nda Savaş Karşıtı Hissiyatın Açık ve Örtük Dışavurumları." *Toplumsal Tarih* 180 (Dec. 2008): 34–41.

———. "Self, Family, and Society: Individual and Communal Reflections on the Armenian Genocide." *Journal of Levantine Studies* 5/2 (2015): 197–206.

———, ed. *Women and the City, Women in the City: A Gendered Perspective of Ottoman Urban History*. New York: Berghahn, 2014.

Marashlian, Levon. "Finishing the Genocide: Cleansing Turkey of Armenian Survivors, 1920–1923." In *Remembrance and Denial: The Case of the Armenian Genocide*, edited by Richard G. Hovannisian, 113–45. Detroit: Wayne State Univ. Press, 1998.

Martin, Ramela. *Out of Darkness*. Cambridge, MA: Zoryan Institute, 1989.

Mazower, Mark. *Salonica: The City of Ghosts*. New York: Alfred A. Knopf, 2005.

Meymerian, Euphoria Halebian. *Housher: My Life in the Aftermath of the Armenian Genocide*. London: Taderon Press, 2004.

Miller, Donald E., and Lorna Touryan Miller. *Survivors: An Oral History of the Armenian Genocide*. Berkeley: Univ. of California Press, 1993.

Muslihiddin, Adil (Taylan). *Alman Hayat-ı İrfanı*. Istanbul: Matbaa-i Amire, 1333 [1917].

Müezzinoğlu, Ersin. "I. Dünya Savaşı Esnasında Yetim ve Öksüz Çocukların Himayesi ve Eğitimi: Darüleytamlar." *History Studies* 4/1 (2012): 399–417.

Nayar, Pramod K. *Colonial Voices: The Discourses of Empire*. West Sussex: Wiley-Blackwell, 2012.

Nichanian, Marc. *Entre l'art et le témoignage: Le roman de la catastrophe*. Vol. 3. Genève: MétisPresses, 2006.

———. *The Historiographic Perversion*. New York: Columbia Univ. Press, 2009.

Nicholson, Colin. *The Longman Companion to the First World War*. Harlow: Longman, 2001.

Nicolle, David, and Raffaele Ruggeri. *The Ottoman Army, 1914–18*. London: Osprey, 1994.

Odyan, Yervant. *Accursed Years: My Exile and Return from Der Zor, 1914–1919*. London: Gomidas Institute, 2009.

Okay, Cüneyd. "War and Child in the Second Constitutional Period." In *Childhood and Youth in the Muslim World*, edited by François Georgeon and Klaus Kreiser, 219–32. Paris: Maisonneuve & Larose, 2007.

Okur, Yasemin. "Darüleytamlar." Master's thesis, Ondokuz Mayıs Univ., 1996.

Onaran, Nevzat. *Emval-i Metruke Olayı: Osmanlı'da ve Cumhuriyette Ermeni ve Rum Mallarının Türkleştirilmesi*. Istanbul: Belge, 2010.

Oran, Baskın, ed. *M. K. Adlı Çocuğun Tehcir Anıları: 1915 ve Sonrası*. Istanbul: İletişim, 2005.

Orga, İrfan. *Portrait of a Turkish Family*. London: Eland, 2002.

Oswell, David. *The Agency of Children: From Family to Global Human Rights*. Cambridge: Cambridge Univ. Press, 2013.

Ölçen, Mehmet Arif. *Vetluga Memoir: A Turkish Prisoner of War in Russia, 1916–1918*. Gainesville: Univ. Press of Florida, 1995.

Özalp, Reşat. *Milli Eğitimle İlgili Mevzuat (1857–1923)*. Ankara: MEB Yayınları, 1982.

Özbek, Nadir. *Cumhuriyet Türkiyesi'nde Sosyal Güvenlik ve Sosyal Politikalar*. Istanbul: Tarih Vakfı, 2006.

———. "Defining the Public Sphere during the Late Ottoman Empire: War, Mass Mobilization and the Young Turk Regime (1908–18)." *Middle Eastern Studies* 43 (2007): 795–809.

———. "II. Abdülhamid ve Kimsesiz Çocuklar: Darülhayr-ı Âlî." *Tarih ve Toplum* 31/182 (1999): 11–21.

———. *Osmanlı İmparatorluğu'nda Sosyal Devlet: Siyaset, İktidar ve Meşrutiyet, 1876–1914*. Istanbul: İletişim, 2006.

Palalı, İrfan. *Tehcir Çocukları: Nenem bir Ermeni'ymiş*. Istanbul: Su Yayınevi, 2005.

Panian, Karnig. *Goodbye, Antoura: A Memoir of the Armenian Genocide*. Stanford, CA: Stanford Univ. Press, 2015.

Panyan, Karnig. *Elveda Antura: Bir Ermeni Yetimin Anıları*. Istanbul: Aras Yayıncılık, 2018.

Peroomian, Rubina. *And Those Who Continued Living in Turkey after 1915: The Metamorphosis of the Post-Genocide Armenian Identity as Reflected in Artistic Literature*. Yerevan: Armenian Genocide Museum-Institute, 2008.

Pignot, Manon. "Entrer en guerre, sortir de l'enfance? Les 'ado-combattants' de la Grande Guerre." In *L'enfant soldat, XIXe–XXIe siècle: Une approche critique*, edited by Manon Pignot, 69–89. Paris: Armand Collin, 2012.

———. *La guerre des crayons: Quand les petits Parisiens dessinaient la Grande Guerre*. Paris: Ed. Parigramme, 2004.

Polatel, Mehmet, and Uğur Ümit Üngör. *Confiscation and Destruction: The Young Seizure of Armenian Property*. London: Continuum, 2011.

Quataert, Donald. *Miners and the State in the Ottoman Empire: The Zonguldak Coalfield, 1822–1920*. New York: Berghahn, 2006.

Sagaster, Börte. *Achmed Talib: Stationen des Lebens eines türkischen Schuhmachermeisters in Deutschland von 1917–1983*. Cologne: Önel Verlag, 1997.

Sakaoğlu, Necdet "Darüleytamlar." In *Dünden Bugüne İstanbul Ansiklopedisi*, 2:558. Istanbul: İletişim, 1994.

Salbi, M. (Aram Sahakian). *Our Cross*. Translated by Ishkhan Chinpashean. Studio City, CA: H. and K. Manjikian, 2014.

Sánchez-Eppler, Karen. *Dependent States: The Child's Part in Nineteenth-Century American Culture*. Chicago: Univ. of Chicago Press, 2005.

Sarafian, Ara. "The Absorption of Armenian Women and Children into Muslim Households as a Structural Component of the Armenian Genocide." In *In God's Name: Genocide and Religion in the Twentieth Century*, edited by Omer Bartov and Phyllis Mack, 209–21. New York: Berghahn Books, 2001.

———. *Talaat Pasha's Report on the Armenian Genocide*. London: Gomidas Institute, 2011.

Sarısaman, Sadık. "Birinci Dünya Savaşında İhtiyat Kuvveti Olarak Kurulan Osmanlı Genç Dernekleri." *Ankara Üniversitesi Osmanlı Tarihi Araştırma ve Uygulama Merkezi Dergisi* 11 (2000): 439–501.

———. "Osmanlı Güç Dernekleri." In *Meslek Hayatının 25. Yılında Prof. Dr. Abdulhaluk M. Çay Armağanı*, edited by M. Abdulhalûk Çay, Atilla Şimşek, and Yaşar Kalafat, 833–46. Ankara: n.p., 1998.

Shamdanjian, Mikael. *The Fatal Night: An Eyewitness Account of the Extermination of Armenian Intellectuals in 1915*. Translated by Ishkhan Jinbashian. Studio City, CA: H. and K. Manjikian, 2007.

Shemmassian, Vahram L. "The League of Nations and the Reclamation of Armenian Genocide Survivors." In *Looking Backward, Moving Forward: Confronting the Armenian Genocide*, edited by Richard Hovannisian, 81–112. New Brunswick, NJ: Transaction, 2003.

———. "The Reclamation of Captive Armenian Genocide Survivors in Syria and Lebanon at the End of World War I." *Journal of the Society for Armenian Studies* 15 (2006): 113–40.

Stoler, Ann Laura. *Carnal Knowledge and Imperial Power: Race and the Intimate in Colonial Rule*. Berkeley: Univ. of California Press, 2010.

Strohmeier, Martin. "Fakhri (Fahrettin) Paşa and the End of Ottoman Rule in Medina (1916–1919)." *Turkish Historical Review* 4 (2013): 192–223.

Şafak, Nurdan. "Darüleytam'da Çocuk Olmak: On Çocuk On Portre." *FSM İlmi Araştırmalar İnsan ve Toplum Bilimleri Dergisi* 2 (2013): 261–84.

Şerifoğlu, Ömer Faruk. *Ressam Mehmet Ruhi Bey'in "Seferberlik Kartpostalları."* Istanbul: Parsan Makina, 2009.

Şişman, Adnan. *Tanzimat Döneminde Fransa'ya Gönderilen Osmanlı Öğrencileri (1839–1876)*. Ankara: Türk Tarih Kurumu, 2004.

Tachjian, Vahé. *Daily Life in the Abyss: Genocide Diaries, 1915–1918*. New York: Berghahn Books, 2017.

———. "Gender, Nationalism, Exclusion: The Reintegration Process of Female Survivors of the Armenian Genocide." *Nations and Nationalism* 15/1 (2009): 71–73.

———. "Mixed Marriage, Prostitution, Survival: Reintegrating Armenian Women into Post-Ottoman Cities." In *Women and the City, Women in the City: A Gendered Perspective of Ottoman Urban History*, edited by Nazan Maksudyan, 86–106. New York: Berghahn Books, 2014.

Tamari, Salim. *The Great War and the Remaking of Palestine*. Berkeley: Univ. of California Press, 2017.

———. *Year of the Locust: A Soldier's Diary and the Erasure of Palestine's Ottoman Past*. Berkeley: Univ. of California Press, 2011.

Tan, Mine, Özlem Şahin, Mustafa Sever, and Aksu Bora. *Cumhuriyet'te Çocuktular*. Istanbul: Boğaziçi Üniversitesi Yayınları, 2007.

Tanielian, Melanie. *The Charity of War: Famine, Humanitarian Aid, and World War I in the Middle East*. Stanford, CA: Stanford Univ. Press, 2017.

———. "Feeding the City: The Beirut Municipality and the Politics of Food during World War I." *International Journal of Middle East Studies* 46/4 (2014): 737–58.

———. "Politics of Wartime Relief in Ottoman Beirut (1914–1918)." *First World War Studies* 5/1 (2014): 69–82.

———. "The War of Famine: Everyday Life in Wartime Beirut and Mount Lebanon." PhD diss., Univ. of California, 2012.

Tashjian Alice A. *Silences: My Mother's Will to Survive*. Princeton, NJ: Blue Pansy, 1995.

Taşkıran, Cemalettin. *Ana Ben Ölmedim: Birinci Dünya Savaşı'nda Türk Esirleri*. Istanbul: Türkiye İş Bankası Kültür Yayınları, 2008.

Tec, Nechama. Introduction to *Children during the Holocaust*, edited by Patricia Heberer, xxi–xli. Lanham, MD: AltaMira Press, 2011.

Thompson, Elizabeth. *Colonial Citizens: Republican Rights, Paternal Privileges, and Gender in French Syria and Lebanon*. New York: Columbia Univ. Press, 2000.

Tongo, Gizem. "Ottoman Painting and Painters during the First World War." PhD diss., Univ. of Oxford, 2018.

Toprak, Zafer. "II. Meşrutiyet Döneminde Paramiliter Gençlik Örgütleri." In *Tanzimattan Cumhuriyet'e Türkiye Ansiklopedisi*, 531–36. Istanbul: İletişim Yayınları, 1985.

Trumpener, Ulrich. *Germany and the Ottoman Empire, 1914–1918*. Princeton, NJ: Princeton Univ. Press, 1968.

Tuksavul, Muammer. *Eine bittere Freundschaft: Erinnerung eines türkischen Jahrhundertzeugen*. Düsseldorf: Econ Verlag, 1985.

Tuna, Serkan, and Eminalp Malkoç. "The Problem of Turkish Captives in Russia from Moscow Treaty to the First Years of the Turkish Renovation." *International Journal of Turcologia* 4, no. 7 (2009): 77–92.

Uşaklıgil, Halid Ziya. *Bir Acı Hikâye*. Istanbul: Hilmi, 1942.

Üngör, Uğur Ümit. "Orphans, Converts, and Prostitutes: Social Consequences of War and Persecution in the Ottoman Empire, 1914–1923." *War in History* 19/2 (2012): 173–92.

van Os, Nicole A. N. M. "Aiding the Poor Soldiers' Families: The Asker Âilelerine Yardımcı Hanımlar Cemiyeti." *Türkiyat Mecmuası* 21 (2011): 255–89.

———. "Gendering Jihad: Ottoman Muslim Women and War during the Early Twentieth Century." In *Jihad and Islam in World War I: Studies on the Ottoman Jihad on the Centenary of Snouck Hurgronje's "Holy War Made in Germany,"* edited by Erik-Jan Zürcher, 153–78. Leiden: Leiden Univ. Press, 2016.

———. "Nurturing Soldiers and Girls: Osmanlı Kadınları Cemiyet-i Hayriyesi." In *Papers of VIIIth International Congress on the Economic and Social History of Turkey*, edited by Nurcan Abacı, 213–18. Morrisville, NC: Lulu Press, 2006.

———. "Taking Care of Soldiers' Families: The Ottoman State and the *'Muinsiz Aile Maaşı.'*" In *Arming the State: Military Conscription in the Middle East and Central Asia, 1775–1925*, edited by Erik J. Zürcher, 95–110. London: I. B. Tauris, 1999.

von der Goltz, Colmar. *Millet-i Müsellaha: Asrımızın Usul ve Ahvali Askeriyesi*. Translated by Mehmet Tahir. Istanbul: n.p., 1884.

Watenpaugh, Keith D. "'Are There Any Children for Sale?': Genocide and the Transfer of Armenian Children (1915–1922)." *Journal of Human Rights* 12 (2013): 283–95.

———. *Bread from Stones: The Middle East and the Making of Modern Humanitarianism*. Berkeley: Univ. of California Press, 2015.

———. "The League of Nations' Rescue of Armenian Genocide Survivors and the Making of Modern Humanitarianism, 1920–1927." *American Historical Review* 115/5 (2010): 1315–39.

Woodall, Carole. "'Awakening a Horrible Monster': Negotiating the Jazz Public in 1920s Istanbul." *Comparative Studies of South Asia, Africa, and the Middle East* 30 (2010): 574–82.

Yalçın, Kemal. *Sarı Gelin–Sari Gyalin*. Istanbul: Bir Zamanlar Yayıncılık, 2005.

Yalman, Ahmed Emin. *Turkey in the World War*. New Haven, CT: Yale Univ. Press, 1930.

Yanıkdağ, Yücel. *Healing the Nation: Prisoners of War, Medicine and Nationalism in Turkey, 1914–1939*. Edinburgh: Edinburgh Univ. Press, 2013.

———. "Ill-Fated Sons of the Nation: Ottoman Prisoners of War in Russia and Egypt, 1914–1922." PhD diss., Ohio State Univ., 2002.

Yıldız, Murat C. "Strengthening Male Bodies and Building Robust Communities: Physical Culture in the Late Ottoman Empire." PhD diss., Univ. of California, 2015.

Zahra, Tara. *Kidnapped Souls: National Indifference and the Battle for Children in the Bohemian Lands, 1900–1948*. Ithaca, NY: Cornell Univ. Press, 2008.

———. *Lost Children: Reconstructing Europe's Families after World War II*. Cambridge, MA: Harvard Univ. Press, 2011.

Zürcher, Erik J. "Between Death and Desertion: The Experience of the Ottoman Soldier in World War I." *Turcica* 28 (1996): 235–58.

———. "Little Mehmet in the Desert: The Ottoman Soldier's Experience." In *Facing Armageddon: The First World War Experienced*, edited by Hugh Cecil and Peter Liddle, 230–41. London: Leo Cooper, 1988.

———. "The Ottoman Conscription System in Theory and Practice, 1844–1918." *International Review of Social History* 43/3 (1998): 437–49.

———. "Ottoman Labor Battalions in World War I." In *The Armenian Genocide and the Shoah*, edited by Hans-Lukas Kieser and Dominic Schaller, 187–96. Zurich: Chronos, 2002.

———. "Refusing to Serve by Other Means: Desertion in the Late Ottoman Empire." In *Conscientious Objection: Resisting Militarized Society*, edited by Özgür Heval Çınar and Coşkun Üsterci, 45–52. London: Zed Books, 2009.

Index

Nazan Maksudyan is an Einstein guest professor at the Friedrich-Meinecke-Institut at the Freie Universität Berlin and a research associate at the Centre Marc Bloch (Berlin). She was a "Europe in the Middle East—the Middle East in Europe" (EUME) Fellow in 2009–10 at the Wissenschaftskolleg zu Berlin and an Alexander von Humboldt Stiftung Postdoctoral Fellow at the Leibniz-Zentrum Moderner Orient (Berlin) in 2010–11 and in 2016–18. From 2013 to 2016, she worked as a professor of history in Istanbul and received her habilitation degree in 2015. Her research mainly focuses on the history of children and youth in the Ottoman Empire during the nineteenth and twentieth centuries, with special interest in gender, sexuality, education, humanitarianism, and non-Muslims. Among her publications are "Foster-Daughter or Servant, Charity or Abuse: *Beslemes* in the Late Ottoman Empire" (2008); "Orphans, Cities, and the State: Vocational Orphanages (*Islahhanes*) and 'Reform' in the Late Ottoman Urban Space" (2011); *Orphans and Destitute Children in the Late Ottoman Empire* (Syracuse University Press, 2014); *Women and the City, Women in the City* (2014); and "Agents or Pawns? Nationalism and Ottoman Children during the Great War" (2016). Maksudyan is among the founders of the Association of Middle East Children's and Youth Studies (AMECYS), and she serves on the board of directors (2017–19). She is also one of the managing editors of the "1914–1918-online: International Encyclopedia of the First World War."